United States Policy on Reducing Juvenile Crime: An Overview of the Issues Related to Reducing Juvenile Crime in the United States

United States Policy on Reducing Juvenile Crime: An Overview of the Issues Related to Reducing Juvenile Crime in the United States

Robert C. Rowland

Communication Studies
The University of Kansas

National Textbook Company
a division of NTC *Publishing Group* • Lincolnwood, Illinois USA

Published by National Textbook Company, a division of NTC Publishing Group.
©1996 by NTC Publishing Group, 4255 West Touhy Avenue,
Lincolnwood (Chicago), Illinois 60646-1975 U.S.A.
Manufactured in the United States of America.

67890 VP 987654321

Contents

Chapter Three: Reducing Juvenile Crime Through Criminal Justice Reform   43

Chapter Four: Social Reform as Means of Controlling Juvenile Crime   81

Chapter Five: Strategic Dimensions in Debating About Juvenile Crime Policy   123

Bibliography   **137**

Introduction

There is no question that juvenile crime represents one of the most important social problems facing the country. While adult crime rates have been falling, juvenile crime rates have been escalating rapidly. And the level of violence found in youth crime also is disquieting. Many of the crimes committed by the young are quite violent; the days where a youth offender was likely to have committed petty vandalism are long gone.

The experts are agreed upon the threat posed by juvenile crime. Terrence Thornberry of the University of Albany, David Huizinga of the University of Colorado, and Rolf Loeber, of the University of Pittsburgh, explain "Youth violence is one of the most serious problems confronting American society today." They continue, "Compared to adolescents in other countries, American teenagers exhibit alarmingly high rates of violence" (B 213). Richard Lerner of Michigan State University emphasizes the magnitude of the problem:

> American is hanging over a precipice. Unless dramatic and innovative action is taken soon, millions of our nation's children and adolescents—the human capital on which America must build its future—will fall into an abyss of crime and violence, drug and alcohol use and abuse, unsafe sex, school failure, lack of job preparedness, and feelings of despair and hopelessness that pervade the lives of children whose parents have lived in poverty and who see themselves as having little opportunity to do better, that is, to have a life marked by societal respect, achievement, and opportunity. (B xiv)

In fact, how we deal with juvenile crime will have a major bearing on the development of the United States in the next century. Meri Pohutsky, Chair of the National Network of Runaway and Youth Services, recently explained the importance of the juvenile crime issue:

> How we treat our young people will have a profound effect on what this country looks like in the not too distant future. Will we be increasingly fearful and isolated because of increasing crime? Will we continue to withdraw from our neighbors and communities, protecting only our own children and not embracing all youth? (D *Hearing Regarding* 87)

In the remainder of this book, I will sketch the state of juvenile crime, describe current policies aimed at curbing it, and discuss alternative policies that might be used to reduce it in the future.

While the juvenile crime topic is undeniably timely, on first consideration, it seems to be quite a narrow area of public policy. The topic states:

Resolved: That the federal government should establish a program to substantially reduce juvenile crime in the United States.

This resolution would seem to focus on criminal justice and other means of reducing juvenile crime. The problem, as I will discuss in more depth in chapter one, is that word "other." An argument can be made that virtually any domestic policy proposal might impact juvenile crime. To take an extreme example, it could be argued that increased funding for the space program would decrease juvenile crime, both because young people need heroes to emulate, and astronauts can function as such heroes, and because space development produces major economic growth, which will provide jobs to many who are unemployed and on welfare, resulting in improved conditions in our urban centers, thus leading to a decrease in juvenile crime. While this example is obviously far-fetched, I am sure that advocates of space development would claim that one of the many benefits of such a development program would be improved economic conditions and decreased crime. The problem, therefore, for the opponent of the resolution is to find means of limiting the topic to proposals that reasonably relate directly to juvenile crime and also to find arguments that can be applied to a variety of proposals for change.

One of the focuses of the remainder of this book will be on answering that problem. My general perspective in accomplishing that aim will be to begin with the core issues involved in the juvenile crime and focus on arguments that have value in the real-world. An advocate who masters the core issues involved with juvenile crime will be prepared to debate more creative approaches to the resolution. For example, against the NASA solves juvenile crime proposal, the negative might argue that the literature does not demonstrate a relationship between increased employment and decreased crime. Nor does it seem likely that most of the jobs produced by space development would be filled by the urban underclass, where juvenile crime is concentrated. Any secondary job effects would relate to service professions, serving the technical specialists working in NASA, and such jobs are currently available. Thus, knowledge of the core issues of the resolution would provide the opponent of change with strong arguments, even against a proposal far out of the core.

I also strongly support the value of real-world arguments. Some object to policy arguments that focus on catastrophic impacts, including environmental collapse, risk of war, and so forth. That is not my objection. In some cases, such "catastrophic" results occur. In the 1970s some labelled as "nuts" scientists who pointed to an ozone depletion threats. Recently, one of those involved in developing the ozone depletion hypothesis was honored with a Nobel prize. The problem is not with the size of the impact, but with unreasonable causal claims or the use of sources who lack knowledge or expertise in an area.

By "real-world" I mean policy positions that experts in the field discuss. "Real-world" arguments are easier to develop and defend, because they are supported by recognizable experts in an area.

A Word About Research

The core research material dealing with juvenile crime is relatively limited. I suggest that four sources or types of sources are particularly useful for exploring the juvenile crime issue. First, a good introduction to many of the issues involved in the resolution can be found in two issues of the *CQ Researcher,* both written by Sarah Glazer. The February 25, 1994 issue, "Juvenile Justice," pp. 169-192 is a good overview to the juvenile justice system and the problems confronting it. In the June 28, 1995 issue, "Preventing Teen Drug Use," pp. 657-680, Ms. Glazer lays out issues relating to both juveniles and drug policy. Second, a good introduction to economic issues that relate to the resolution can be found in the book, *Reducing Poverty in America: Views and Approaches,* edited by Michael R. Darby (Thousand Oaks, CA: Sage, 1996). The book is not focussed on juvenile crime directly, but it discusses anti-poverty policies that are one means of confronting the conditions that lead to such crime.

The third and fourth suggestions for research relate to types of sources, rather than particular works. One means of gaining an understanding of the social science research on juvenile crime is to systematically review recent issues of important academic journals in the area, including *Journal of Research in Crime and Delinquency, Crime & Delinquency,* and *Criminology.* In the main, articles in these journals are clearly written and they provide the researcher both with up to date scientific findings and citations to earlier research. Finally, Congressional Hearings are an especially useful research source on juvenile crime issues. Hearings generally include the testimony of a number of experts in the area.

Conclusion

In the remainder of this book, I will describe the crucial policy issues relating to juvenile crime. The first chapter will discuss the meaning of the resolution and lay out the variety of policy options included within it. The second chapter will consider the magnitude of juvenile crime, its characteristics and causes, and current policies dealing with it. The third chapter will consider alternative criminal justice policies for reducing juvenile crime, including proposals to increase or decrease punishment for juveniles, and alternative policing. The fourth chapter will discuss a wide variety of social service and alternative policy means of decreasing juvenile crime. In that chapter, I initially will consider social service programs targeted at juveniles and then analyze a broad array of social programs that arguably could decrease conditions leading to juvenile crime. In the last main section, I will consider other proposals for eliminating the causes of juvenile crime such as drug legalization, regulation of the television and music industries, and gun control. In the final chapter, I will describe the characteristics of an effective affirmative and negative strategy and conclude with a number of outlines of potential affirmative and negative arguments.

Throughout the book I have relied on an internal citation scheme for referencing material in the bibliography. I have divided the bibliography into four sections: books and book chapters (B), Congressional Record (CR), documents (D), and periodicals (P). For every source that I cite, I include a reference indicating the type of source, the author's name (or title of the work, if there is no author), enough of a citation to find the source in the bibliography, and (if relevant) a page number. So the source (P Glazer "Juvenile" 173), refers to page 173 of the Sarah Glazer essay on "Juvenile Justice" in the *CQ Researcher*. In this instance, I included enough of the title for the reader to be able to tell which essay by Glazer I was referencing. The reader should find the bibliography a useful resource for researching the status of U.S. juvenile policy.

1 Debating the Parameters of Federal Juvenile Crime Policy

Debate resolutions serve the functions of focusing debate on a timely issue, dividing ground between the proponent and opponent of change, and narrowing research burdens to manageable levels.

The second and third purposes both mean that a particular debate resolution should be neither too broad, nor too narrow. An excessively broad resolution will leave little ground for the opponent of change, because so much of the policy universe is included within the resolution. Similarly, an excessively broad resolution will produce research burdens that are almost insurmountable for the negative. This, in turn, will result in a situation in which the affirmative wins a disproportionate percentage of debates.

On the other hand, a well-crafted debate resolution also should not be too narrow. An excessively narrow resolution will provide little ground for advocating the resolution. And the negative will be able to prepare in such depth that the proponent of change will have a very difficult time being competitive. Moreover, extremely narrow resolutions also often produce dull debate, because the same issues are discussed again and again.

The problem area and the specific topic dealing with juvenile crime pose problems in relation to the second and third purposes of topicality. The problem area asks:

How should the federal government reduce juvenile crime in the United States?

The topic states:

Resolved: That the federal government should establish a program to substantially reduce juvenile crime in the United States.

There is no question that the topic is timely. As I noted in the introduction, juvenile crime is a crucial issue facing the country.

On the other hand, there is danger that the topic could be interpreted in an extremely broad manner, thus producing excessive and unfair research burdens on the negative, and reducing the quality of clash. The difficulty is that there are a wide variety of potential means of influencing juvenile crime. To be successful, the opponent of change will need some means of limiting the resolution to a focus on policies that are aimed directly at juvenile crime.

Debating Topicality

Arguing about "topicality" in academic debate is similar to the way that courts and others argue about the meaning of terms in statutes, contracts, and so forth. In the real world, we debate about topicality at any time in which the meaning of words is at issue. That happens a lot.

The first step in preparing to debate topicality is research. The prepared advocate should gather definitions from all of the major dictionaries, as well as from specialized dictionaries. In particular, legal dictionaries, including *Black's Law Dictionary or Corpus Juris Secundum (CJS),* are quite useful. Legal dictionaries are especially valuable because they often provide a number of different definitions of a term as it was used in court cases. These definitions are most useful when they can be matched to the context of the resolution. For example, a definition of how the term "substantially" was used in a court case dealing with juvenile justice treatment programs would be especially valuable, because it is from the context of juvenile justice.

In addition to researching general and specialized dictionaries, debaters also should do contextual research. This means constantly being on the alert for definitions found in the literature on juvenile justice. Such contextual material may be found in a definitional section at the beginning of Congressional legislation, in statements about intent found in Congressional Hearings and Reports, and, randomly, when definitional issues are discussed in any type of source material.

Contextual definitions are especially useful, because they show how a term is used in a particular context area. We all know that the meaning of a term varies by context. For example, the phrase "substantially reduce" could have different meanings, depending upon the area in which it was used. Unfortunately, there is no section of the library titled "Contextual Definitions Found Here." However, a wise debater who keeps his/her eyes open inevitably will find a number of them, over time.

The second step in preparing to debate topicality is to actually structure the argument. Many debaters simply read definitions and then assert that the affirmative proposal does not meet them. It is a better approach to both present the definition and explain why it makes the affirmative plan non-topical. The easiest way to do this is to include within the topicality argument a statement of its "impact." This "impact" is the reason that the affirmative definition should be viewed as illegitimate. A complete topicality argument might be structured as follows:

A. Definition of the term in the resolution
B. Explanation of why the affirmative definition is illegitimate
C. Explanation of why the negative interpretation of the resolution is
    superior to that of the affirmative

Rather than structuring topicality arguments in this manner, some divide the issue between discussions of violation and standards for assessing the violation. I don't think that approach is useful, because arguments about standards for assessing meaning need to be applied specifically. This is accomplished in the organization I suggest.

In developing the B and C points, the opponent of change should keep in mind the following basic principles. First, the most important principles for distinguishing among competing definitions are all tied to the three purposes of resolutions, which I discussed earlier. In particular, the opponent of change should consider whether the affirmative interpretation is overly broad and/or unfairly divides ground.

Second, in preparing topicality arguments, the advocate should consider how the resolution could have been worded in order to make arguments about its meaning. For example, the resolution calls upon the federal government to establish the program dealing with juvenile crime. The affirmative might argue that they should be allowed to include state efforts within their broad policy approach, because federal government is not capitalized. When capitalized, the term refers to the national government in Washington. Thus, by considering an alternative wording (in this case capitalization) debaters may be able to develop a strong topicality position.

Third, debaters should consider whether an interpretation of the resolution makes one or more terms in the topic meaningless. For example, some definitions of the word "substantially" are so vague that they do not add specificity to the meaning of the resolution. To satisfy them, all the affirmative has to do is meet the meaning of "reduce." However, such a definition has the effect of making the word "substantially" meaningless. It no longer serves a function in the resolution. In this instance, the negative should argue that every word is in the resolution for a purpose and that the affirmative proposal does not satisfy the definition of substantially.

The process of developing arguments and responding to topicality for the affirmative is very similar to what I have described for the negative. The affirmative should demonstrate that their definition is reasonable, while that of the other side is not.

The previous discussion does not serve as a complete guide to the theory and strategy of debating about topicality. It does, however, serve as a necessary introduction to debating about federal policies dealing with juvenile crime.

Federal Policies Aimed at Reducing Juvenile Crime

Once again, the resolution states:

Resolved: That the federal government should establish a program to substantially reduce juvenile crime in the United States.

Federal government

The first important term in the resolution is "federal government." The relevant definition in *Webster's New Twentieth Century Dictionary* says "designating, of, or having to do with the central government of the United States. *Black's Law Dictionary* defines federal government as "The system of government administered in a nation formed by the union or confederation of several independent states." And *CJS* says that Federal "In American law, belonging to the general government or union of the states, founded on or organized under the constitution or laws of the United States."

Therefore, federal government seems to refer to the central government of the United States in Washington, including the executive branch, the Congress, independent agencies, and the Courts. In addition, the advocate of change could argue that "federal government" also includes within it the union of the fifty states. If this is the case, then the affirmative arguably can implement their proposal through the states as well as central government action. Such an approach might be superior to uniform national policy by allowing for state to state experimentation.

In addition, if "federal government" includes state action within it, negative counterproposals for dealing with the issue at the state level are arguably topical. In other words, a negative counterplan to have the states implement a juvenile justice reform proposal would not be legitimate, because the states are included within the "federal government."

Against the view that the states are included within the resolution, the negative might argue that such an interpretation is illegitimate, since it denies them the right to advocate non-federal policy options. The negative also might argue that the states may act in two different ways in relation to a social problem. When they act as part of a federal government solution, they do so in a generally uniform manner by following a national law. On the other hand, sometimes the states act on their own, independently of the central government. This second kind of action is arguably not within the jurisdiction of the federal government.

The negative also might make a completely different sort of topicality argument using the words "federal government." They could argue that when those words are used to refer to the central government they are capitalized. For example, the Webster's definition that I cited earlier includes the following notation, before the actual definition "[usually F-]." In other words, when referencing the central government, as opposed to the union of states, the term should be capitalized. If this is the case, then the topic does not allow action by the central government (since the term federal government is not in capitals), but only cooperative action by the states.

However, there are good reasons to reject the view that the lack of capitalization means the affirmative is precluded from advocating action by the central government. First, in the context of juvenile justice policy, the term federal government (without capitalization) is often used to refer to the central government. For example, Feyerherm notes how the requirements of the Juvenile Justice and Delinquency Prevention Act of 1974 (as amended) require the states to take certain action or risk loss of "federal funds" (B 4).

Second, while Federal is "usually" capitalized when referring to the central government, that is not always the case. If the framers of the resolution had meant to forbid central government action then they would have worded the resolution to say that "a confederation of states" should act. They did not do so.

Third, the argument that the failure to capitalize federal government precludes central government action, is unreasonable. It has the effect of outlawing consideration of how the United States as a unified country can confront juvenile crime. That makes no sense.

In summary, there are strong reasons to believe that the term federal government encompasses both the central government and also a union of states acting under the general direction of the central government

Should

The second important term in the resolution is should, which, by longstanding agreement in debate, means "ought to, but not necessarily will." In other words, debate focuses not on what the federal government will do, but on what it ought to do. This means that the affirmative need not prove that their plan will be passed by Congress. Nor is it legitimate for the negative to argue that public opposition means that the affirmative plan will be repealed. That would be what is known as a "should-would" argument.

While the negative cannot argue political feasibility, the presence of "should" in the resolution does not rule out negative arguments concerning the effect of a proposal on public opinion. For example, the negative might argue that the result of a proposal to legalize drugs would be enormous public backlash, which in turn would cause the Congress to repeal the measure legalizing drugs. Since this argument concerns the result of plan action, it is not sufficient for the affirmative to label it as a "should would" argument. It is a public backlash position that avoids the should-would principle.

Establish

The next important term in the resolution is "establish." The relevant definitions in *Webster's New Twentieth Century Dictionary* include:

1. to make steadfast, firm, or stable; to settle on a firm or permanent basis; to set or fix unalterably;
4. to found permanently; to institute or settle; to set up (a government, nation, business, etc.; as to establish a colony or an empire.

The *Oxford American Dictionary* defines establish to mean "to set up (a business or government etc.) on a permanent basis." Black's cites similar definitions including "To make or form; as to establish uniform laws governing naturalization or bankruptcy." and "To found, to create, to regulate."

Thus, the word establish would seem to allow the affirmative to implement a program dealing with juvenile crime. However, the negative might argue that the term only gives the affirmative the right to "found" a new program. Thus, the affirmative is precluded from expanding upon a current effort, because that program already has been "established."

This interpretation of establish, while at first consideration sensible, is not in fact legitimate. Initially, there are several definitions of establish which put the meaning as broader than "found." Establish also can mean to confirm, or organize a program. Second, given the many different programs out there dealing with juvenile crime, it would be unreasonable to require the affirmative to come up with a completely new program. If we require the affirmative to establish a program that has never been tried anywhere, that will put a nearly impossible burden on them. Such a view also has the unfortunate effect of forcing the affirmative to focus on completely untried policy options.

Third, any new proposal for creating a federal program would still meet the meaning of establish, even if similar current programs exist, because the affirmative is still advocating the establishment of a new program. The new program would be an expansion or correction of the previously existing policy. That new program would be "established" in the same way that the older programs had been created.

Thus, the term establish should not be of much import in the resolution. The term merely grants the affirmative the right to put their program into place.

"A"

The next important term in the resolution is the article "a," which is used in relation to program. According to *Black's Law Dictionary,* a means "'one' or 'any.'" In other words, the affirmative is allowed to implement their specific program.

The negative could argue, however, that "a" is singular. *Black's* notes that "It is placed before nouns of the singular number, denoting an individual object or quality individualized." Thus, the affirmative must be limited to "a" single program. If the affirmative advocates several policies, they are, in this view, violating the singular nature of "a" and are not topical.

The argument that the presence of "a" in the resolution limits the affirmative to advocacy of a single policy option is misguided. The presence of "a" in the resolution says nothing about the type or complexity of the program defended by the advocate of change. And the term program, as I will note in a moment, is broad enough to include a variety of policy proposals tied together in a single package.

Moreover, the argument that the affirmative may implement only a single change is unreasonable, since virtually every policy proposal contains multiple parts. In the context of juvenile justice policy, for instance, the literature is filled with arguments for the creation of a comprehensive approach to the problem. A comprehensive approach is one that attacks juvenile crime in several ways at different points in the system. Crucially, the negative interpretation of "a" as limiting the affirmative to a single policy change, obviously rules out a comprehensive approach. That, in turn, means that the affirmative is limited to defending non-comprehensive (inferior) policy options. Surely, that makes no sense.

Program

According to the *Oxford American Dictionary,* a program is "a plan of intended procedure." *Webster's New Twentieth Century Dictionary* provides a similar definition: "an outline of work to be done; a prearranged plan of procedure; as, the program of the administration." Interestingly, neither *Black's,* nor *CJS* defines the term.

Clearly, program is a broad term. In the context of the resolution, it refers to the proposal that would be implemented by the government. It is important to note that a "program" can refer to a wide variety of policies that are grouped together under a label. Note, the reference by Webster's to the "program of the administration." This means that the affirmative can include a number of different provisions within their program.

"To"

The next important term in the resolution is to. To designates the goal or aim that must be served by the affirmative proposal. *CJS* notes that "to" "is a flexible term, having no specific and no settled legal meaning, and its signification is to be ascertained from reason and the sense in which it is used." *CJS* continues "as commonly used, the word 'to' conveys the idea of movement toward and actually reaching a specified point or object, and the meaning is not satisfied unless the point or object is actually attained." But it also can "be used merely to express direction" (*CJS*). It is also "sometimes employed as indicating intention, purpose, or end" (*CJS*). *Webster's New Twentieth Century Dictionary* cites similar definitions. They define "to" as "in the direction of; toward" and as "for the purpose of; for; as, they came to our aid."

Oddly enough the word "to" is at the core of resolutional interpretation. There are two issues relating to the term. First, and much less importantly, the negative might argue that "to" requires the affirmative to actually attain their objective of decreasing juvenile crime. Recall the definition from *CJS* specifying that one must actually reach the objective. This would mean that the affirmative must have 100% proof of solvency or their proposal would not necessarily meet the "to" standard.

The view that "to" requires the affirmative to eliminate juvenile crime is not reasonable. First, it obviously would not be possible for any affirmative to eliminate all juvenile crime. Since that result is not feasible, it would be absurd to require the affirmative to meet an impossible standard, in order to fall within the resolution. Second, from the context of the sentence, the meaning of "to" in the resolution would seem to be "for the purpose of" or "in the direction of." To designates that the aim of the affirmative proposal must be to substantially reduce juvenile crime. As long as the affirmative meets that purpose, they satisfy the word "to" in the resolution. Moreover, it would be illegitimate to require the affirmative to prove the solvency of their proposal as defense of topicality. Topicality arguments concern the meaning language in context. That definition of meaning cannot depend upon an event taking place after the fact.

The second argument concerning the meaning of "to" is more important. The negative must be prepared to argue that the affirmative proposal must be "for the purpose of" reducing juvenile crime, as opposed to for some other purpose, but also resulting in such a decrease in crime. If the affirmative is allowed to defend any policy proposal that arguably could reduce juvenile crime, then there are essentially no limits on the policies included within the resolution.

Therefore, in order to fulfill the resolution, the aim of the program must be to reduce juvenile crime. In this view, it is not enough for the program to produce the effect of reducing juvenile crime; its primary purpose must be to achieve that end. This topicality position can be justified as a means of providing appropriate limitation to the resolution. Absent the "for the purpose of" approach, there is danger of abuse. Would, for instance, a program to reduce teen pregnancy be a legitimate means of reducing youth violence. Clearly, a successful anti-pregnancy program would reduce violence by youths. If there are fewer juveniles, it seems intuitively obvious that there will be less violence. By this standard, anything that effects the number of juveniles, their economic standard, their place in society, and so forth, legitimately would fall within the topic, which then would include aspects of virtually every domestic policy proposal.

Consider the following illustration of how far the resolution could be stretched. Professor James Johnson of the University of North Carolina argues that:

> There is strong evidence that the federal government's effort to create a laissez-faire business climate to facilitate the competitiveness of U.S. firms in the global marketplace has drastically altered the structure of economic opportunity in American society. (B 339)

In chapter two, I will cite experts who believe that lack of economic opportunity is a crucial factor in some youth violence. Based on this logic, a program strengthening anti-trust regulation would be topical, since it would reduce business control of the economy, resulting in improved economic conditions for workers, which in turn would improve the conditions for many poor families, creating better family conditions for kids, producing a decrease in juvenile violence. As this example indicates, if "to" is defined merely as "in the direction of" reducing youth violence, the resolution will be extremely broad.

Thus, the negative should argue that the word "to" requires the affirmative to defend a proposal that is designed, as part of its fundamental purposes, to substantially reduce juvenile violence. Programs directly relating to juvenile violence, some proposals for expanding or decreasing social programs, including welfare reform, options relating to television violence, among others would fit into the resolution. But policy proposals that indirectly might improve conditions that some believe lead to youth violence would not be within the resolution, because those policies are not primarily "for the purpose of" substantially reducing juvenile violence.

Against the view that resolutional action must be "for the purpose of" reducing juvenile violence, the advocate of change can make a number of powerful arguments. Initially, there are good contextual definitions suggesting that any number of social programs serve the purpose of reducing juvenile crime. For example, Terrie Moffitt, a psychologist at the University of Wisconsin, notes, "I'd put my money on public health programs to improve infant health and prenatal care as the best ways to prevent delinquency" (qtd. in P Bower 233). Judge Frank Orlando takes a very similar view, "The solution [to juvenile violence] is prevention and early intervention in the home and community, access to quality health care, teen-pregnancy prevention, intensive in-home social and medical services, and, most of all, full funding of Head Start, would be a beginning" (D *Juvenile Courts* 5). Representative Bruce Vento says that recreation and park programs serve the purpose of reducing crime. He notes that "The Urban Park and Recreation Programs under this Committee's jurisdiction are an *essential* part of the Federal Government's response to the epidemic of crime in America" (D *Urban Recreation* 9). Thus, there is good contextual evidence indicating that many social programs do serve the purpose of substantially reducing juvenile crime.

Second, the affirmative should argue that public policies often serve multiple purposes. Thus, a program of welfare reform may serve the purposes of reducing welfare spending, decreasing dependence on the system, cutting poverty, and reducing juvenile crime. In relation to this position, the affirmative should note that there is nothing in the resolution that limits them to advantages relating only to juvenile crime. It is perfectly legitimate to advocate positions that are aimed at reducing juvenile crime, as well as achieving other goals as well.

Third, the affirmative should argue that the "for the purpose of" definition is inferior to the "in direction of" definition, since the latter definition is more specific. How can one identify "the purpose" of any proposal? As a general rule, policy proposals often serve multiple purposes. Different people may identify different purposes for the program. Therefore, rather than relying on a definition of "to" as "for the purpose of," it makes sense to define the term as indicating the general direction in which the affirmative must act.

Of course, the negative should respond to the "in the direction of" response by claiming that it is so vague as to be useless for limiting the resolution. They also should note that the "in direction of" response, again combines the burdens of solvency and topicality and that such combination is not legitimate.

Fourth, the affirmative should argue that the "for the purpose of" topicality position is both overlimiting and unacceptably vague. It is overlimiting in that it restricts the affirmative to policies that are perceived to be for the purpose of reducing juvenile crime. It is arbitrary in that there may be no agreement on the purposes served by a given program. Thus, it makes sense to reject the position.

As long as the affirmative can defend their policy position as clearly related to the juvenile crime problem, they should have little trouble meeting the definition of "to." With this said, however, the "for the purpose of" interpretation of "to" should be a mainstay of a general negative strategy. The argument is needed if the negative is to limit the affirmative to proposals that are relatively directly related to the juvenile crime issue.

Substantially

The next important term in the resolution is "substantially." The word designates the goal of policy change, a major decrease in juvenile crime. *CJS* defines substantially as "A relative and elastic term which should be interpreted in accordance with the context in which it is used." *CJS* continues that the term means "in the main; essentially; solidly; actually; really; truly; competently." *CJS* also cites a case which defines substantially as "Strongly; for the most part." *Black's* cites similar definitions including "essentially" "in the main" "in substance."

Based on these definitions, the negative could argue that the affirmative must defend a policy producing a truly major decrease in juvenile crime. One approach is to look for definitions of substantially that specify the meaning of the term in a particular context. For example, *Black's Law Dictionary* defines the term "substantial performance" as meaning "no willful departure from the terms of the contract, and no omission in essential points." By analogy, the term "substantially" requires the affirmative to make truly major reductions in juvenile crime.

There are several problems with a topicality argument stating that the term substantially requires the affirmative to essentially eliminate juvenile crime. First, as *CJS* noted, there is considerable ambiguity about what the term means. A 5% reduction in juvenile crime may seem pretty substantial if you would have been victimized by someone in that 5%. Second, the resolution does not call for a substantial reduction in juvenile crime, it calls for establishment of a "program to substantially reduce juvenile crime." Therefore, the affirmative need not prove that their program in fact will make a major reduction in juvenile crime, only that it serves the purpose of substantially reducing juvenile crime or moves in the direction of accomplishing that aim. Thus, the advocate of change could argue that failure of the proposal to achieve the aim of producing a major reduction in juvenile crime has no bearing on whether that proposal falls within the resolution.

Third, in most cases the proponent of change will be claiming that their proposal will result in a major reduction in juvenile crime. Fourth, again this topicality position combines topicality and solvency arguments. The affirmative should argue that their proposal is aimed at producing a major reduction in juvenile crime and that solvency questions are irrelevant to the topicality debate.

Reduce

Reduce means "to lessen in any way, as in size, weight, amount, value, price, etc.; to diminish" (*Webster's New Twentieth Century Dictionary*). Thus, the affirmative must defend a policy aimed at a significant reduction in juvenile crime.

Reduce is unlikely to play a major role in debating the boundaries of the resolution. I already have explained that the affirmative need not prove that their proposal in fact will produce a substantial reduction in juvenile crime. Rather, they only need to indicate that it is aimed at producing that reduction.

In theory, the negative could argue that a proposal was not topical because it aimed at eliminating, rather than reducing, juvenile crime. However, it seems unlikely that any proposal actually could eliminate all juvenile crime. Moreover, the total elimination of juvenile crime still would seem to be a reduction of it. It would be intellectually absurd to reject a program, because it did "too good" a job of curtailing juvenile crime.

Juvenile Crime

The next important term in the resolution is "juvenile crime." These words specify the type of crime, which is to be reduced. Juvenile is defined by *Webster's New Twentieth Century Dictionary* as "pertaining to, characteristic of, or suited for children or young persons." *Black's* is even clearer, defining a juvenile as:

> A young person who has not yet attained the age at which he or she should be treated as an adult for the purposes of criminal law. In some states, this age is seventeen. Under the federal Juvenile Delinquency Act, a 'juvenile' is a person who has not attained his [or her] eighteenth birthday.

In general, juvenile is defined as synonymous with child. In an essay on "Juvenile Courts," *American Jurisprudence* notes, "The purpose of juvenile court legislation is to provide for the disposition of delinquent, dependent, neglected, and abandoned children by providing a complete scheme for treatment" (B 1052). So who is a child in the context of the juvenile courts? The simplest answer is that a juvenile is an underage law violator (B "Juvenile Courts" 1062). Usually, then a juvenile criminal is someone under a particular statutory age (generally 17, 18 or 21), who has committed a crime. *American Jurisprudence* notes in this regard that either the 18 or the 21 standard can be used: "A statute providing that an accused minor over 18 years of age, but under 21 years of age, may, but need not, be treated as a juvenile, does not deny equal protection of the law" (B "Juvenile Courts" 1063).

Crime is "a positive or negative act in violation of penal law" (*Black's*). It also "may be defined to be any act done in violation of those duties which an individual owes to the community" (*Black's*).

The obvious meaning of the words "juvenile crime" is to specify the type of crime that is to be reduced. There are several topicality positions that come out of these words. First, it could be argued that the affirmative proposal must be aimed at reducing juvenile crime and not some other type of crime. By this logic, for instance, a program to expand community policing would not be legitimate, because it would be aimed at reducing all crime, not just juvenile crime.

The view that the affirmative must focus exclusively on juvenile crime is misguided. The resolution requires the affirmative to establish a program "to substantially reduce juvenile crime." It in no way says that the program cannot produce other benefits as well.

The negative also might argue that the words "juvenile crime" mean that so-called "status offenses" lie outside the resolution. Senator Kohl of Wisconsin refers to status offenders within the juvenile justice system as committing behaviors such as drinking or skipping school "that would not be considered criminal if they were over 18 years old" (D Status 1). Thus, the negative might argue that it is illegitimate for the affirmative to focus on status offenses, since they really aren't crimes.

The claim that status offenses do not fall within the resolution is clearly misguided. It is true that status offenses do not apply to adults, but that is irrelevant, because they are crimes for juveniles. Perhaps status offenses should not be criminalized, but they have been and, thus, it is legitimate for the affirmative to advocate a proposal that would substantially reduce them.

Third, the negative could argue that given changes in state laws, much of what previously was defined as juvenile crime is no longer in that category. In chapter two I will describe the trend toward placing juveniles in adult courts. The negative could cite that trend and argue that the term "juvenile crime" should be used only in relation to people who are not treated as adults.

This argument is important, but the stronger view probably supports defining juvenile crime as an illegal act committed by someone under the age of 18 (or even 21). The fact that someone is tried in an adult court does not deny that the person is a juvenile criminal. All it means is that we have extended the application of adult laws to that person.

Finally, the negative should be prepared to argue that the reduction in juvenile crime must be a real decrease, rather than the result of a definitional change. For example, an affirmative program that eliminated status offenses could be defended as substantially reducing juvenile crime, since status offenses that previously had been labelled as criminal, no longer would be included in that category. But the reduction in crime only would be definitional, not real. There still would be just as many kids skipping school, illegally buying liquor, and so forth. We merely wouldn't be labeling them as criminals. Thus, the negative should argue that in order to provide appropriate negative ground, the affirmative must implement a program that actually reduces the criminal act, rather than defining it away.

The primary trouble with this topicality position is that affirmatives will be able to argue that programs redefining who is a juvenile will work at both a definitional and a policy level. Thus, for instance, a program to eliminate status offenses would be topical, not merely by eliminating the category, but also because eliminating status offense, would reduce the number of juveniles going to prison and allow the criminal justice system to focus on truly dangerous juvenile criminals.

In sum, juvenile crime refers to a criminal act committed by someone under age 18 or 21, who is still labelled by the law as a child.

in the United States

The final words of the resolution "in the United States," specify where the juvenile crime is to be reduced. In other words, the affirmative must defend a program that will reduce juvenile crime in the United States, as opposed to some other nation. It, therefore, would be illegitimate for the affirmative to advocate a foreign aid program to reduce juvenile crime in Russia.

Clearly, the words "in the United States" are unlikely to be important in most discussion of the juvenile crime resolution. It is hard to imagine the advocate of change choosing to focus on juvenile crime elsewhere in the world from the United States.

Conclusion

The juvenile crime resolution is both narrow and broad. It is narrow in the sense that the core area included within it is discrete and easily researchable. It is broad in the sense that virtually all domestic policies arguably impact juvenile crime.

In preparing to debate the resolution, the opponent of change should try to limit the affirmative to proposals directly relating to the juvenile crime issue. The key is to develop a strong position arguing that the word "to" requires the affirmative to defend a program directly aimed at reducing juvenile crime.

The remaining terms in the resolution will be important only in rare cases. There may be instances in which the opponent of change can argue that the affirmative program is aimed at producing an "insubstantial" reduction in juvenile crime. But, clearly the most important topicality issue relates to the meaning of "to."

2 The Magnitude and Characteristics of Juvenile Crime and a Consideration of Current Control Programs

This chapter sets the stage for an analysis of means of substantially reducing juvenile crime. Before the various policy alternatives for dealing with juvenile crime can be considered, it is necessary to understand the problem and present system responses to it. Therefore, in the first section of this chapter, I lay out the magnitude of and characteristics defining juvenile crime. In the second main section, I consider the various factors that have been cited as causes of juvenile crime. In the final section, I summarize the development of the legal system's approach to juvenile justice and describe status of current anti-juvenile crime efforts.

The Scope of Juvenile Crime

There is no question that juvenile crime poses a major threat to this nation. FBI figures indicate that two million juveniles were arrested in 1993, accounting for 17% of all arrests (B Howell, Krisberg and Jones 1). These figures provide only an indication of the impact of juvenile crime. Despite the fact that juvenile criminals apparently commit less than 20% of all crimes in this nation, they are responsible for a disproportionate percentage of violent crime. According to Representative George Miller, "perhaps 60% of the violent crimes are committed by young people between the ages of 10 and 20 years old" (D *Urban Recreation* 1).

The effect of this crime on children in our society is enormous. A recent Harris poll found that 40% of kids knew someone who had been shot by a gun (P Jourdan 20). Moreover, the problem is especially serious in the inner city, which is in turn the breeding ground for more juvenile crime. Minerbrook cites the experience at Chicago high schools: "A 1992 study of South Side Chicago high school students between the ages of 13 and 18 reported that 47% had seen a stabbing, 61% had witnessed a shooting, 45% had seen someone get killed and 25% had experienced all three" (P 37). Representative Major Owens notes the effect on the minority community, observing that "homicide is the leading cause of death among African-American males and females aged 15 to 24" (D *Joint Hearing* 1). Thus, juvenile crime plays a major role in creating horrible conditions in impoverished urban areas.

Unfortunately, the juvenile crime problem continues to escalate. In the first five years of the 1990s, juvenile arrests were up 12% (P Simons 20). The problem is still worse for crimes of violence. Juvenile arrests for violent crimes were up

27% between 1980 and 1990 (P Kotlowitz 40). More recent statistics indicate a
still faster pace. According to Lattimore, Visher, and Linster, "The latest statistics
from the Federal Bureau of Investigation (FBI) *Uniform Crime Reports* indicate
that arrests for violent index crime by youth under age 18 increased 47% between
1988 and 1992" (P 55). In that period, murder increased 51% and arrests for
carrying weapons were up 66% (P Lattimore, Visher, and Linster 55).

The trend away from minor crimes, such as vandalism, toward much
more serious crimes is quite clear. While as late as 1986, most cases in the New
York City Family Court were misdemeanors, by 1992 about 90% were felonies (P
Lacayo 61). This trend is quite apparent in FBI reports on arrest data for persons
under eighteen:

	1985	1990	1994
Murder	1,193	2,508	2,982
Robbery	28,688	33,582	45,046
Aggravated assault	32,809	50,425	64,648

(in P Morganthau 40).

The increase in violent juvenile crime since 1990 is especially disturbing, since
it comes at a time in which adult violent crime is no longer increasing (P LaVelle
85).

To make matters worse, the official figures may understate the problem. One
commentator estimates that juveniles actually commit 4,000 homicides and that
the number will rise to 5,000 (views of James Fox cited in P Morganthau 41). John
Calhoun, Executive Director of the National Crime Prevention Council, puts the
fantastic increase in violence into perspective:

> In 1929, Al Capone's men murdered seven of Bugs Moran's gang. This, the Saint
> Valentine's Day Massacre, became the stuff of American yore. It is referenced in the
> World Almanac. Seven deaths: that's the number of murders in DC over a long
> weekend. (in D *Hearing Regarding* 105–106)

Twenty years ago, young criminals vandalized cars or stole hubcaps. Now they
commit murder.

The long-term trend is particularly discouraging. According to the U.S. Department of Justice Family Research Council juvenile violent crime arrest rates per
100,000 have increased dramatically in the last thirty years, from 1341 in 1965, to
2741 in 1975, to 4200 in 1992 (in P Tapia 47). Some, including Hugh Price of the
Urban League, believe that the rate of juvenile crime could double again over the
next decade (cited in Herbert "Trouble" A15).

To make matters worse, it is possible that an increased juvenile crime wave is
inevitable, because of the population structure. As Gest and Friedman note,
"Population trends beyond the control of any politician will fuel the wave, and
even a multibillion dollar war on crime may fall way short of curbing it" (P 26).
They go on to quote James Alan Fox, a criminologist at Northeastern University,
"not only are violent teens maturing into even more violent young adults, but they

are being succeeded by a new and larger group of teenagers" (P 26). Mortimer Zuckerman, editor of U.S. News puts this ominous trend into perspective, noting that "In the next five years there will be at least 500,000 more males in the dangerous age range" (P 96). Thus, violent juvenile crime may get much worse in the future.

The problem is not just the increasing rate of violent juvenile crime. Of equal significance is the increasing severity of such violence. One sign of that severity is found in the number of violent acts now being committed by ten to fourteen year old children. One commentator notes that "Homicide arrests of kids ages 10 through 14 increased from 194 to 301 between 1988 and 1992" (P Lacayo 61). This development is reflective of a trend toward more and more serious and cold-blooded violence. Scott Minerbrook of *U.S. News* writes that we now have "A generation of stone killers" (P 33). Michael Marris of *Newsweek* agrees, characterizing youth criminals as "Young, Angry and Lethal" P 122).

This trend toward greater violence is reflected in a vast increase in youth murder. Since the mid 1980's, murder arrests for juveniles have more than doubled (P Gest and Friedman 26). The arrest rate apparently reflects the actual rate of commission. Bob Herbert notes, "the rate of known homicide offenders aged 14 to 17 has climbed from 16.2 per 100,000 youngsters in 1990 to 19.1 in 1994" (P "Trouble" A15).

The escalating trend toward youth violence has had a natural effect; more kids are in prison or a detention facility of some kind than ever before. On an average day about 100,000 juveniles are in prisons, jails, or some other sort of juvenile facility (P Lacayo 91). Over the course of a year, this means that more than a half million juveniles are placed in secured detention (B Howell, Krisberg and Jones 3). This rate reflects a one third increase "between 1983 and 1991" (B Wiebush et al 171).

Keeping juvenile criminals in prison is costly for society. First, the monetary expenditures required to keep juveniles in prisons and jails are enormous. Gregory McDonald of the General Accounting Office notes that in 1988 it cost $1.7 billion to hold youths in custody, a figure that surely has increased substantially since then. That works out to a cost of $29,600 per person, per year, which "was more expensive than sending a child to Harvard, Yale, or Princeton for a year" (D *Youth Violence Prevention* 11).

But there are other costs as well. Holding juveniles in overcrowded jails may make it difficult for them to leave a life of crime. In that regard, it is important to understand that conditions in juvenile detention centers, jails, and secure confinement facilities (juvenile prisons) vary considerably. In some areas, conditions are generally quite good. But in many instances, conditions are simply terrible. One study found that by 1989, about half of juveniles in such facilities were held in overcrowded conditions (B Schwartz and Willis 16). David Steinhart described a detention facility in San Francisco as "a cheerless building with water leaking from the ceilings, patches of paint and plaster missing, poor heating and ventilation, and a documented asbestos problem" (B 47). Keeping young offenders in such conditions can do little to rehabilitate them.

While most experts believe that juvenile crime is a serious and growing problem, not all agree with this conclusion. Initially, some theorists argue that delinquent juvenile behavior should not be viewed as dangerous in and of itself. In fact, there are experts who see delinquency as "a form of adaptive, problem-solving behavior, usually committed in response to problems involving frustrating and undesirable social environments" (P Brezina 39). By that, experts mean that delinquent behavior may help the child deal with a very difficult societal environment.

Others argue that the impact of juvenile crime has been overstated. For example, according to the Office of Juvenile Crime and Delinquency Prevention, only about 100,000 of 2.3 million arrests of juveniles in 1991 were for violent crimes (in D *Hearing Regarding* 34). Howell, Krisberg and Jones back up this view, by noting that "The vast majority of arrested juveniles in America are arrested for property crimes and other less serious offenses—not crimes of violence" (B 2).

Some experts even argue that the rate of juvenile crime is quite consistent with the average for all crime in our society. In this view, since juveniles are 13% of the general population and committed 13% of all violent crimes (B Howell, Krisberg and Jones 1), it could be argued that the juvenile crime problem is merely a reflection of the general crime problem in the country.

However, the arguments that juvenile crime is not a serious problem are not very strong. Initially, while delinquency may not be harmful in and of itself, the same cannot be said of violent acts. And juveniles may be committing many property crimes, but they also are committing a disproportionate percentage of crimes of violence in this country. Moreover, since the juvenile population includes kids under the age of ten, who commit very few violent crimes, the claim that juveniles commit only their population percentage of violent acts is clearly wrong.

In summary, the juvenile crime problem has been growing substantially, both in terms of numerical increase and in relation to severity. At this point, the best data indicates that these trends are likely continue or even expand in the future.

Characteristics of Juvenile Crime

In this section, my goal is to lay out salient characteristics that define juvenile crime.

Dangerous Offenders

While the juvenile crime problem has grown in leaps and bounds, that increase is not tied to a rapidly increasing delinquency problem. Instead, the escalation in juvenile crime is linked to a relatively small group of juveniles. According to the Office of Juvenile Justice and Delinquency Prevention, about 18% of delinquents can be labelled chronic offenders. This group commits over 60% of all offenses and approximately two-thirds of violent offenses (in D *Hearing Regarding* 23). Thus, most of the juvenile crime problem can be traced to the actions of a relatively small group of youths.

Crime in Schools

Much juvenile crime occurs in schools. Ronald D. Stephens, of the National School Safety Center, writes that "Nearly 3,000,000 thefts and violent crimes occur on or near school campuses every year" (P 29). The vast majority of these crimes undoubtedly are carried out by juveniles. The result is a situation in which many students feel that they must carry a weapon for self defense. According to Senator DeConcini, "About one out of every 5 high school students now carries a firearm, knife or club to school on a regular basis" (D *Youth Violence: A Community* 5).

It is important to note that while much crime occurs in school, that does not necessarily make schools the most dangerous place in the community. In many instances, according to Victor Herbert, a superintendent in the Phoenix area, schools are "the safest places in their [kids} lives" (D *Youth Violence: A Community* 53).

Status Offenses

A status offense is an act that would not be a crime if committed by an adult, but is a crime for a child. Included in the category are truancy, not obeying parents, staying out past a curfew, and so forth. The number of juveniles arrested for status offenses is down dramatically, largely because of changes in court practice and Federal law. With this said, there are still many juveniles who are punished for status offenses. Senator Kohl reports that in 1991, "On any given day in this country, some 3,000 status offenders and nonoffenders who are just abused or neglected kids are locked up, and most often they are locked up because there is no room in community programs" (D *Status* 1).

Moreover, even where status offenses have been all but eliminated, the judicial system may find a backdoor means of punishing youths. Recently, Randall Beger, of the University of Wisconsin-Eau Claire, found that Illinois judges were using contempt orders to "force nondelinquent status offenders to comply with routine court directives" (P 54). Beger argues that these acts are inconsistent with the law governing use of contempt citations (P 54, 65-66). This inconsistency, however, has not stopped judges from using contempt power. Barry Feld of the University of Minnesota notes that "Several courts have approved the use of the criminal contempt power to 'bootstrap' status offenders into delinquents who may then be incarcerated" (D *Juvenile Courts* 171).

On the other hand, it is easy to exaggerate the problem of status offenders. Under the Juvenile Justice and Delinquency Prevention Act, the Federal Government has led an initiative in which the states have deinstitutionalized status offenders (B Feyerherm 3). This initiative largely has been successful. According to Senator Biden, between 1974 and 1988 the states reduced the number of status offenders held in "secure detention facilities" from 187,000 to 10,000 (D *Status* 6-7). And by 1991, according to the Office of Juvenile Justice and Delinquency Prevention, only about 3% of all juvenile offenders in public juvenile facilities were status offenders, although the figure was disproportionately high for girls, 12.9% (in D *Hearing Regarding* 21).

Sex

There are far more violent female juvenile offenders now than in the past. We no longer live in an era when fighting is almost exclusively male. With this said, the juvenile crime problem, especially in relation to murder and other violent crimes, is still primarily one relating to boys (Office of Juvenile Justice and Delinquency Prevention in D *Hearing Regarding* 35).

One surprising fact is that girls often are sentenced to longer periods in juvenile facilities than their male counterparts, and for less important offenses. The reason for this is that the courts often give girls much longer sentences for status offenses than they do boys (P Anderson 13). This undoubtedly reflect societal stereotypes about proper gender roles. Thus, a drunken or truant girl is viewed as more deviant than a drunken or truant boy. Because of a dearth of community-based facilities, girls committing status offenses (including drunkenness or truancy) often are placed in institutions (P Anderson 14). Thus it is not surprising that while girls "accounted for only 13.8% of the total detention center population, females made up just under 50% of all status offenders in detention centers in 1989" (B Schwartz and Willis 18).

Minority Group Treatment

One aspect of the juvenile crime problem that has received a great deal of consideration is the degree to which minority group members are treated equitably in the juvenile justice system.

In considering this issue, it is important to recognize that juvenile crime is an endemic problem in urban areas possessing a high percentage of minority group members. The level of juvenile crime in such areas is reflected in the increase in the murder rate for black youth from about 71 per 100,000 in 1978 to almost 115 in 1989 (P Stevens "Treating Violence" 30). Fox and Pierce of Northeastern University note that "Black males aged 15–24, while only one percent of the U.S. population, constitute 14% of the victims of homicide and 19% of the perpetrators" (P 25).

Given the magnitude of the juvenile crime problem for minority youths (both committing it and suffering from it), it is unsurprising that a very high percentage of those prosecuted for juvenile crime are minority group members. In fact, some experts believe that minority youths may comprise "more than half of all the juveniles incarcerated" in the United States (Ira Schwartz of the Hubert Humphrey Center cited in B Feyerherm 7).

In percentage terms, this places minority youths at much greater risk of prosecution than white kids. One study indicates, for example, that Hispanic youths are between 2.3 and 2.6 times more likely to be incarcerated than white male youths (B Feyerherm 8). Similar studies could be cited for African American youths. The result is that a disproportionate percent of incarcerated youth offenders belong to a minority group. For example, Welsh, Harris, and Jenkins cite research in Pennsylvania which "found that minority youths aged 10 through 17 constituted 75% of all those confined in secure detention facilities, even though minorities comprised only 12% of the state juvenile population" (P 77). Moreover, minority youths are most likely to be sent to the most prison-like facilities (views of Barry Krisberg of the National Council on Crime and Delinquency, cited in B Feyerherm 8).

It appears that the overrepresentation is not tied to the seriousness of the act committed by the juvenile. A study conducted at the University of Colorado found that for the same level of delinquency, black juveniles were twice as likely to be arrested as white youths (cited in B Feyerherm 10). One recent study argues that "fear" of violent crime and the perception that minority youths are more dangerous than white youths is the primary explanation for the differential treatment (see the study of Washington State conducted by Bridges, Conley, Engen and Price-Spratlen 148). Frazier and Bishop argue that one reason for the overrepresentation is that state officials misperceive that drugs and family problems are more prevalent in minority than white communities. They recommend improved record keeping and diversity training to deal with these problems (B 42–43).

While it is clear that in terms of percentages there are far more minority juveniles in prison than their percentage in the population, there is disagreement about whether prejudice is the cause of this disparity. Some argue that most of the disparity is caused by higher rates of criminal activity among minority youth, than among juveniles overall. According to Bridges, Conley, Engen and Price-Spratlen, a review of the literature found that 37% of the studies on ethnic characteristics of juveniles found no significant differences in treatment (of course 63% found such differences) (B 129). Moreover, research on the most serious crimes does not indicate differential treatment (B Leonard and Sontheimer 101).

Even where differential treatment is found, the disparity may not be that significant. For example, research in Florida found that for the crime of simple battery against a person, the difference in the percentage of white and black youths who will be recommended for processing into the system was 7% (54% versus 47%) (B Frazier and Bishop 25). The difference in the detention rate was between 16% and 12% (B Frazier and Bishop 25). While the authors of this study conclude that these differences are significant, they are nowhere near the enormous disparity in imprisonment rates cited earlier.

Moreover, some justify the disparate sentencing of white and black juveniles as justified by the need to control violent crime in impoverished areas. In this regard, the attitudes of black Americans can be cited to justify harsh treatment of black juvenile offenders. Sarah Glazer notes that a survey conducted by researchers at the University of Michigan

> found that African American parents have much tougher attitudes toward juvenile criminals than other racial or ethnic groups—including white parents. The majority favors adult trials and terms in adult prisons for juveniles who commit violent crimes. African American parents tend to be keenly aware that the violence is increasingly black-on-black and that juvenile violence most likely claims the lives of young, black males. (P "Juvenile" 176)

Moreover, recent research indicates that the perceived certainty of punishment in the black community is higher than that in the white community (see P Yu and Liska). This "unfairness" might have a positive effect. The perceived greater degree of certainty of punishment should help keep down black on black crime rates and thus protect the black community from even more serious crime problems.

In addition, the present system has taken steps to address the disparities. Under 1989 guidelines established by the Juvenile Justice and Delinquency Prevention Formula Grant Program, states must plan means to reduce overrepresentation in order to "continue receipt of federal funds" (B Feyerherm 4). With that said, programs to reduce disparities between the treatment of white and minority group youths in the juvenile justice system are, however, in an early stage of development and are not widespread across the United States (P Welsh, Harris, and Jenkins 77).

The bad news is that even if it were clear that the disparity in arrest and imprisonment statistics reflected pure prejudice, it would not necessarily be easy to reduce the disparity. Some believe that the overrepresentation of minority groups in the juvenile justice system is tied to decisions of the police about which individuals to bring into the system. For example, Wordes and Bynum have found that the police disproportionately target minority youths (B 62) The problem is that the "supply" of minority youths for potential confinement is much higher than the "supply" of non-minority youths (see B Feyerherm 5). Given the supply imbalance, it is arguable that the disparity in treatment cannot be solved via reform of the legal system alone.

On the other hand, some believe that the disparities are related to racism. A survey in Florida found that some of those who deal with juvenile crime believe that the differential treatment can be traced to "institutional racism" (B Frazier and Bishop 35). Obviously, the systemic problems associated with this form of racism may be extremely difficult to solve.

Moreover, reforming one aspect of the present system may lead to a backlash in another part of the system, thwarting the reform effort. This problem has been refereed to as systemic homeostasis. The idea is that systems have a tendency to respond to potential reforms in such a way that little change occurs. According to Feyerherm: "Most systems have some form of quasi-stationary equilibrium around which they fluctuate. An effort to change a system in one area is likely to produce a counterbalancing reaction, even though that reaction may not be consciously intended as racist" (B 6).

In sum, minority group youths are arrested and sentenced to secure detention facilities at a much higher rate than white youths. On the other hand, they also commit far more crimes, a fact which explains part, but not all, of the disparity. Some see the remaining disparity as proof of institutional racism; others see it as the result of a reasonable crime fighting strategy. In any case, it is not clear that either programs existing in the present system or other systemic reforms—for example, the use of sentencing guidelines and training workshops (see B Pope 208-209)—will have much effect in reducing the disparity.

Gang Violence

Most experts agree that the gang violence problem is growing. First, gangs are spreading across the country. According to the FBI, Los Angeles gangs such as the Crips and Bloods have spread to 45 cities in the west and Midwest (P Howell 509; also see B Howell "Gangs and Youth Violence" for a review of the literature). Gangs also may be spreading to smaller cities, largely due to family relocation (P Howell 509). Senator Kohn of Wisconsin has observed that while only 23 cities reported gang activity in the middle 1960s, currently more than 700 do so (D *The Gang Problem* 1). And the gang problem may be spreading even to rural areas (testimony of St. Louis police sergeant Michael Nichols in D *The Gang Problem* 19–20).

Second, the violence problem has followed the geographical pattern of gang dispersal. Senator Hatch reports that even in Utah, the rate of gang violence has been escalating rapidly. Between 1992 and 1993, the number of gang-related offenses tripled from a little over 1700 a year to almost 5,500 (D *The Gang Problem* 4). Apparently, the level of violence also is increasing (P Howell 509).

At the same time, not all evidence supports the view that gang violence represents an escalating problem. Initially, the impact of gang violence may be overstated, since much of it is internally directed at those who also are members of a gang. Howell notes, for instance, that "Most gang violence appears to be related to turf disputes" (P 510). Stevens supports this view, noting that only 3% of U.S. murders are committed by gangs and that most of them are linked to "revenge for insults or previous violence" (P "Treating Violence" 25).

In addition, gang membership may not be as great as some estimate. Research by Esbensen and Huizinga puts the percentage of urban youths who are involved in gangs at between 3% and 7%, depending upon the study and age of the youths (P 581). They conclude that "even in a sample of high-risk urban youths, gang membership is a statistically infrequent phenomenon" (P 581). It also is important to recognize that many gang members are young adults, not juveniles. According to Senator Hatch of Utah, only about 35% of gang members are juveniles (in D *The Gang Problem* 4).

Thus, while the gang problem is clearly increasing, the gang problem is not as serious as some news reports suggest.

Juvenile Drug Use

Another important characteristic defining juvenile crime is drug use. Recently, rates of drug use among juveniles have increased. According to Sarah Glazer, who writes for *CQ Researcher,* a recent survey found that the percentage of eighth graders who admitted to using marijuana in the previous year, doubled from 1991 to 1994, reaching 13% (P "Preventing" 657). Other studies find a similar pattern of increase. The National Parents' Resource Institute for Drug Education (PRIDE), has "reported significant increases among teenagers for crack, cocaine, heroin, LSD, non-LSD hallucinogens, inhalants, and marijuana" (Senator Coverdale in CR "Department of Commerce" 7 December 1995 S18167). Thus, drug use is one area in which juvenile crime is increasing. It is, as I will explain later, also a factor that many have identified as important in the overall escalation of juvenile crime.

Summary of Characteristics

In the previous section, I have noted seven important characteristics of juvenile crime. First, violent juvenile crime is linked to relatively few, extremely dangerous offenders. Second, much juvenile crime occurs in schools. Third, while most status offenders have been removed from the criminal justice system, there are still thousands who are processed through the system. Fourth, most violent juvenile offenders are male, but females are sentenced disproportionately to detention facilities. Fifth, there are enormous disparities in the treatment of minority and white youth offenders. Sixth, gang violence is increasing rapidly. Finally, drug crime among juveniles recently has increased dramatically.

The Causes of Juvenile Crime

In this section, I discuss a number of different factors that have been proposed as causes of juvenile crime. It is especially important for advocates to be aware of the debate about causation, since any juvenile crime program must be able to overcome the causal factors in order to be effective.

However, before considering the causes of juvenile crime, it is important to note that kids don't suddenly decide to be a juvenile criminal. Rather, there are distinct developmental paths which lead to escalating patterns of juvenile crime.

Experts believe that juvenile delinquency develops in three main ways. In the *authority conflict pathway,* it develops from stubborn behavior, to defiance or disobedience in the home and elsewhere, to authority avoidance, including truancy and staying out late. In the overt pathway, delinquency begins with minor aggression, such as bullying, and the progresses to fighting and finally to violence. In the covert pathway, it begins with a minor covert criminal act such as shoplifting, and then progresses to property damage (vandalism, for instance) and then to more serious covert actions, including burglary (see B Thornberry et al 222–223).

It is important to keep these pathways in mind when considering the factors causing juvenile crime. Society is most concerned with those juveniles who follow the overt pathway. These individuals commit a high percentage of juvenile crimes of violence. Unfortunately, the causal factors that lead youths into the overt pathway may be especially hard to confront.

The Growth of Gangs as a Causal Factor in Escalating Violence

Earlier, I cited information on the growth of gangs. It seems intuitively obvious to many that this growth of gangs is a primary cause of youth violence. The argument is simply that gangs recruit kids into a life of drugs and violence. While this is a common perception, the best evidence does not support it.

Rather than gangs being a major cause of juvenile violence, it seems more likely that their development reflects the other factors causing that violence. Quite a lot of evidence supports this view. Initially, it is important to understand that gangs are not a new phenomenon. Perhaps the foremost researcher on gangs, Irving Spergel, has documented their existence throughout American history and in other societies as well (B 3-11). This point is important for policy analysis. If gangs have been common at earlier times in American history (when juvenile crime was much lower than today) that indicates that some other factor than gang membership may be responsible for the recent rise in juvenile crime.

Moreover, research indicates that gangs per se are not necessarily a key factor in juvenile crime, even in drug sales. In the context of drug crime, for instance, individual gang members, but not gangs per se, are involved in drug distribution. For example, Esbensen and Huizinga note that drug sales was not "an organized gang activity involving all gang members" (P 582). An argument could be developed that these individuals would be involved with drugs, regardless of their link to gangs (P Howell 509).

Nor are gangs always harmful. Goldstein and Glick argue that some gangs apparently act as "prosocial" institutions (B). This is a key point. Juveniles join gangs not primarily as a vehicle for starting a criminal career. They join the gang in order to become part of a strong culture, which serves many of the functions of a family. The gang provides support and friendship. There is an argument that the growth of gangs in impoverished urban centers is a sign of the terrible conditions in these places. Thus, some argue that it is not the gang that causes juvenile crime, but, rather, gang membership is a reflection of the social conditions that actually are the proximate cause of the crime.

Drug Crime

Many experts believe that drug use has played a major role in increasing rates of juvenile crime. For example, one recent study found that crack cocaine use leads to increased robberies, a small increase in murder, but no increase in burglaries (P Baumer 311). Thus, the movement in the middle 1970s of juvenile drug users away from marijuana toward cocaine may explain part of the increased rate of juvenile crime. In this regard, Sarah Glazer notes that "The unprecedented surge in violent youth crime coincided with a dramatic increase—over 700 percent—in the juvenile heroin and cocaine arrest rate during the 1980s, according to the Justice Department" (P "Juvenile" 171). The obvious inference is that increasing drug use caused the increase in crime.

Changes in drug use and drug sales may account for a large part of the vast increase in youth crime and violence. For example, the National Drug Strategy document speculates that the recent doubling of the youth homicide rate, when the adult rate has not changed, may "relate to the nature of illegal drug markets, the predatory practices of drug dealers, and the inability of the juvenile justice system to adequately deal with violent juvenile offenders" (D *President's Drug Control* 30). This conclusion is supported by the words of one commentator, who concludes that drug dealing has "fueled a prodigious arms race on America's streets" (P Minerbrook 37). A similar judgment has been made by the Parent Resource Institute for Drug Education (PRIDE), which found that "students who bring guns to school, participate in gang activities, threaten a teacher or another student at school, contemplate suicide, or are in trouble with the police, are more likely to use drugs than are students who do not engage in these behaviors" (D *President's Drug Control* 30).

Relative drug usage rates among the young also may play a role in the increased rates of juvenile crime. While about one in three of all Americans have used an illicit drug (D *President's Drug Control* 9), the rate of use among youth is much higher (D *President's Drug Control* 9) The report notes that "The activities of the chronic, hardcore drug user directly and indirectly account for high rates of crime, violence, and negative health consequences in this country" (D *President's Drug Control* 9–10). This may explain why between 1985 and 1989, those detained in delinquency cases related to drugs increased by over 250% (Office of Juvenile Justice and Delinquency Prevention in D *Hearing Regarding* 22).

While there is strong evidence that drug use, especially changing patterns of drug use and increased use of firearms relating to drug marketing, has played a role in escalating levels of youth violence, there is also data denying that conclusion. It should be noted that overall use of drugs is way down from historic highs that occurred in the late 1970s. For example, in 1979 about 23 million people used illicit drugs in a given month. By 1993, the figure was approximately 12 million (see figure 2-2 D *President's Drug Control* 19). Cocaine use is down from a peak of over 5 million monthly users to less than 2 million (D *President's Drug Control* 19; also see P Glazer "Preventing" 658).

The fact that drug use is not nearly as high in the middle 1990s as it was in the 1970s could be cited to deny that drug use has played a crucial role in causing juvenile crime. It is important to remember that juvenile violence has increased dramatically since the late 1970s when drug use peaked. Juvenile crime increased dramatically at a time when juvenile drug use was decreasing. It, therefore, may not be sensible to blame juvenile crime on the recent surge in drug use.

Clearly, drugs and juvenile crime are related. The best argument concerning that relationship may be that from the late 1970s to the early 1990s, violence related to drug sales gradually escalated in a pattern similar to an arms race in the international arena. Since many of those involved in drug sales were juveniles, the result was a major increase in the violence level found in juvenile crime.

Decline of the Family

There is little doubt about the third factor that is often cited as a cause of juvenile crime, decline of the family. Virtually all experts agree that the decline of the family as a strong institution, especially in impoverished central cities, has played a major role in rising rates of juvenile crime. Several different types of data support the conclusion that weakened family structure has led to escalating youth violence.

First, research strongly supports the conclusion that dysfunctional family life often leads to juvenile delinquency and crime. For example, in a study of youth offenders in California, Lattimore and her colleagues found that "evidence of family violence, parental criminality, and parental neglect or poor supervision significantly increased parolees' risk of rearrest for violent crimes" (P 77). A closely related point concerns severe childhood maltreatment. Research now indicates that maltreatment correlates to delinquency and that more serious maltreatment and more serious delinquency also are related (P Smith and Thornberry 451). Professor Eisenman explains in this regard that "Dysfunctional families frequently are found when the backgrounds of youthful offenders are investigated" (P 27). A study of juveniles on death row, found that 12 out of 14 had been seriously abused (P Minerbrook 36).

Second, evidence indicates that the decline of strong two-parent families has led to greater rates of youth violence. Juvenile crime is most prevalent in single parent families (P Gest and Friedman 26).

Third, the problem is not limited to single-parent or dysfunctional families. Some researchers believe that many parents simply are not spending enough time with their kids. Conservative commentator and Watergate felon Charles Colson writes "Today parents spend 40% less time with their children than their own parents did" (P Tapia 46). One result may be increased juvenile delinquency.

The consensus of opinion seems to support the view that a variety of problems in family life have created conditions which lead to juvenile crime. According to Patrick Fagan of the Heritage Foundation, "There is a wealth of evidence in the professional literature of criminology and sociology to suggest that the breakdown of the family is the real root cause of crime in America" (P 157). Mort Zuckerman of *U.S. News* also emphasizes the centrality of the family. He says simply that "the root cause of their [juvenile] alienation is the destruction of the family" (P 96).

Poverty

Poverty is a fourth factor that often is cited as causing juvenile crime. The argument is quite simple. Poor children grow up in deprivation. In order to get both basic needs and the luxuries that they see others consuming, these deprived kids turn to crime. Moreover, poor kids are routinely provided with inferior education and health care; they often are abused and certainly do not share the varied opportunities that middle and upper class children receive every day. In this environment, increased crime seems a logical result.

There is no question that poverty is a major problem for America's children. Senator Dodd notes that 26% of kids under three in the United States are growing up in poverty, which makes us the worst industrialized society in the world for taking care of children (in D *Hope For Tomorrow* 11). And research does suggest a link between poverty and crime. The American Psychological Association reports, "Many social science disciplines, in addition to psychology, have firmly established that poverty and its contextual life circumstances are major determinants of violence" (qtd. in P Gitlin 93).

As poor kids grow into adolescence, they may perceive that they have no chance to achieve the kind of affluent life style that they see others leading. According to Fox and Pierce, "A growing number of teens and pre-teens see few attractive alternatives to violence, drug use, and gang membership. For them, the American Dream is a nightmare. There may be little to hope for and live for, but plenty to die for and even kill for" (P 25).

Additionally, some argue that poverty is associated with other economic problems that also may be tied to juvenile crime. For instance, a great deal of research suggests that crime and unemployment are strongly related (see P Hagan 465). Carl Pople notes that "members of the underclass [who rarely are employed] comprise the bulk of juvenile and adult institutionalized populations and represent the most frequent clients of the criminal justice system" (B 213). Thus, unemployment and other factors causing poverty, also may be factors involved with juvenile crime.

Drug use also interrelates with poverty as a factor causing juvenile crime. Crack use is clearly related to poverty. According to Johnson, Golub and Fagan, "Many crack sellers came from households where three generations or more had been on welfare or lived below the poverty line (excluding their illegal income) for their entire lives" (P 286). This conclusion is supported by Baumer's judgment that "economic deprivation" is a "source of high levels of illicit drug use" (P 322). Therefore, high rates of drug use are associated with poverty and may be one factor in the recent increases in juvenile crime.

Others argue that a variety of economic circumstances that are related to poverty, including industrial downsizing, cuts in social programs, declining value of the minimum wage, and so forth, have created a social setting that leads to youth (especially gang) violence (see P Rodriguez 607).

While there is strong evidence that poverty and other forms of economic deprivation influence levels of juvenile crime, there are also strong counter arguments to this conclusion. Some experts argue that increased crime rates have not tracked poverty or unemployment rates. Professor Norman Brill, formerly of UCLA School of Medicine, explains:

"It is of interest that the dramatic increase in violent crime in the U.S. in the first half of the 1970's (when it seems to have started) was not associated with any increase in poverty or unemployment." He adds, "During the depression in the 30's with its huge unemployment and poverty, one could walk city streets without fear and there was no need for armed guards in schoolhouse halls" (B 17).

Clearly, Brill's argument that levels of youth violence and economic growth and unemployment have not been strongly correlated is a good one, but the stronger argument is on the other side. It is undeniable that poor children are more prone to juvenile crime. And there are several strongly plausible explanations for how poverty and juvenile crime might be related. Moreover, Brill seems to answer his own argument when he explains the rise of juvenile crime based on disorder in the larger society (B 18-19). But that disorder in the larger society is the explanation behind the historical anomalies cited by Brill. Juvenile crime did not skyrocket in the 1930s, because of the strong family and other institutions in society, With the breakdown of such institutions, there are no longer forces preventing poor kids from becoming criminals. Thus, poverty and economic deprivation are in all likelihood very important factors in the increase in youth crime.

Racism

A fifth factor cited by some in the rise in youth crime is racism. For example, Spergel notes evidence that racism is one of the factors leading to the growth of gangs (B 161-163). Of course, racism also may be an indirect cause of juvenile crime by limiting the opportunities that minority group members have to make it in society.

While it is plausible that racism is a factor in juvenile crime, especially because it acts to limit economic opportunity for minority youths, there are counterarguments that also need to be considered. For example, youth crime has risen dramatically in the same period that racism as a general problem in society has been decreasing. I am not denying the continued impact of racial prejudice in our society, but surely all would agree that there is far less prejudice in 1995 than there was in 1965 or 1955. The thirty years since 1965 have seen the development of an African-American middle class and the success of many people of color in the larger society. Yet, at the same time that economic and other opportunities have been growing, youth crime also has been increasing. If racism were the primary cause of violent juvenile crime, we should have a much reduced juvenile crime problem today than in the past.

Moreover, the suggestion that juvenile crime is caused by racism ignores the significant increases in juvenile crime among white youths. Racism is not the cause of the drug use of Bobby and Betty Suburbia. Thus, there are good reasons to doubt whether racism is a primary cause of the rise of youth violence.

Genetics

A sixth factor cited by some in the rise of youth crime is that criminals possess a genetic predisposition for crime. Criminals generally possess substantially less intelligence than other Americans. According to Bruce Bower, "Research consistently places the average IQ of convicted lawbreakers at 92, some 8 points below the population average and 10 points below the average for law-abiding folks" (P 232). He goes on to note that repeat offenders have even lower IQs (P 232). Research also indicates that juvenile delinquents are likely to act impulsively and have poor verbal skills (P Bower 232).

The claims that criminal possess lower skill levels than other Americans and often have genetic problems that predispose them for deviant behavior seem quite strong. Yet, genetics clearly is an inadequate explanation for the increase in juvenile crime. The genetic structure of the U.S. population did not change radically in 1980 at about the time the rise in juvenile crime began. The fact that genetics have remained constant, while juvenile crime has increased, is strong evidence that genetics are not a primary cause of increased juvenile crime.

Strain

A final explanation for the recent increase in juvenile crime can be found in strain theory. Strain theory pulls together several of the factors already discussed and places them in a coherent framework. One variant of the approach says that "strain" is related to delinquency and is produced by three factors: inability to achieve desired results, loss of valued objects, and negative stimuli (summarized in P Paternoster and Mazerolle 235). The argument is that these three factors create pressures that push juveniles into crime.

Recent empirical research supports strain theory to some degree (P Paternoster and Mazerolle 235-263). The idea that the "strain" on children in impoverished areas plays a role in pushing them into crime is also supported by the research of James Garbarino, of the Erikson Institute, who has been cited as arguing that kids in the inner city show many of the same symptoms that you might find in children from a war-torn country, such as Bosnia (P Minerbrook 33).

While there seems to be some significant support for strain theory, it is important to recognize the weakness of the approach. It is undoubtedly true that potential juvenile criminals are under more strain than other kids. Almost by definition, kids in supportive, non-threatening environments, rarely become criminals. The difficulty is in defining the sources of the strain that oppresses some youths. Without identifying those specific sources, strain theory is not very helpful.

Summary of Causal Factors

In sum, a variety of factors play a crucial role in the development of juvenile crime. The best evidence seems to support the argument that poverty (along with a general lack of economic opportunity) and decline of the family have been the most important factors in the recent rise in youth crime.

The Status of Juvenile Crime Programs

Before one rationally can consider the alternatives for reforming the juvenile justice system, it is important to understand the status of current programs in that system. In this section, I first sketch the development of juvenile law and consider issues relating to how juveniles currently are treated in the juvenile justice system. I then describe current state efforts to control juvenile crime and conclude with a discussion of the evolution of Federal programs aimed at reducing youth violence.

The Development of Juvenile Law

Until the last part of the 19th century, juveniles were treated in much the same way as adults. Beginning with the first juvenile court in Chicago in 1899, however, the nation moved rapidly toward establishing a separate justice system for juveniles in which the primary goal was treatment. The legal work, *American Jurisprudence,* summarizes the philosophy of the juvenile court system that developed:

> the philosophy of juvenile court laws is that the juvenile is to be considered and treated not as a criminal, but as a person requiring care, education, and protection. A fundamental aim of the juvenile laws is the prevention of delinquency of children. Consequently, such laws are not punitive, but are corrective and protective in that their purpose is to make good citizens of potentially bad ones. In other words, the welfare of the child lies at the very foundation of the statutory scheme. (B "Juvenile Courts" 1052)

In order to achieve its purposes, juvenile courts have utilized simpler procedures than adult courts (B "Juvenile Courts" 1053). *American Jurisprudence* continues: "The juvenile court's purpose is more reformative than punitive. Thus, in juvenile court, technicalities and formalities are largely done away with. . ." (B 1055). Records often are sealed in the juvenile court context (B "Juvenile Courts" 1054).

Historically, juvenile defendants were governed by the *parens patriae* doctrine, under which the court exercised broad discretion better to protect the child. One result was that traditional protections of trial rights were not extended to children (P Sanborn 599; also see B Guarino-Ghezzi and Loughran 6-7). Moreover, the juvenile court had control over a a wide range of acts that were not considered crimes when committed by adults. These "status offenses" included truancy and a variety of "lifestyle issues" relating to sexuality and other behavior (B Guarino-Ghezzi and Loughran 6).

The juvenile system was designed to protect the child, but it often produced precisely the opposite result, oppression. Juvenile courts did not protect the due process rights of children. They could impose extremely long sentences for the purpose of "rehabilitating" the child. And the treatment of status offenders was obviously unfair, since adults were not punished for similar offenses. These problems in the juvenile system led both the Congress and the Supreme Court to reform it.

In the 1967 case, In re Gault, the Supreme Court guaranteed that juvenile courts must provide meaningful hearings for juveniles who wanted them. In 1970, the Court held that "juvenile court adjudications had to be based upon proof beyond a reasonable doubt" (*In re Winship,* see P Sanborn 599). However, the courts also ruled that the juvenile was not entitled to a trial by his peers and that a non-adversary process could be appropriate (P Sanborn 599, 600). In these cases, and others that followed, the Court applied a due process revolution to the juvenile courts, while still maintaining some differences in formality from adult courts. "As a result of the due process revolution, juveniles in court now have legal rights that run parallel to adults in most areas of the law, although juvenile courts operate with less formality" (B Guarino-Ghezzi and Loughran 13–14).

Due Process Protection

While the courts have imposed due process protection standards upon the juvenile justice system, these standards are not always enforced. Two commentators note that "It is apparent from anecdotal as well as systematic evidence that due process protections are highly uneven across juvenile courts" (B Guarino-Ghezzi and Loughran 97). One recent survey of those who work in the juvenile court system concluded that "some juvenile courts have retained some characteristics of parens patriae, which was the dominant philosophy of the pre-*Gualt* era" (P Sanborn 612).

A variety of factors may cause the system to act in a manner that is not procedurally fair. Some experts argue that due to excessive case-load, a lack of concern for juvenile rights, or too great an emphasis on treatment, many appropriate safeguards are not provided for juveniles (see P Sanborn 600–603).

One area of particular concern is whether juveniles are provided with attorneys. Some experts believe that juveniles often are not given the benefit of counsel and that, as a consequence, their rights are not fully protected. Barry Feld argues that in Minnesota about 45% of juveniles do not receive counsel (D *Juvenile Courts* 163–164). Feld says that national data indicates that this is a general problem across the United States (D *Juvenile Courts* 167). Crucially, Feld argues that juveniles are not competent to waive counsel, because they often do not understand the consequences of such waiver (D *Juvenile Courts* 168–170). If only about half of juveniles receive counsel and if juveniles are not competent to waive counsel, then there is a major due process problem in the juvenile justice system, which could result in juveniles receiving harsher sentences than they deserve (Feld in D *Juvenile Courts* 172–173).

One solution to the problem of juveniles representing themselves would be for the Federal government, under the juvenile justice act, to forbid waiver of counsel (testimony of Feld in D *Juvenile Courts* 165). In other words, states would not receive Federal grants, unless they guaranteed juveniles access to counsel (testimony of Gary Melton in D *Juvenile Courts* 224).

Some support for systemic reform to address the due process problem. Doctor Gary Melton, of the University of Nebraska, argues that significant safeguards should be added to juvenile courts. He also believes that "the juvenile court should be just one part of a comprehensive system for advocacy and protection of children's interests" (D *Juvenile Courts* 223). Melton suggests that the Federal government should use grants to encourage the states to establish an Office of Ombudsman for Children. He claims that such offices have been effective in protecting the rights of children in Norway, New Zealand, Israel and South Australia and that there would be similar results in this country (D *Juvenile Courts* 224).

Other experts agree that minor reform can solve the due process problem. For example, Sanborn argues that several reforms significantly could improve the situation. He calls for greater training for attorneys and judges working in the area, adding protections to guarantee that delinquency records are not available to the court prior to trial, and establishing procedures so that the same judge does not hear the same defendant in multiple cases (P 612).

Feld takes a more radical approach. Given the trend away from rehabilitation, toward an emphasis on punishment, he believes that the proper solution is to abolish the juvenile courts and provide juveniles with the same safeguards that are found in the adult courts (D *Juvenile Courts* 163–164, 188–189). Feld writes, "Without a juvenile court an adult criminal court that administered justice for young offenders could provide children with all the procedural guarantees already available to adult defendants and additional enhanced protections because of their vulnerability and immaturity" (D *Juvenile Courts* 189).

Why is a consideration of procedural fairness relevant in relation to programs designed to reduce juvenile crime? There are two answers to this question. First, crime control programs, especially those that increase punishment, may impact procedural fairness. Thus, it is important to understand that due process protections provided in the present system.

Second, some claim that perceived fairness is needed for successful deterrence of crime. Lawrence Sherman of the University of Minnesota argues that "Procedural justice (fairness or legitimacy) of experienced punishment is essential for the acknowledgement of shame, which conditions deterrence; punishment perceived as unjust can lead to unacknowledged shame and defiant pride that increases future crime" (P 445). In this view, one reason the present system often fails to deter criminals is that the system is perceived to be unfair. If the system could be reformed, then it more effectively would act as a deterrent to crime. If Sherman is correct, reform of due process requirements would fit within the topic of juvenile crime control as a means of improving deterrence.

Against the position that better protection of due process is a viable means of implementing a program to reduce crime, the negative might argue that procedural fairness is adequately guaranteed in the present system. On the most important issue, access to an attorney, for instance, some argue that juveniles are not provided with counsel only in relatively trivial cases. Even Feld admits that for more serious crimes, counsel is more likely to be provided (testimony of Feld in D *Juvenile Courts* 167). Judge David Mitchell of Baltimore says that juveniles are essentially always represented by counsel in his court and in Baltimore in serious cases (D *Juvenile Courts* 149).

More generally, research indicates that in most instances the juvenile justice system produces a just result. Three-quarters of professionals surveyed by Sanborn concluded that "defendants could receive fair trials in juvenile court" (P Sanborn 611).

Second, the negative could argue that the claim that there is a strong relationship between procedural fairness and juvenile crime is not clearly supported. Over the last thirty years, the Supreme Court has increased the due process requirements that must be met in juvenile courts. It is in precisely this period that juvenile crime has soared. Moreover, the claim that street thugs ignore the law because they think that court procedures for juveniles are unfair is implausible at best. It is hard to see why they would make such a calculation. And there is also an argument that juveniles are harder to deter than other criminals, because they are less calculative and more spontaneous in their criminal actions. In addition, one would expect a lack of procedural fairness to improve (not decrease) the deterrent effect of the juvenile system. If kids perceived the system as procedurally unfair that should make them more resolved to stay away from crime.

The opponent of change also might argue that reform could be very costly. For example, , Sanborn admits that to implement the changes which he advocates could be "prohibitively expensive, both financially and conceptually" (P 613). I will discuss specific cost disadvantages in the final chapter.

Finally, greater procedural formality might not help juveniles. In a study of juvenile courts in Minnesota, Barry Feld found that "more procedurally formal urban courts sentence more severely than do their rural counterparts" (B 66). Only about 20% of rural delinquents were incarcerated, versus one-third in the urban environment (B Feld 68). Thus, greater procedural protection could have the effect, not of better safeguarding the rights of juveniles, but merely of increasing their punishment.

Trends in State Policies Toward Juvenile Justice

Juvenile crime control is primarily a state and local responsibility. In fact, the Federal Government prosecutes only a very small number of juveniles in a given year. According to Senator Ashcroft of Missouri, in the peak year of 1990 there were only 197 juveniles prosecuted in the Federal courts (CR "The Violent" S13657). This does not mean that the Federal Government plays an inconsequential role in juvenile justice. The Department of Justice and other agencies provide grants to support state and local programs and draft guidelines that must be followed in order to be eligible for funding. I will discuss these programs in a moment. But the dominant role in the juvenile justice system is that played by the states and localities.

Since the 1970s, two trends in juvenile justice have emerged. One trend, reflected in the experience of Massachusetts and several other states, has been toward deinstitutionalization of juveniles. The contrary trend is toward harsher sentences and treatment of juveniles in the adult courts. This second trend has been informed by what is known as a "just deserts" philosophy of punishment (see P Glazer "Juvenile" 182).

In relation to the movement toward deinstitutionalization, a number of states have closed large training schools or reform schools and replaced them with smaller, community-based facilities. Such programs have been aimed at both placing kids in an environment that maximizes the chance for rehabilitation and saving money. Massachusetts led the way in carrying out a deinstitutionalization program, which ended up producing savings of more than $10 million a year. Other states, including Utah, Pennsylvania, Maryland and Florida have taken similar action (Office of Juvenile Justice an Delinquency Prevention in D *Hearing Regarding* 24).

While some states have moved toward taking kids out of large institutions and placing them in the community, the more important development has been toward stricter punishment for juveniles. As the rate and seriousness of juvenile crime have increased, state law makers have grown weary of releasing apparently brutal teens into community treatment programs. In many states they have stopped doing so.

There are several aspects of the movement toward a "just deserts" approach to punishment. For example, forty-six states have judicial waiver statutes under which the juvenile court judge can transfer jurisdiction for a particular case to a criminal court judge. Moreover, 18 states have a legislative waiver policy, under which the juvenile is automatically transferred to the criminal court if he/she meets certain standards. For example, in some states a juvenile who is 16 (or even 14) automatically will be transferred to an adult court if he/she is accused of a violent felony (P Jense and Metsger 97). And laws passed in Georgia, Florida, Tennessee, and Oregon mandate fixed sentences in adult prisons for youths without an age requirement (P Brazemore and Umbreit 296).

The trend toward toughness also has been reflected in stricter curfew enforcement against juveniles. According to Ruefle and Reynolds, 59 of the 77 cities with populations over 200,000 now have curfews and 26 of these cities adopted the curfew for the first time after 1990 (P 347). The move toward curfews has occurred despite expert opinion that they do little to stifle crime and are discriminatory. For example, the Board of Trustees of the National Council on Crime and Delinquency has called for the abolition of curfews (P Ruefle and Reynolds 347).

The overall changes in the system have led some commentators to refer to the current system as a "criminalized" juvenile court (P Brazemore and Umbreit 297).

The Development of Federal Programs Dealing With Juvenile Crime

The Federal Government has been involved in fighting juvenile crime for almost a half century. The Staff of the House Committee on Natural Resources notes the evolution of that role:

> Initiatives to combat juvenile delinquency at the federal level began around 1953 and culminated in the passage of the Juvenile Justice and Delinquency Control Act of 1974. This Act created the Office of Juvenile Justice and Delinquency Prevention (OJJDP) in the Justice Department to administer grants for the improvement of the juvenile justice system and the prevention of juvenile delinquency. The Act required states to separate juveniles from adults in secure facilities and placed an emphasis on diverting youth from the legal system into community based treatment centers. Subsequent reauthorizations included new themes such as removal of juveniles from adult detention centers and a mandate for strengthening and maintaining family values. The 1988 reauthorization contained in the Anti-Drug Abuse Act established grant programs within OJJDP for prevention and treatment relating to juvenile gangs, drug abuse and drug trafficking. (D *Urban Recreation* 4)

The 1992 authorization of the Juvenile Justice and Delinquency Control Act put into place "incentive" grants to encourage coordination of state and local programs and emphasized the importance of prevention programs (staff report of the House Committee on Natural Resources in D *Urban Recreation* 4).

The grant programs of the Justice Department are also notable for their impact on the system. The Office of Juvenile Justice has supported programs both to separate juveniles from adults in jail settings and to have them held in separate facilities altogether. These two goals have been "achieved [with] a relatively high degree of success" (B Feyerherm 3).

It is important to recognize that not all Federal grant programs dealing with juvenile justice are housed in the Department of Justice. Currently, there are many programs dealing with juvenile issues at the Federal level. And these programs are spread across a number of different departments and agencies. According to Senator Glenn, "We have some seven departments of Government and 17 separate agencies that deal with delinquency and at-risk youth, and there are some 260 programs spread across the length and breadth of Government that deal with these problems" (D *Youth Violence Prevention* 2).

Some view these programs as quite disorganized. The Attorney General as head of a Coordinating Council on Juvenile Justice and Delinquency is supposed to deal with any coordination difficulties. Not everyone agrees that the coordination effort has been successful. According to the General Accounting Office, "The Coordinating Council does not have a strategic plan to address the problem of youth violence" (D *Youth Violence Prevention* 82).

Gregory McDonald explains how the grant programs were organized in the period after the 1988 reauthorization of the Juvenile Justice and Delinquency Control Act:

these [Justice] programs spent approximately $4.2 billion in 1989, the most recent year data were collected. Most of this money supported services to reduce general risks that youth face, in particular through things like job training.

Programs targeted to treating delinquents or to directly preventing crime accounts for a total of $760 million; 82% of this money went to combat alcohol and drug abuse. Our analysis found that only 4%, or $28 million in Federal funding specifically targeted violence. About half of this was for HHS's youth gang prevention program. (D *Youth Violence Prevention* 12)

McDonald goes on to note that discretionary money available to the Office of Juvenile Justice and Delinquency Prevention for fighting youth violence "is quite limited" (D *Youth Violence Prevention* 12).

Several major policy changes have occurred during the Clinton administration, impacting the Federal role in confronting juvenile crime. In 1993, the Office of Juvenile Justice and Delinquency Prevention of the Department of Justice issued a report endorsing the following basic principles: the importance of strengthening the family, the value of relying on core community institutions such as schools and churches in fighting delinquency, the importance of delinquency prevention, the need for immediate intervention to deal with delinquent behavior, and the value of identifying the core group of serious offenders so they can be dealt with (in D *Hearing Regarding* 25). Clearly, this report represents a shift toward prevention and away from the "just deserts" philosophy. Of course, absent funding for prevention programs and a shift in state and local law enforcement and sentencing practice, such a report means relatively little.

The other important development in the fight against juvenile crime was passage of the 1994 crime bill. That legislation allocated $30.2 billion to prison construction, hiring additional police, prevention programs and other anti-crime spending. The money for the legislation was placed in a trust fund and was to be generated from savings produced by cutting the Federal work force.

The bill attacked crime by allocating almost $9 billion to assist localities in hiring 100,000 additional police officers over six years. It also provided almost $8 billion in grants to states for prison construction. About half of the money for prison construction was to be given to states that enact tough sentencing laws, requiring violent repeat offenders to serve at least 85% of their sentence. The bill also authorized the death penalty for certain Federal crimes and enacted the so-called "three-strikes" provision, under which a third felony criminal conviction results in life imprisonment. Perhaps the most controversial provision was a ban on the manufacture and possession of assault weapons (for a summary of the legislation see P Masci "The Modified" 2490; Dewar A14; P Neil Lewis A6).

The bill also included $150 million to support alternative forms of incarceration for youth offenders, such as boot camps (P Neil Lewis A6). One legal change was aimed directly at juvenile crime. The legislation altered standards so that kids 13 and older could be tried as adults if charged with certain violent crimes (P Masci "The Modified" 2490).

In addition to the funding for law enforcement programs and changes in Federal law, the legislation provided almost $7 billion in crime prevention programs. Not quite $2 billion of the prevention money was allocated for a "Violence Against Women" program." Another roughly $1 billion was provided "for drug courts, which seek to rehabilitate first-time or non-violent drug offenders with intensive treatment and supervision rather than incarceration" (P Masci "The Modified" 2490). The remaining prevention money, approximately $4 billion, included a variety of anti-crime programs, some aimed directly at juvenile crime. For example, $567 million was included for "midnight basketball" leagues and after-hours programs . Another $243 million was provided in funds for school programs to help young offenders (see P Neil Lewis A6). Roughly $90 million was allocated for funding a crime coordination and prevention program called "Ounce of Prevention" (P Neil Lewis A6). And approximately $80 million was provided for residential schooling of offenders and anti-gang training (P Neil Lewis A6). On the other hand, the final bill cut $900 million that had been proposed to provide job training for youths who promised not to use drugs or commit crimes.

In crafting the legislation, Congress combined thirteen previously existing grant programs into a $380 million block grant program (P Masci "The Modified" 2490; also see P Dewar A14). Under the block grant approach, the Federal government would give money to states and localities with fewer strings attached. Rather than Congress specifying how each dollar included in the appropriation would be spent, Congress would provide states with large (block) grants that they then could use as they saw fit within certain guidelines.

While the crime bill passed, there was major opposition to it. Republicans opposed the 1994 act on two main grounds. First, many rejected the ban on assault weapons. Conservative Republicans were unwilling to accept any new limitation on gun ownership. That point will be relevant when I discuss gun control issues in chapter four. Second, and more important in relation to juvenile justice issues, many felt that the legislation contained a great deal of "pork" (see P Dewar A14). In particular, they felt that the prevention programs were just more wasteful social spending.

Consequently, after they became the majority party in both houses of Congress, following the 1994 election, Republicans pushed for major modification in Federal crime policy. Both the Senate and House passed bills that made significant changes in the 1994 law. In the end, the conference legislation would have shifted Federal support for controlling crime away from specific mandates, such as the Clinton plan of adding 100,000 police to the nation's law enforcement forces, to a block grant approach. Clinton vetoed that bill on December 19, 1995 and at this writing a final resolution of the dispute has not been reached. Congress and President Clinton also have not been able to agree on a bill funding the Justice department, including its law enforcement and prevention programs (see "Issue: Crime" 40-41).

Conclusion

The focus of this chapter has been on two main points. In the first half of the chapter, I described the magnitude, defining characteristics, and causes of juvenile crime in the United States. In the second half, I discussed the development of juvenile law, trends in state and local treatment of juvenile offenders, and the evolution of Federal programs responding to the juvenile violence problem.

The foregoing analysis has important implications both for those advocating change in this nation's juvenile policies and those opposing any modification in policy. First, the evidence on the impact of juvenile crime is overwhelming. No negative team is going to be able to deny that juvenile crime is a significant problem. This suggests that it is not wise for the opponent of the resolution to allocate significant time to denying that there is a juvenile crime problem. He/she should attempt to minimize the problem isolated by advocates of change, but anything more than that is not likely to be useful.

Second, the data on factors that cause juvenile crime is important because the existence of alternative causes of youth violence can be used to deny that any given policy is likely to be effective.

Third, the confusing set of Federal juvenile anti-crime programs provides ground for the advocate of change to rationalize the organization of those programs. In so doing, he/she may claim that a particular policy approach would not in fact cost money, but would save costs.

3 Reducing Juvenile Crime Through Criminal Justice Reform

The focus of this chapter is on means of reducing juvenile crime that fit within the criminal justice system. I begin by considering proposals first to increase and second to shift punishment of juveniles to a graduated sanctions model. In the third main section I consider alternative sentencing schemes for dealing with juvenile crime. The fourth section discusses police programs that might be used to reduce juvenile crime. The final section of the chapter focuses on drug enforcement alternatives as a means of confronting the epidemic of youth violence.

Proposals to Treat Juveniles More Harshly

The dominant reaction of ordinary citizens and our political leaders to the escalating juvenile crime problem is that tougher action is necessary. If juvenile offenders are dangerous, perhaps we should put them away for longer. While this is the most common response to juvenile crime, it is not, as I will argue throughout this section, one that is backed up by the strongest arguments.

Treat Juveniles as Adults

The most obvious means of controlling juvenile criminals is to place them in the adult criminal justice system and deal with them in precisely the same fashion that we deal with any dangerous criminal. Clearly, the present system has been moving rapidly in the direction of treating juveniles as adults. Forty-six states already have waiver procedures under which juveniles can be transferred to adult courts (P Lavelle 86).

Before a state can transfer a youth to an adult court, the state must satisfy a set of standards established by the United States Supreme Court. In procedural terms, a full investigation must be carried out, followed by a hearing in which the child is guaranteed counsel. The transfer is allowed only if after full consideration of the records, the court concludes it is justified. In the hearing the court is to consider the age of the child, the chance of successful rehabilitation, and possible consequences of the transfer (the standards are summarized in B Spergel 222).

In addition to the discretionary transfer policies, there is a trend toward automatically moving teens to adult courts if they commit a certain class of crime and are above a minimum age (see P Glazer "Juvenile" 176).

There is no doubt that both the discretionary and the automatic transfer policies have had an effect. Increasingly, juveniles are being treated as adults, a trend which distinguished author Alex Kotlowitz refers to as the "adultification" of juveniles (P 40). The trend toward treating juveniles as adults in part can be traced to public pressure, since about 75% of the public, according to poll results, favors

43

such a policy (P Kotlowitz 40). According to the Office of Juvenile Justice and Delinquency Prevention, 200,000 or more juvenile offenders currently are processed in the criminal courts. Moreover, between 1985 and 1989, waivers to adult courts increased over 75% and the number of juveniles admitted annually to prison increased to almost 12,000 (in D *Hearing Regarding* 20). Since the report of the Office of Juvenile Justice was issued in 1993, one would suspect that these trends have accelerated.

Despite the trend toward treating juveniles as adults, some still argue that current laws are not restrictive enough. For example, Sarah Glazer cites the example of an eighteen year old juvenile in Washington, D.C., who was being released after serving two years for homicide. The teen told an official in the D.C. justice system that he had hired another kid to shoot someone for him. Even with this admission, the two year sentence was the maximum allowed by law (P Glazer "Juvenile" 171). In many such cases, according to advocates of tougher sentencing, current law is not nearly tough enough. Norman Brill concludes that many juvenile offenders receive inappropriately light sentences. He writes, "Generally the juvenile criminal who commits a brutal act of random violence must receive the least restrictive punishment" (B 29).

The conclusion that we are not imposing adequately restrictive punishment on brutal juvenile offenders is backed up by interviews with juveniles in jail for homicide in Washington, D.C. A study by Claire M. Johnson discovered that the offenders

> have little understanding of alternatives to their actions and are not interested in changing their lifestyles or behavior or the probable course of their lives. They seem not to have a sense of remorse for the murders they have committed and accept the certainty of a very dismal and limited future. (qtd. in P Glazer "Juvenile" 186)

The study concluded that the perception that juveniles would not serve long sentences was a factor encouraging them to commit crimes (P Glazer "Juvenile" 176).

Even black liberal Senator Carol Moseley-Braun of Illinois favors tightening Federal law to allow juveniles to be tried as adults. She notes that in some cases in the current system juveniles "can shoot someone with impunity at 14 years of age" (qtd. in P Glazer "Juvenile" 173). Moseley-Braun means that juveniles know that they will not be given adult punishment for committing a murder and so they are undeterred from carrying out the act.

The obvious solution to the failure to deter juveniles is to try them in adult courts. One approach would be to follow the suggestion of Barry Feld, which I discussed in the last chapter, and simply abolish the juvenile courts. A less radical option would be to automatically transfer certain classes of crime to adult courts. Then, juveniles would be required to face the same punishment as adult criminals. Some argue that juveniles receiving an adult sentence still should be put in a special facility, designed for juveniles. Colorado is taking that approach (P Glazer "Juvenile" 176).

The proponent of applying adult sentences to juveniles can claim three possible benefits of such a policy. First, it could be claimed that violent juvenile offenders simply deserve the punishment. This "just deserts" perspective is based on the idea that a person who cŏmmits a terrible crime deserves to pay a terrible price. Second, the advocate of tougher punishment could argue that such action will deter juvenile criminals. They will know that criminal actions will put them in prison for a very long time and abstain from such actions. Third, some argue that putting violent juveniles in prison is beneficial, even if it does not deter other potential offenders. It is beneficial because the violent offender will not be able to harm society while in prison. By "incapacitating" the offender society may protect itself.

As I will explain in a moment, the juvenile-specific data available on these issues strongly suggests that a tougher approach will not work. For a review of the general literature on deterrence, just deserts, and incapacitation see an earlier book in this series (Robert C. Rowland, *Behind Bars: The Problems Plaguing Our Correctional System* (Lincolnwood: National Textbook, 1989).

While there are undoubtedly some juvenile offenders who could be deterred by the threat of prosecution in adult courts and others who simply deserve such prosecution, the weight of evidence does not support expansion of current waiver efforts.

First, as I already have explained, waiver procedures are available for use in important cases and their use is increasing. It is hard to see that there is much need for action in the area of waiver.

Second, it is not clear that juveniles are being treated more leniently in the present system than they would be in adult courts. A fundamental change in philosophy of juvenile courts occurred in the 1980s that makes them more like adult courts. "During the 1980s and into the 1990s, juvenile courts became more offense-oriented and less offender-oriented, and responding to the 'needs' of the child was no longer the first priority" (B Guarino-Ghezzi and Loughran 101). According to Barry Feld, of the University of Minnesota, recent "formal changes and actual practices eliminate most of the differences between juvenile and adult sentencing" (D *Juvenile Courts* 186).

The conclusion that adult and juvenile courts are not very different is backed up by the literature on sentencing. A study by the Rand Corporation found that in California juvenile drug offenders received 20 month sentences, while adults received sentences of about 12 months (P Glazer "Juvenile" 176). In contrast, a second California study found that only a little over 10% of juveniles transferred to adult court received jail time in California (P Glazer "Juvenile" 177; also see Howell, Krisberg and Jones 14-16). Several other studies have found that juvenile courts are not necessarily more lenient than adult courts (Office of Juvenile Justice and Delinquency Prevention in D *Hearing Regarding* 37). Thus, if juveniles already are being treated as harshly as adults in juvenile courts, there is little reason to alter the present system.

In actuality, there is a very strong argument that transfer occurs too often in the present system. It has been reported, for example, that 57% of those transferred in

1992, were for property and/or drug offenses (B Howell, Krisberg and Jones 19). Similarly, Alex Kotlowitz has found that there is a trend toward transferring kids to adult courts, even for trivial crimes (P 40). There clearly is an argument that a violent fourteen year old, who has committed a murder, should be transferred to the adult system. It is hard to see the same rationale for transferring a fourteen year old petty thief.

Third, one very good reason not to treat juveniles as adults is that they are not adults. For example, Alex Kotlowitz argues that many of those charged in the adult courts are functionally children, who do not understand their acts and have grown up in awful personal situations (P 40). The point is not only that it is immoral to apply adult standards to someone who is still a child, but that adult penalties cannot deter offenders, who neither know what the penalties for a given crime are or even understand their own criminal act.

In this regard, James Fox and Glenn Pierce argue that the trouble with a general transfer is that deterrence theory does not apply to young kids. Simple incarceration

> can not be counted on for dissuading kids from the temptations and thrill of street crime and gang membership. No matter how punitive society becomes and what kind or how strong of a message is sent out to the street, teens who are attracted to crime always will turn a deaf ear to deterrence. Besides, by the time a juvenile offender has 'graduated' to murder, it is likely too late to reach him. (P 26)

If deterrence theory does not apply to juvenile offenders, the rationale for adult transfer becomes quite problematic.

On similar grounds, an automatic waiver policy can be treated as fundamentally unfair. In this regard, Michael Saucier, chair of the Coalition for Juvenile Justice, argues that automatic waiver is not rational, since a few identifiable offenders are committing 75% of the juvenile crimes (in D *Hearing on Juvenile Crime* 36). If this tiny majority is committing most of the crime, it hardly seems fair to severely punish a much larger class of juveniles.

Fourth, research on transfers to the adult system indicates that such a policy is not effective and may be counterproductive. Saucier notes

> Experience and research show higher recidivism rates for young people tried in adult courts compared to those tried in juvenile courts for the same offenses and with similar personal backgrounds. There is no research that we have identified to show any positive result in crime prevention when young people are tried as adults in adult court. (in D *Hearing on Juvenile Crime* 31)

Jeffrey Fagan of Rutgers cites comparable results. He did research comparing similar juveniles in New Jersey, which uses juvenile courts, and New York, which uses adult courts. He found that criminal courts were much more likely to place the offender in prison than were the juvenile courts (B "Separating" 248), but he did not find that the harsher sentences were effective in deterring crime. In fact, he found the opposite. Fagan writes:

Comparing overall crime rates for the 1981-1982 cohorts, recidivism rates appeared
to be higher for criminal court cases, their rearrests occurred more quickly, and their
return to jail was more likely. Recidivism among the juvenile court cohort also
appeared to be no more serious than that among the criminal court cohort. Rather
than affording greater community protection, the higher recidivism rates for the
criminal court cohort suggests that public safety was, in fact, compromised by
adjudication in the criminal court. Moreover, the data hint that increasing the
severity of criminal court sanctions may actually enhance the likelihood of recidivism. (B "Separating" 254)

In a study of legislative waiver standards in Idaho, Eric Jensen and Linda Metsger
found no effect on crime (P 96). They note that this result is consistent with
previous research from New York State (P 102). And former Judge Frank Orlando
argues that transfer to adult courts has been more common in Florida than
elsewhere and that it has failed to deter crime (D *Juvenile Courts* 10). Thus, strong
data on the effects of treating juveniles as adults suggests that such a policy is not
productive.

Fifth, transfer to an adult institution also may be a bad idea. Saucier explains that

Juveniles in adult institutions are five times more likely to be sexually assaulted,
twice as likely to be beaten by staff, and 50% more likely to be attacked with a
weapon than youths in a juvenile facility. Furthermore, it is well documented that
adult institutions rate much lower in availability of counseling programs, efforts to
improve family relations, and medical care, while the juvenile facilities were rated
much higher in promoting social and personal development through youth and staff
interaction. (in D *Hearing on Juvenile Crime* 37)

Such findings explains the judgment of Howell, Krisberg and Jones, that "juveniles incarcerated in adult prisons are more likely to recidivate following imprisonment" (B 23).

In fact, some argue that not only does prison not deter juvenile offenders; it
becomes an advanced school for the criminal. Glazer notes that conviction in the
adult courts can have the unfortunate side effect of "sending them [the offender] to
schools for crime or handing them over to adult sexual predators" (P Glazer
"Juvenile" 176). Or as Spergel argues, imprisonment in adult institutions produces
"unintended criminogenic effects" (B 223). Ira Schwartz, former head of the
Office of Juvenile Justice and Delinquency in the Justice Department, concludes
that the "'criminalizing effects of adult prison' may explain why youths commit
more crime" (qtd. in P Glazer "Juvenile" 176).

Finally, it is important to recognize that a move to get juvenile cases into the
adult system could have unintended consequences. Such a policy action might
snowball and become in the words of James Bell, an attorney with the Youth Law
Center, "'the first step toward abolishing the juvenile justice system" (qtd. in P
Glazer "Juvenile" 173).

Of course, the advocate of change could argue that abolishing the juvenile
justice system would be good, not only because it would better control juvenile

crime, but also because the system is fundamentally unfair to juveniles. It also is important to recall from the last chapter the point that some experts believe that perceived procedural fairness is related to successful deterrence of crime. If that theory is correct, then abolishing the juvenile courts would strengthen deterrence.

Of course, the relationship between procedural fairness and deterrence is quite speculative. As I explained in the previous chapter, juvenile crime began increasing steadily at precisely the time that the Supreme Court was guaranteeing juvenile rights. Thus, there are good arguments against the claim that improved procedural fairness will result in crime decrease. It also seems likely that someone like Barry Feld would not prefer to have all juveniles treated harshly in the adult system.

Rather than simply transferring all juvenile offenders of a certain type to the adult system, it probably makes more sense to maintain the current system for assessing the need for transfer.

Tougher Penalties in General

A second proposal for reducing juvenile crime calls for making the penalties facing juvenile criminals more strict. Senator Ashcroft of Missouri argues that one reason for the juvenile crime problem is excessively weak sentences. He cites several horrendous examples of juveniles committing terrible acts and then receiving light punishment. In one case, a murder was punished with a two year term in a detention facility, In another case, a convicted killer can be held only until he is 21. Ashcroft explains the problem in this way:

> For its part, the current juvenile justice system reprimands the crime victim for being at the wrong place at the wrong time, and then turns around and hugs the young criminal, whispering ever so softly into his ear, 'Don't worry, the State will protect you.'" (CR "The Violent" S13657)

A number of commentators agree with Ashcroft. Richard Lacayo describes a question and answer session between Los Angeles District Attorney Gil Garcetti and a juvenile, in which the offender asked questions about what his punishment for a given crime could be. The strong implication was that tougher laws might deter the offender (P 62).

Ashcroft proposes what he describes as a "comprehensive approach" to juvenile crime. The first aspect of his program is tougher sentences for juveniles. He explains:

> This legislation provides Federal funds to States and local governments to assist them in reforming their juvenile justice systems. The bill identifies violent and hardcore criminals, imposes stiffer penalties, and deters crimes. (CR "The Violent" S13657)

Ashcroft believes that tougher sentences will deter juvenile criminals, "Studies show repeatedly that punishment reduces both frequency and seriousness of offenses by young criminals and is most effective when it is consistently imposed for every offense" (CR "The Violent" S13657).

Additional research backs up Ashcroft's judgment. A recent study focused on what happened to youths in Massachusetts after a juvenile correctional institution was closed. The researchers compared the recidivism rates of youths who were released into a non-institutional program and those who remained incarcerated. Denise Gottfredson and William Barton conclude that "The postclosing group's recidivism was significantly higher than that of the institutionalized groups for serious crimes. . ." (P 604). In other words, those who were kept in prison committed fewer crimes, thus supporting the view that harsher punishments act as a deterrent factors. One expert believes that harsher punishment could have a major effect on juvenile crime. Norman Bill believes that "incarcerating young recidivists for a year would result in a 50% reduction in the crime rate" (B 31).

The second main provision of the Ashcroft bill calls for establishing specific standards for when juveniles should be transferred to adult courts. In Ashcroft's view, serious crimes such as murder, forcible rape, serious drug offenses and so forth, should result in automatic transfer for youths of 14 or older (CR "The Violent" S13657).

Third, the Ashcroft legislation calls for consistent record keeping about juveniles and transfer of those records to the FBI to assist in controlling crime (CR "The Violent" S13658). He also advocates providing juvenile criminal records to judges at sentencing. In support of such a policy, he cites an example where because a judge lacked knowledge of an offender's previous record, the juvenile offender was sentenced to probation and let back on the streets (CR "The Violent" S13658). The problem of judges sentencing without adequate knowledge of an offender's record may be significant. Sarah Glazer cites a survey which found that about half of prosecutors say that in most cases they do not receive the juvenile record of serious adult offenders (P "Juvenile" 174). The Ashcroft legislation would confront that problem by providing both schools and local law enforcement agencies with access to juvenile records (CR "The Violent" S13658).

Finally, Ashcroft argues for Federal funding of Serious Habitual Offender Comprehensive Action Programs (SHOCAP) in which police, schools, prosecutors and others "utilize their collective resources to identify serious, violent, habitual juvenile offenders" (CR "The Violent" S13659). This approach is aimed at the 2-3% most dangerous juvenile offenders. According to Ashcroft, SHOCAP has proved its potential effectiveness in a pilot test in Oxnard, California. After implementation of the program, the violent crime rate dropped 38%, rape decreased 30%, and murder declined by 60% (CR Ashcroft "The Violent" S13659).

Of course, Ashcroft's plan is not the only possible one for increasing the severity of punishment of juvenile offenders. It is, however, the most detailed major plan on the public agenda today. While Ashcroft has crafted a well thought out comprehensive plan for imposing greater punishment on juveniles and otherwise strengthening the judicial system's response to youth crime, the balance of evidence suggests that his approach would not be beneficial.

There are a host of reasons not to support stricter sentences for juveniles. First, it is difficult to argue that we are not putting enough juveniles in prison or juvenile facilities. As early as 1992, there were 53,000 juveniles held in facilities on any given day (Senator Fowler in D *The State* 2). The number of offenders in juvenile facilities increased by almost 50% from the mid 1980s to 1990 (Office of Juvenile Justice and Delinquency Prevention in D *Hearing Regarding* 21). Moreover, only about 19% of those confined in juvenile facilities were violent offenders (Office of Juvenile Justice and Delinquency Prevention in D *Hearing Regarding* 21). It would seem that we are not coddling juveniles, a conclusion that is also backed up by information cited previously about tough treatment in the adult courts and increasingly high sentences for them in juvenile courts.

The fact that juvenile crime has sky rocketed at precisely the same time that imprisonment rates also have been increasing casts doubt upon Ashcroft's proposal. There are very good reasons to doubt whether his bill would produce any deterrent effect. Initially, tougher sanctions may be far less effective in the context of juvenile than adult law, because few kids are aware of the law and calculate its effects (P Lacayo 62). Curtis Artis, a member of the Police Chief's Youth Task Force and former gang member and drug dealer, testifies:

> People don't care about getting locked up. They are more scared to live than they are to die. It sounds crazy but it's the truth. There are a lot of people in jail, young'uns, that got 15-life, 45-life. They don't care, and they didn't care when they were on the street. Most young'uns coming up now, all they know is you are not a man until you do 5-to 15. You are not a man until you bust a block up on somebody. (D *Youth Violence Prevention* 28)

Some gang members even believe they will have fun in jail (testimony of Mark Wilkins of the Police Chief's Youth Task Force in D *Youth Violence Prevention* 28).

Moreover, for many kids, prison may offer a better life (Senator Cohn citing Jesse Jackson in D *The Gang Problem* 36). It is also important to recall information cited in reference to proposals that transfer juveniles to the adult court system. There is strong evidence that many juveniles simply lack the maturity to understand either the crime they have committed or the likely punishment structure for their crime.

In addition to questions of psychological maturity, there is solid evidence indicating that stricter punishment is unlikely to produce any deterrent effect. Andres Tapia writes. "A central irony in the debate is that while the U.S. prison population has increased four-fold since the 1960s, violent crime has gone up 560%" (P 46). This data suggests no correlation between tougher treatment and crime reductions. Based on a review of relevant materials, Senator Simon argues that the theory that putting more people in prison for longer periods will deter crime is not well supported. In building this argument, he draws a distinction between what amateurs (politicians) think and what experts in the field believe. Simon argues that experts know that prison does not work to reduce crime (CR "The Pros Know" S17928-S17929).

Particular research studies back up this claim. In a national study funded by the National Science Foundation, Anne Schneider considered the relative effects of incarceration, probation and restitution. She concluded that

> the overwhelming evidence for all groups included in the research is that incarceration had no discernable effect on perceptions of certainty and severity of punishment. Instead incarceration and detention increased remorse, but also damaged the individual's self-image. These effects of punishment offset one another, leaving punishment policies with about the same results as less coercive programs such as restitution and probation. (B 4)

And, as I mentioned earlier, the general literature on deterrence does not support the claim that increased severity will substantially reduce crime.

In fact, the consensus of opinion seems to deny deterrence theory. According to American Correctional Association President Bobbie Huskey, an "'overwhelming consensus' exists among wardens that 'incarceration, in and of itself, does little to reduce crime'" (qtd. in an Op Ed essay by Coleman McCarthy from the *Washington Post* included in CR "The Pros Know" S17929). Senator Simon reports on a poll of prison wardens:

> Eight-five percent of the wardens said that most politician are not offering effective solutions to crime. Instead of building more prisons and passing mandatory minimum sentencing laws, the wardens overwhelmingly favored providing vocational— 92 percent—and literacy—93 percent—training to prisons, and 89 percent support drug treatment programs in prisons. Congress has been quick to defund these programs . . . (CR "The Pros Know" S17929).

It is important to understand that there are two dimensions of punishment involved in deterrence: severity and certainty. In particular, the evidence strongly denies that greater severity produces a deterrent effect. One reason is the so-called maturation effect. Typically, many criminals "lose their enthusiasm for crime as they belatedly mature in their 30s" (P Marris 122). As a consequence, long prison sentences may have the effect of keeping people who are no longer criminals in prison, but serve no other function (P Eitzen 471).

Third, tougher sentences also may produce a stigmatization effect, which causes the humiliated juvenile to turn more toward crime, because his/her ties to the community have been severed. Moreover, by making it more difficult for the juvenile to find a job, tough sentences may push the offender toward a life of crime (P Brazemore and Umbreit 300).

A related problem is the fact that prison can serve as a sort of school for crime. Based on stigmatization and the school of crime effect, one commentator notes simply that "The prison experience tends to increase the likelihood of further criminal behavior" (P Eitzen 471).

Fourth, harsher sentencing programs that keep people in prison for longer periods of time may accomplish that aim only by kicking other people out of prison earlier than their sentence states (see CR Simon "Time To Face" S13549).

A good illustration of this problem can be found in literature on "three strikes" laws that exist in many states and the Federal system. Under the approach, a criminal convicted of a third "strike" is sent to prison for a very long period, often twenty-five years to life. These laws have produced some major side effects. In California, for instance, defendants are refusing to plea bargain and demanding a trial, because they have nothing to lose by doing so. The result is massive overcrowding in the jail and judicial systems. The situation is so bad that it has been reported that prosecutors are "ignoring" new strikes and judges reducing felony charges to misdemeanors (P Smolowe "Going Soft" 63). Why are they reacting in this way? The answer is that three strikes and other harsh sentencing legislation has the effect of putting some people in prison for much longer periods of time. That, in turn forces the prison system to release other prisoners at an earlier time, in order to free up the cell.

Fifth, tougher sentences also may produce unfair treatment for people of color. Howell, Krisberg and Jones note that "Many of today's get-tough proposals would exacerbate existing disparities [between white and non-white defendants]" (B 17). In other words, the law could be used to disproportionately punish black and Hispanic defendants.

Finally, any program of harsher sentencing could require massive new spending programs at the state, local, and Federal levels. It is very simple. In order to keep people in prison for longer time, society will need to build many more prison cells, because the longer-serving criminals still will be taking up a cell, when they otherwise would have been released. I will discuss funding issues in chapter five.

In sum, the best data suggests that proposals for harsher treatment of juveniles are based more on a glandular reaction to juvenile violence, than they are to close analysis of the deterrence literature.

Boot Camps and Shock Therapy

The third major alternative for increasing punishment of juveniles would be to rely on boot camps or other forms of "shock therapy." Here, the argument is that by placing a first-time juvenile offender in an environment such as a booth camp, society has a chance to "shock" him or her out of a life of crime. This argument for boot camps as a form of shock therapy is built on two principles. First, the shock of incarceration in a harsh environment combines with the hard work in the boot camp to build self-esteem. Second, the sentences in boot camps are relatively short in duration. As a consequence, youths do not suffer the same negative effects as in more traditional prison settings.

There have been many experiments with boot camps across the country. According to one source, 29 states and the Federal Government have opened 46 boot camps and there are about 7500 beds in boot camp programs nationwide (P MacKenzie and Piquero 224). Of course, it would be possible for the Federal Government to provide grants to assist states in creating additional boot camp program.

There is some reason to believe that an expanded boot camp program might be quite effective. For example, a study conducted by the University of South Alabama of a boot camp in Mobile country found that juveniles who went through the program were arrested for 30% fewer felonies and 70% fewer misdemeanors than those who were assigned to other correctional facilities (P Simons 20). If the Mobile experience could be generalized, juvenile crime would plummet.

However, there are good reasons to believe that the Mobile experience could not be generalized and that an expanded boot camp program would do little good and might do significant harm. First, as I noted earlier, boot camps already are in operation across the United States. There is certainly no barrier to state expansion of those programs in the present system.

Second, the rationale behind "shock" incarceration is unclear. If lack of economic opportunity and loss of family structure are the main causes of escalating youth violence, it is hard to see how boot camps could do much about these problems. A boot camp won't give a juvenile the life skills that he/she needs. Nor will the boot camp provide family support programs.

Third, research suggests that boot camps have, in many cases, not been successful at all. A review of boot camps in eight states found that there was no clear overall relationship between such programs and recidivism rates. In some cases, the boot camps seemed to result in a reduction in recidivism. In at least one instance, (Georgia) the recidivism rate was higher for participants in the boot camp than for a corresponding group in the prison system. After four years of experience with boot camps in Georgia, the recidivism rate was about 50%, as compared to one third or less for offenders initially sentenced to probation, and 56% for those sent to prison (P Glazer "Juvenile" 181). This study seems to indicate that probation is the most effective method of deterring juveniles from commission of crime.

Other data supports this conclusion. Doris Layton MacKenzie, of the University of Maryland, reviewed boot camps for the Department of Justice and found that they had no effect on recidivism (P Glazer "Juvenile" 180). One reason that boot camps work in the military is that following their completion, the soldier gets a job and the chance for advancement. Following completion of a juvenile boot camp, however, the offender is placed back in the same violent society in which he/she had been living.

Fourth, there is some evidence that boot camps may make things worse, by actually creating delinquency (P Glazer "Juvenile" 175). According to Howell, Krisberg and Jones, "Deterrence programs, such as shock incarceration and those based on encounters with hard-core prisoners actually had negative effects; that is youths who received these treatments had higher recidivism rates than did those who did not receive them" (B 28).

Fifth, boot camps may produce counterproductive "net widening." Net widening occurs when a program is used, not to target a particular population for punishment, but as a means of increasing the total number of people who are punished altogether. In the case of boot camps, one problem is that many of those sent to such institutions otherwise would be put on probation. Under the rules of boot camp programs, participants must complete the program or be remanded to prison. Since about 30-40% of boot camp participants drop out, the result is a sentence to prison for a population that prior to the boot camp simply would have been released. One impact may be to increase prison overcrowding (see P Glazer "Juvenile" 181). Another would be to increase crime by stigmatizing juveniles who should have been put on probation.

On balance, the literature does not suggest that boot camps could do much to control juvenile crime in the United States. On the contrary, the literature indicates that boot camp programs may well be counterproductive.

Punish Parents

The final main proposal for using increased punishment to reduce juvenile crime is to punish parents when their children disobey the law. Thus, if a teenager continued to commit crimes, his/her parents could be confined as punishment. There are several cases in the United States, where judges have taken this tact with parents. In one instance, a woman was sentenced to a 100 day term and her children placed in foster care, because a daughter had been truant for over fifty days (P "Should Good" 14). The trend toward such action has been increasing. John Leo writes "Hundreds of exasperated communities, large and small, are holding parents responsible for curfew violations, graffiti damage and crimes by their children. Often they impose fines or community service and sometimes require attendance at basic classes on how to parent" (P 18).

The Federal Government could encourage the expansion of current programs for punishing parents by offering incentive grants to encourage the states to implement the approach.

The idea of holding parents responsible for kid's behavior is, at first glance, appealing (especially to their children), but a second look suggests that it is not a very good idea. First, there is a basic principle of jurisprudence that only the person guilty of the crime should be punished for that crime. To punish parents for the actions of their children violates this principle.

Second, the obvious assumption of this legislation is that the threat of punishment will force parents to control their kids. But, if kids are alienated from society, then it is hard to see how a parental responsibility approach could work. The kids will simply ignore the parents.

Third, some argue that jailing parents will only make the situation worse, because it removes the source of discipline and support from the household. Chicago School Superintendent Argie Johnson says that such punishment "may simply add to the burden some families face in trying to successfully raise their children" (qtd. in P "Should Good" 15).

Summary of Increased Punishment Options

In the previous sections, I have outlined four main alternatives for increasing punishment of juvenile offenders. One proposal is to channel juveniles into adult courts in order to better control crime. A second approach calls for systematically tightening enforcement against juveniles. The third approach relies on boot camps in order to shock juveniles about a life of crime. And the final approach is to punish the parent for the sins of the child. While good arguments can be made for each of these perspectives, far and away the strongest arguments oppose their use.

Graduated Sanctions

The graduated sanctions approach is built on the premise that truly dangerous youth offenders need to be placed in secured facilities (prisons), but other youths need to be rehabilitated. Advocates of graduated sanctions also call for increased support for prevention programs.

The Clinton administration advocates a variant of graduated sanctions. John Wilson of the Office of Juvenile Justice and Delinquency Prevention argues for a three tiered program, in which different punishments are applied to delinquent youths at each tier level. This approach, which draws on the "social development model," "has been demonstrated to be effective in preventing serious and violent juvenile delinquency" (Office of Juvenile Justice and Delinquency Prevention in D *Hearing Regarding* 23). In their 1995 book, *Balancing Juvenile Justice,* Susan Guarino-Ghezzi and Edward J. Loughran defend a similar approach, which they call a "balanced model" of juvenile justice. An essentially equivalent perspective has been endorsed by The National Council on Crime and Delinquency (B Krisberg et al 142).

A system of graduated sanctions is built around five points: risk assessment, support for prevention, low level punishment in combination with rehabilitation programs, mid-level punishment with rehabilitation programs, and high level punishment for the most dangerous offenders.

Before turning to a discussion of the system itself, it is important to note that nothing like such a scheme has been implemented nationally, although many pilot programs have been implemented. Krisberg et al put it simply, "There is no graduated sanctions system in operation today that one can point to as a perfect model" (B 142).

Before considering the three stages of graduated sanctions, it is important to understand that key element in a graduated sanctions approach is the use of clear standards for placing juveniles into each tier of the punishment/rehabilitation system. Those standards are necessary to get the juvenile into the right part of the system. Wiebush and his colleagues explain that:

any system predicated on graduated, differential interventions must have:

    * Clearly specified selection criteria for the various programs and levels of intervention

    * Adequate methods for assessing the degree to which individual youth meet those criteria

    * A selection process that ensures that youth targeted for intervention at each level of the system are those who in fact are served at that level. (B 172)

Without such a system, the graduated sanctions and prevention programs will not be applied to the right youths.

Fortunately, there is good evidence that clear and rational standards can be established. Wiebush et al write:

> A core set of variables has been identified repeatedly in the research literature as recidivism predictors for juvenile offenders. These include age at first referral/ adjudication, number of prior referals/arrests, number of out-of-home placements or institutional commitments, academic achievement, school behavior and attendance, substance abuse, family stability, parental control and peer relationships. . . (B 178)

There is also empirical data indicating that standards can be defined effectively. Under the system used in Detroit, juvenile offenders labelled "high-risk" were found to have a 76% recidivism rate, while medium risk offenders had a 39% rate and low-risk a 19% rate (B Wiebush et al 177). It seems likely that a more sophisticated system, based on the research variables I mentioned, could do an even better job of assessing offenders.

The second aspect of a graduated sanctions system is support for prevention programs for youths who suffer from the most "risk factors." Risk factors are individual and community characteristics that put a youth "at risk" of becoming a criminal. This risk factor approach is based on "more than 30 years of research" (B Krisberg et al 143) and models exist to assess the need for prevention. Hawkins and Catalano have identified a number of major risk factors falling in four main areas: community risk factors, family risk factors, school risk factors, and individual and peer risk factors, along with a number of protective factors (this is summarized in B Wiebush et al 184). After those risk factors have been identified, Federal grants could be provided to support "community interventions" "that are designed to strengthen protective factors, thereby mitigating the influence of risk factors" (B Wiebush et al 184).

I will discuss prevention programs in the next chapter, but it should be recognized that one highly defensible approach to juvenile crime would be to include an emphasis on prevention in a comprehensive program including the use of graduated sanctions. However, it also would be possible for an advocate of graduated sanctions to leave out the prevention provision and concentrate on alternative forms of punishment. That approach would avoid disadvantages associated with support for prevention programs.

The third facet of a graduated sanctions program is a first level punishment program for the least serious offenses. For kids who commit minor first offenses,

John Wilson proposes "constructive sanctions" including "informal probation, mediation, restitution, outpatient drug treatment programs peer juries, and the like" (D *Hearing Regarding* 9).

At this first level, it may make sense to implement an "immediate sanction" program, in which the youth receives intensive contact with a case worker. The idea is that at-risk youths can be saved if they are dealt with immediately. In order to achieve that aim, the youth must receive intensive contact with case workers who can check on his/her progress and provide appropriate educational and other support. For example, in a program in Bethesda, Pennsylvania, youths are placed in a day school and/or after-school program, including individualized education and

> individual, group, and family counseling; drug/alcohol counseling; life skills development; and employment opportunities. Work experiences are provided for all clients of working age, who are required to contribute the majority of their paychecks to pay restitution, court costs, and fines. (B Krisberg et al 154)

Research indicates a tiny 5% recidivism rate for participants in this program (B Krisberg et al 154).

Similarly, a program of intensive in-home counseling in Baltimore has been quite successful. In the program case workers visit kids three to five times a day. According to Gest and Friedman, "73% of them [juveniles in the Baltimore program] had avoided further trouble six months later—a record better than that of most traditional corrections programs" (P 28).

In addition to immediate sanctions, broad community based programs might be applied to offenders at this first level. Rather than place the youth in an institution, he/she is diverted to a community program run by a church, social services agency, and so on. The literature generally supports the value of such programs. According to Krisberg and his associates, "Taken together these studies [a summary of the literature on community sanctions] show that community-based programs can serve as safe, cost-effective alternatives to incarceration for many youths" (B Krisberg et al 146).

Probably the strongest support for community-based programs for first-level offenders can be found in the Massachusetts deinstitutionalization experience. In chapter two I noted that Massachusetts has implemented a program that deinstitutionalized the vast majority of youth offenders into community-based programs, with only the most dangerous 15% going to "secure facilities" (B Krisberg et al 146). Studies have demonstrated that the Massachusetts system has resulted in a decrease in "offending" behavior following admission to the system and has produced "recidivism rates that were as good or better than those for most other jurisdiction" (B Krisberg et al 146). In addition, the program has resulted in savings of approximately $11 million per year (B Krisberg et al 146).

The second level of a graduated sanctions system would involve use of somewhat harsher sanctions, applied to juvenile offenders who had committed somewhat more serious acts and possessed other characteristics that made them more of a threat to the community. For dealing with repeat offenders, serious or violent offenders, John Wilson, of the Office of Juvenile Justice and Delinquency Prevention, proposes sanctions "such as weekend detention, alcohol and drug abuse treatment, which can be inpatient, a range of community-based residential programs, electronic monitoring, boot camps and many other alternatives" (D *Hearing Regarding* 9-10).

Some data supports the efficacy of such intermediate sanctions. Krisberg and his colleagues have studied a number of successful intermediate sanction programs that are operating in various areas around the country. For example the Family and Neighborhood Services (FANS) program in South Carolina has used "principles of multisystemic therapy" in "a highly individualized family- and home-based treatment" (B 158). The program has been effective, with youths in it experiencing "slightly more than half as many arrests as the usual services controls" (B Krisberg et al 158). And a program in Broward County, Florida also was effective in reducing the number of juveniles in secure detention by increasing use of alternatives, such as home detention, "without experiencing an increase in failures to appear or subsequent offending by youths on detention status" (B Barton, Schwarts and Orlando 84). Another approach is to emphasize restitution programs. Anne Schneider argues that "Community-based restitution and work-service programs were more effective in reducing illegal behavior than traditional probation" (B 4).

The third level of a graduated sanctions program would deal with the most dangerous juvenile offenders. In all likelihood, a third level program would distinguish between offenders who were essentially untreatable and those who potentially could be salvaged. The most dangerous offenders, those who were apparently untreatable, would be placed in adult prisons (D Wilson *Hearing Regarding* 10).

Those who were treatable would be transferred from prisons and jails to community correctional facilities. According to Wilson, "Studies show that from one-third to one-half of the juveniles who are in detention and correctional facilities are not a threat to community safety and can be appropriately treated in the community or while living at home" (D *Hearing Regarding* 10). Similarly, research in Alabama, New Hampshire and Nebraska indicate that between 20 and 50% of those institutionalized are actually "low risk" offenders, who do not need to be confined in an institutional setting B Guarino-Ghezzi and Loughran 166). This problem is especially prevalent for female offenders (B Guarino-Ghezzi and Loughran 167) and drug offenders. One study found that "the vast majority of juvenile offenders currently housed in long-term state correctional facilities have been committed for nonviolent offenses" (B Howell, Krisberg and Jones 15). This means that only a relatively small percentage of third-level juvenile offenders would be placed in adult institution.

For kids who have committed serious crimes, but do not fall into the most dangerous categories, advocates of graduated sanctions argue for use of "small community-based facilities and programs that provide intensive therapy" as a transition back to community-residential programs (Wilson in D *Hearing Regarding* 10).

The Office of Juvenile Justice and Delinquency Prevention has identified a number of programs that have been effective in curbing delinquency and crime and, therefore, could serve as models for future third level programs. For example, the Violent Juvenile Offender (VJO) program places offenders "in small, secure facilities" and then gradually reintegrates them "into the community thorough community-based residential programs followed by intensive supervision in their neighborhoods" (B Krisberg et al). A review of the program revealed that "VJO youths had significantly fewer and less serious rearrests than did the control group when time at risk was taken into account" (B Krisberg et al 164).

In defending a graduated sanctions model, an advocate can claim to achieve the advantages of both high and low level punishment. Most offenders would receive relatively low levels of punishment, thus avoiding the negative effects of imprisonment, which I already have discussed. On the other hand, truly dangerous offenders would be placed in adult prisons and given long sentences. Focussing attention on these offenders, who commit the vast majority of juvenile crimes, is sensible. Howell, Krisberg and Jones support this judgment, noting that about 5% of offenders at each age level are labelled "serious violent offenders" (B 11). Amazingly, each of these offenders commits approximately 8 serious violent offenses and 132 delinquent offenses each year (B Howell, Krisberg and Jones 11). Howell, Krisberg and Jones note that the system often does not get to these kids until "It is too late for early intervention" (B12).

Use of a risk assessment system would help identify the dangerous offenders early and free up resources to help those offenders who can be treated. Baltimore Judge David Mitchell explains, "No juvenile court system is going to be effective unless and until a shift in focus occurs in the treatment of offenders. Earlier identification and concentration of resources is the key" (D *Juvenile Courts* 150). Previous research indicates that a risk assessment system could be used to place high risk offenders in an appropriate prison or jail and release others to lesser sanctions. For example, in Sacremento use of a risk assessment system "resulted in a 45% decrease in the number of detention beds required" (National Council on Crime and Delinquency cited in B Wiebush et al 193).

The system of graduated sanctions that I have described is only one of the options available, although it is the most developed and easily defensible approach. Other proposals are quite similar. For example, some argue for greater use of so-called "intermediate sanctions," (including house arrest, community service and so forth). Another method is to better link probation/imprisonment decisions to the risk posed by the offender to the community. A recent study conducted in Austin, Texas, found that a Client Based Management Classification System, built on interviews, was an effective means of predicting probation risk (P Harris 154).

There is more support for a graduated sanctions system than for any other comprehensive approach to juvenile crime. Use of such a system has several advantages. First, it is easy to combine the graduated sanctions approach with prevention programs. In this regard, Wilson argues that a comprehensive program, encompassing prevention and law enforcement programs has the best chance of being successful (D *Hearing Regarding* 10). Second, a graduated sanctions approach has the best chance of effectively deterring, incapacitating and rehabilitating offenders because the various programs are tied to the characteristics of the juveniles and the risks they pose to the community. Krisberg and his colleagues note that "Studies of the most well-structured graduated sanctions programs have shown them to be more effective than incarceration. In addition, community-based programs often cost significantly less than their traditional counterparts" (B Krisberg et al 145).

Third, a graduated sanctions approach may make it easier to provide appropriate and equitable punishment to all offenders. One strong argument for decreased penalties for low-risk offenders is that such a reduction makes it easier to provide more certain punishment. Recent research on deterrence theory explains the failure of many studies to find a deterrent effect based on inadequate certainty of punishment. In this view, where the certainty of punishment is below a given level, which is usually estimated at between 25 and 40%, the criminal is not deterred. If, however, the certainty of punishment reaches that level, which is referred to as the "tipping point," then there will be a significant deterrent effect (P Yu and Liska 447-464). A graduated sanctions approach would allow the juvenile justice system to provide an appropriate punishment for every offender, rather than the almost random use of probation and imprisonment in the status quo.

Graduated sanctions also may be more equitable for minority groups, since the punishment will be based on relatively objective standards. Such an approach would seem to provide far less room for subjective and biased determinations.

Fourth, the graduated sanctions approach is difficult to attack, because the present system is also a graduated sanctions system, albeit not a very well designed one. The point is that the present system attempts to provide appropriate punishment and rehabilitation, depending upon the threat posed by the offender. Thus, the advocate of change can argue that disadvantages to the approach are both non-unique and actually solved by the restructured graduated sanctions system.

The graduated sanctions proposal is the best thought out comprehensive approach to juvenile crime in the literature. Admittedly, conservatives generally oppose its use as soft on crime. However, if the proponent of such a system can prove that their system for rating the dangerousness of the offender will be accurate, then the system will be anything but soft on the serious offender. In fact, proof of an effective method of predicting dangerousness can be used to defeat virtually all arguments against the proposal. Of course, like all systems, there ar objections against graduated sanctions.

In order to defeat a graduated sanctions program, the opponent of change must either deny that risk assessment is feasible or present a disadvantage to its use. There are a number of problems that relate to the risk assessment stage. Initially, it should be noted that there undoubtedly will be many errors. Wiebush et al note that "Even the best risk assessment instruments still result in substantial prediction errors. Many identified high-risk offenders never go on to commit another crime, whereas many low-risk offenders do" (B 177). There are only two possible ways to deal with this problem. The system can err on the side of releasing the youth or it can err on the side of protecting the community. If the second choice is made then many youths who are not a threat to the community will be placed within the justice system unnecessarily. On the other hand, if the system errs on the side of protecting individual rights then it is inevitable that many dangerous kids will be let back on the street. The only answer to this dilemma is to defend the accuracy of a particular risk assessment system, a point that will be considered in a moment.

The prediction problem is still greater when risk assessment is applied to predicting what individuals need intensive prevention (B Wiebush et al 185). Many youths come from situations that often lead to delinquent or criminal behavior, but do not become delinquents or criminals. Use of a risk assessment approach to target prevention programs is, therefore, fraught with difficulty.

What is the impact of the problems with risk assessment. First, there is some danger that the risk assessment system could be used in a discriminatory manner. Many of the risk factors are correlated with race. It is easy to imagine certain localities applying the system in a way that would be unfair to minority groups. This is especially important since some of the risk factors (at both the prevention and the correctional stage) relate to situations that are not inherently criminal. If a kid with family problems is more likely to recidivate, does that make it fair to punish that child more harshly? The family situation is not his/her fault. Of course, the opponent of change should keep in mind that a well-designed risk assessment system will diminish the problem of racism.

Second, the risk assessment system must be accurate. If it is not accurate, then little will have changed from the status quo, where graduated sanctions are available, but not consistently applied. In opposing graduated sanction, one should argue that the present system has no incentive not to use the best available risk assessment system. The failure of risk assessment in the present system is, therefore, an indication that a new program also might fail.

It also might be argued that it will be difficult to take academic research on risk and transform it into a nationwide risk assessment system. One crucial point is that risk assessment always depends upon judgments about subjective factors, the degree to which a youth seems to want to improve his/her life, for example. This means that a pilot study of risk assessment may have succeeded, not because of the inherent value of the system, but because of the insight of those working in the study.

Third, the negative may want to argue that some variants of risk assessment violate the equal protection clause of the Constitution. There are two arguments here. First, risk assessment that takes into account variables which are correlated with race in making a judgment about where to place an offender, is arguably discriminatory. Second, it could be argued that risk assessment denies juveniles both due process and equal protection, because not all risk factors relate to the crime they have committed. A youth from a broken family is more likely to recidivate than a youth from an upper middle-class home. But the kid from the broken family may have committed precisely the same crime as the rich kid. Is it fair to sentence the rich kid to stage one and the poor kid to stage two of the graduated sanctions system? If the program violated the Constitution in any of the ways that I have mentioned, it would be struck down by the Court.

Note two additional points about the constitutional issues. It is not "should would" to argue that the Court would strike down the plan. A "should would" argument is one that denies the plan would be implemented, based on political factors. It would be "should would" to argue that Congress would never pass a graduated sanctions plan. But the Constitutional argument deals with a result of the plan; it says nothing about the plan's initial implementation. Second, when running the Constitutional argument, the negative should claim a value disadvantage in violating the terms of the Constitution. In this way, you argue both that the Court would strike the plan down, and more importantly, should do so.

Fourth, there is a danger that the risk assessment system might be used by actors in the criminal justice system to bring still more youths under social control. In other words, a youth who committed a minor crime, but who possessed high risk factors, might be given a harsh sentence. Of course, the goal of graduated sanctions is precisely the opposite of this situation. However, it is important to remember that the people enforcing the system will be the same prosecutors, judges, social workers, and so forth, who work in the current system. Given the punishment mindset of the present day, there is a significant risk of "net widening." In that case, the intermediate sanctions would be used for those who today are not prosecuted at all or receive probation. If that were to happen, the result would be to drastically increase the number of people receiving punishment. This is not far fetched. One research study found that the community approach "actually tripled the proportion of persons under state control" (P MacKenzie and Piquero 223). Studies in a variety of other contexts have found a similar result (P MacKenzie and Piquero 223). If this research is correct, the move to a "graduated sanctions policy" would not produce a system in which sanctions are applied in a graduated manner. When a new program was implemented in San Francisco, for example, the initial reaction of many workers was to override the program and keep kids in jail, who, by program standards, should have been released. According to David Steinhart, "more than half of referred youth in San Francisco who scored nine or fewer points were nevertheless detained because the probation officer ignored or 'overrode' the score" (B 58).

It also should be mentioned that allocation of prevention dollars based on a risk assessment system creates a perverse incentive for cities to not deal with problems. If they solve problems, their prevention needs score will decrease and so will their funding.

In sum, there are a number of ways that the negative can attack the risk assessment system at the heart of a graduated sanctions policy. That risk assessment system is both the strength and the greatest weakness of the graduated sanctions approach. If you successfully can attack it, then you have a very good chance of defeating the approach.

A second major position against graduated sanctions is to argue that intermediate sanctions and treatment programs can do little to reduce juvenile crime. The problem is that it is very difficult to take a criminal and turn him/her into a good kid. Thornberry and his colleagues explain:

> Our results, however, suggest that treatment programs have an uphill battle. By the time most serious delinquents are identified by and receive intensive treatment from the juvenile justice system, they are well into their delinquent careers. For example, the National Youth Survey found a substantial gap between the peak ages of involvement in serious violence and processing by the juvenile justice system. Moreover, a substantial number of chronic offenders, based on self-reported data, are never arrested and treated. (B 233)

Thornberry et al conclude that "a policy strategy focused on a treatment orientation will be unresponsive to a large proportion of the serious delinquent acts that are committed" (B 233).

There also are problems with second level punishment. For example, probation may not be an effective alternative. Georgia Judge Glenda Johnson notes that in her state the typical probation officer has a case-list of about 90 (D The State 57). Given caseloads of this magnitude, it may be quite difficult for probation officers to keep track of all their clients. Judge Michael Malmstadt agrees with that judgment. He notes that in Milwaukee the average juvenile will see a probation officer only once a month and that the only information the probation officer will have will come from the juvenile (D *Juvenile Courts* 3).

Of course, one could increase the contact with the system, as has been done in the Bethesda program, which I described. However, to do so would require a massive commitment of resources. In the present system, probation officers see their clients once a month, because they are terribly overworked. To provide an intensive sanction for all who could use it would be immensely expensive.

In addition, it is not clear that an intensive sanction program (or other variants of the intermediate and graduated sanctions approach) would be successful if expanded to a nation wide program. Pilot programs often produce great results, but then do not lead to the same results when expanded nationwide. The pilot program is run by committed, well-trained and idealistic staff. Oftentimes, participants for the program are hand picked. When such a program is expanded, however, it takes on the characteristics of the entire system. Thus, neither the staff nor the participants will be of the same quality as in the pilot study.

It is also important to note that even in the case of the Bethesda program, there are significant questions. Krisberg et al point out that the findings in regard to the program "must be taken with extreme caution because the sample size was very small (n = 20) and the study did not incorporate a control group" (B 154).

While there are very strong arguments against a graduated sanctions policy, probably the stronger arguments lie on the other side. Remember that the present system must make judgments about relative risk in making prosecution decisions.

It is hard to see how a graduated sanctions policy could do a worse job. One key to effectively defending such an approach is to find appropriate models upon which to base both the risk-assessment and the intermediate sanctions portions of the program. By basing those aspects of the policy on real-world examples, the advocate can claim that the proposed approach has empirical support. Moreover, the supporter of graduated sanctions should claim that the other side must cite evidence dealing with their specific models for risk-assessment and intermediate sanctions. Absent that evidence, the affirmative could claim that more general negative material simply was not relevant.

Sentencing Reform

A number of potential means of dealing with juvenile crime fall into the category of sentencing reform. In a sense the policies that I already have discussed also fit within sentencing. However, the essence of those policies was to increase or moderate punishment. The point of sentencing reform is to make punishment more certain and equitable. In this section, I will describe policy options relating to mandatory sentencing, restorative justice, and drug sentencing.

Mandatory Sentencing

A mandatory sentencing policy requires judges to follow specific guidelines in setting a sentence for a juvenile offender. The goal is that by using objective standards, written into a sentencing grid that takes into account all relevant factors in the sentencing decision, disparities in sentence can be minimized. For example, Pope argues for the use of sentencing guidelines similar to those found in the Federal courts as a means of reducing disparities in the treatment of minority youths. Such "guidelines could reduce discretion in reaching outcome decisions and help to ensure equity in processing" (B 211).

Another option would be to alter the system used by parole boards. Lattimore and her associates at the National Institute of Justice and the U.S. Department of Justice conducted a study of almost 2000 youths paroled in California. They concluded that variables such as prior criminal history, socioeconomic status, and so forth can be used to predict the likelihood of rearrest (P 54). In particular, Lattimore found that "threats, aggressive acts, or other institutional infractions [in prison or the juvenile facility] are strongly associated with the risk of rearrest for violence" (P 76). If criteria, such as those identified by Lattimore, could be made part of a parole system, the effect could be to reduce juvenile crime. Those juveniles who were most likely to commit new and violent crimes would be incarcerated for longer periods, thus reducing crime. On the other hand, those who were least likely to commit crimes would be let out sooner, reducing the negative effects of prison life upon them.

Mandatory sentencing policies conceivably can reduce juvenile crime in one of three ways. By reducing disparities in sentencing among different juveniles, they can reduce the perception that the juvenile justice system is corrupt. By changing that perception, they might be able to improve the deterrent effect of the law. Second, mandatory sentencing laws can be used to increase the certainty that a youth will receive a punishment. Higher certainty could produce better deterrence. Third, they could be used to set a minimum standard for punishment in relation to particular crimes. Used in this fashion, mandatory sentence laws are primarily a vehicle for increasing punishment.

While good arguments can be made for mandatory sentencing, once again the strongest arguments are on the other side. First, mandatory sentencing laws often are merely a vehicle to increase punishment. In that case, many of the arguments which I discussed previously are relevant. Second, the claim that increased equity will decrease crime is problematic. Underclass youths are becoming criminals because they have little economic opportunity and live in a social structure that is destructive. Their criminal behavior has very little to do with gaps in sentencing among defendants for a given crime.

Third, mandatory sentencing laws are extremely costly because they require more people to go to prison. Later, I will discuss cost issues, but suffice it to say that the potential for cuts in important programs or other negative economic effects from a major investment of money in mandatory sentencing is significant.

Fourth, there are good reasons to believe that mandatory sentencing will not work in deterring crime. A host of mandatory sentencing laws were passed in the 1970s and 1980s, at just the time when crime was beginning to shoot up. The recent overall decline in crime does not seem to be correlated with sentencing policy. Moreover, research on earlier mandatory sentencing suggests that such a program is unlikely to be successful in reducing crime. For example, a recent study found that laws setting mandatory prison sentences for people using guns had little or no effect on crime rates (P Marvell and Moody "The Impact" 247).

Fifth, mandatory sentencing programs have been used in many states and, in the form of Federal Sentencing Guidelines, in the Federal system. Many argue that such programs are counterproductive, because they force early release of some violent offenders. By setting a mandatory punishment of X years, the guidelines may have the result of driving up the prison population. At that point, rules regarding overcrowding may force prison officials into early release programs or, alternatively, the overcrowding may press prosecutors to be more lenient in bringing charges against someone (P Griset 546).

Restorative Justice

Another sentencing alternative is restorative justice. A restorative justice approach "emphasizes the need for active involvement of victims, the community, and offenders in a process focused on denunciation of the offense, offender acceptance of responsibility (accountability), and reparation, followed by resolution of conflict resulting from the criminal act and offender reintegration" (P Bazemore and Umbreit 302). Such an approach emphasizes restitution, community service, and various programs in which the offender confronts his/her responsibility for the crime (P Bazemore and Umbreit 308).

While there have been a few courts that have tried such an approach, for "the most part, restorative practices remain on the fringes. . . ." (P Bazemore and Umbreit 310). Thus, implementation of a restorative justice approach, either through Federal standards or via an incentive program, would be a major change in policy.

The advocates of a restorative justice approach point to successful use in Europe, Australia and New Zealand (P Bazemore and Umbreit) and claim that the program likely would work in the United States as well. In the Australian and New Zealand "family group conference" model, for example, the victim and his/her supporters are given the opportunity to speak about how they have been affected by the crime and to condemn the behavior of young offenders. The offender, his/her family or community surrogates, a trained facilitator/mediator, and the victim then participate in designing appropriate ways for the offender to make amends to the victim and the community. This begins a reintegrative process for the delinquent in which members of the family and community take responsibility for monitoring offender compliance and facilitating community healing. (P Bazemore and Umbreit 311)

While the restorative justice approach sounds good in theory, it does not seem well-adapted to the juvenile violence problem in the United States. Put simply, the United States is a much more violent society than Australia or New Zealand and attempts to make the offender face his/her guilt are less likely to work here.

Second, the opponent of restorative justice should argue that it will be difficult to implement a restorative justice approach, because of the strong societal support for the current retributive model. Remember, a restorative justice approach would have to be implemented by the same prosecutors, judges, and social workers who manage the retributive approach of the present system. Since a restorative justice approach would involve many discretionary judgements, there would be great opportunity for these individuals to block the successful application of the model. One possibility is "that such programs will simply expand and strengthen social control, either by net widening or by adding to current requirement imposed on offenders" (P Bazemore and Umbreit 309). In that case, the restorative justice approach would not achieve its objective and instead would be counterproductive.

Third, the opponent of restorative justice could argue that the model is merely a variant of the intermediate sanctions approach and then apply similar arguments to it. For example, restorative justice implicitly depends upon risk assessment practices, since not all offenders are reachable via a restorative justice approach. And failure of previous intermediate sanctions model projects is strong evidence that intermediate sanctions, even within a restorative justice approach, are unlikely to be successful.

Fourth, implementation of a restorative justice model similar to that used in Australia and New Zealand would be quite expensive. The description cited earlier included meetings among the victim, social workers, rehabilitative professionals, and the offender. After the punishment had been determined, appropriate supervision would be required. Clearly, we do not currently have the resources to provide that level of supervision over the offender. To provide such resources would be expensive. Moreover, the expense might be much higher in the United States than in other nations, due to the nature of our legal system. It is hard to see how a restorative justice system could be implemented without adding appropriate legal protections. Those protections would add expense and also bureaucratize the program, in all likelihood making it less effective.

Finally, the restorative justice system requires monitoring of the offender by the community. Obviously, that will be much more difficult to do in the United States than in the other nations that have applied the model. It is hard to see how a monitoring program could be established in impoverished urban areas that would be acceptable both to the victim and the offender. Given the racial disparities in juvenile arrests, a monitoring system easily could be perceived by inner city residents as white imperialism into their communities. In that instance, there would be some chance that a restorative justice system could spark additional violence. On balance, the restorative justice approach seems too idealistic to work in contemporary America.

Fair Drug Penalties

The final sentencing program to be considered as a means of controlling juvenile crime relates to drug penalties. A strong argument can be made that current drug penalties are unfair because they are so much stricter for crack cocaine, which is used by mainly black inner-city youths, than for powdered cocaine. It is because of this disparity that the U.S. Sentencing Commission has recommended reducing penalties for crack (cited in CR "Drugs Legislation" S13738).

Once again, this version of sentencing reform could reduce juvenile crime for the same reason that other attempts to increase procedural fairness might reduce crime. It is arguable that a system of drug sentencing that was perceived to be more equitable than the present system also would be a system that better would deter drug crimes. If that were the case, then the sentencing reform would result in less crime overall and less drug crime in particular.

There is also an argument that reform of drug sentencing laws would reduce juvenile crime by definition. Depending upon how the law was written, it might change the definition of a crime so that not as many people would be considered to be criminals.

While there is a lot of support for equalizing sentences between crack and powdered cocaine use, this is not one of the stronger proposals for reducing juvenile crime. Most importantly, the relationship between inequitable sentencing laws and juvenile crime is unclear at best. I already have explained that the claim that procedural justice is related to low crime rates is not one that is supported by historical examples. Moreover, it is hard to see how decreasing penalties for crack could decrease crime. Why would people be more deterred by lower penalties?

Perhaps, the redefinition would result in more people being charged with misdemeanors, but the overall crime rate would not necessarily drop. And the negative would be on strong ground in arguing that a claim of topicality based on a decrease in crime brought on by redefinition of the nature of the crime is illegitimate. The negative would argue that there was no "real" program to decrease, but only a redefinition of terms.

Second, the negative would argue that the proposed change actually would result in increased cocaine use and, therefore, is the antithesis of the resolution. On the danger of increased use, Senator Abraham argues that proposal to lower sentences for crack to make them consistent with powdered cocaine would result in significantly lessened sentences and that would send "entirely the wrong message" (CR "Drugs Legislation" S13738). By sending the wrong message, the affirmative would create the preconditions for expanded use.

A related justification for the current penalties is the comparative dangerousness of crack and powdered cocaine use. Abraham argues that crack is more dangerous than powdered cocaine and is "associated with systemic violence to a greater degree than powder cocaine" (CR "Drugs Legislation" S13739). Representative Bereuter notes that "Crack is by far the more dangerous product because it fuels gang warfare, drive-by shootings and the breakdown of inner-city families. Cheap and potent crack is ripping apart black neighborhoods in Omaha and elsewhere across the country" (CR "Bereuter E2249).

Abraham favors increasing the sentence for powdered cocaine to eliminate any inequity. Of course, the negative could not advocate increasing the sentence, because it arguably would be a topical act, designed to decrease powdered cocaine use among teens and others.

In sum, there are good reasons to believe that a program to equalize drug sentences is either not related to juvenile crime or would result in increased, not decreased crime. It certainly is hard to see how such a proposal would be considered on its face "a program to substantially reduce juvenile crime."

Police Programs

There are three main police programs that could be defended as a means of reducing juvenile crime: community policing, anti-gang programs, and projects aimed at reducing violence against women. .

Community Policing

Community policing has been referred to as the "watchword" for American law enforcement and is now favored by virtually everyone in the law enforcement system (P Rosenbaum and Lurigio 299). At the same time, there is major disagreement about what the term means. A number of different strategies for police work are included under the general label. Eck and Rosenbaum note that "ombudsmen, coordination councils, mobile and stationary mini-stations, enforcement crack-downs, advertising campaigns, problem-solving efforts and foot patrols" are just some of the techniques often included in the concept (B 5). This is a key point. The advocate of community policing needs to be able to defend a specific approach to community policing that is flexible enough to be applicable across the United States. That is a tall order.

Advocates of an expanded community policing program argue that the present system only gives lip service to the concept. As a consequence the approach has not yet been widely implemented (P Rosenbaum and Lurigio 299). The advocate of community policing should claim that Federal standards could be established requiring that states implement community policing programs or lose their eligibility for certain grant programs. The Federal Government also might provide grants to assist localities in implementing the concept.

Proponents of community policing see a number of benefits flowing from the approach. First, they argue that community policing improves the relationship between the police and the community. Strong evidence exists, for instance, that both the police and residents are generally favorable toward community policing (P Rosenbaum and Lurigio 299).

Second, community policing improves officer morale and better empowers them to proactively solve problems in the community. A recent study of community policing in the 72nd precinct in Brooklyn found that in general officers favored the program and that it assisted them in developing "effective methods for solving neighborhood problems" (P Pate and Shtull 384).

Third, the advocate should argue that community policing effectively reduces crime. For example, New York City has been quite effective in reducing crime by using "more effective and aggressive policing-stopping suspects, frisking them, confiscating guns, locking up more offenders, engaging in direct and random patrols in areas of higher risk" (P Zuckerman 96). The result has been a significant decline in crime: a 40% drop for murder and a 30% drop for all serious crime (P Zuckerman 96). On the crime control value of community policing, Senator Kerry of Massachusetts has argued that such a strategy can make an enormous difference for the community:

> I was in a housing project where you now have community police officers on bicycles who ride around and through the entire community, who walk around and play with the kids, who started basketball with the kids. The kids run up to them when they come into the area, instead of running away from them, which is what they used to do. These officers have helped literally to provide that community hope. (CR "Department of Commerce" 28 September 1995 S14512)

In Lowell, Massachusetts, a Federal grant allowed for opening a branch station and as a result "The druggies are gone, the prostitutes are gone, the community has been reclaimed, and it is coming back to life" (Senator Kerry in CR "Department of Commerce" 28 September 1995 S14512).

While there is a groundswell of support for community policing, there are good arguments that the concept is so vague that there is no certainty that future expansion of the program will produce the same level of success, as in the past.

First, there is a strong argument that community policing is not a "juvenile crime" program. Rather, it is an anti-crime program. Again, the negative should argue that if general police programs are included within the topic, then the resolution has grown overly broad and the negative is denied legitimate ground.

Second, the opponent of change could argue that community policing already has been implemented (or is in the process of being implemented) where it can prove valuable. One survey conducted in 1993 found that 50% of police officials in towns of over 50,000 said that they already had implemented community policing and 20% more said that it was in the works (P Grinc 437).

Not only have many communities already implemented a community policing program, but it seems likely that many which have not done so, are opposed to the concept. It will be difficult to overcome this opposition. Remember, that community policing is quite a vague concept. A police chief opposed to the concept easily could establish programs that "seemed" to implement community policing, but, in fact, would not do so. The idea that the police might try to circumvent a community policing proposal is quite credible. It is important to recognize the skepticism that many in the police have expressed to ideas such as increased foot patrols (P Lurigio and Skogan 315). That skepticism could lead to the program being blocked.

Fourth, research indicates that it will be very difficult to increase community involvement via community policing (P Grinc 437). This only makes sense, especially in neighborhoods that are most impacted by juvenile crime.

Fifth, there are good reasons to believe that community policing would not be effective in reducing juvenile crime. A recent review of studies on the effectiveness of community policing found that in three of six studies there was "no preventive effect on crime itself" (B Brewer, Hawkins Catalano and Neckerman 127) and in only one of the six studies did the evidence seem to support a decrease in the victimization of the population (B Brewer, Hawkins Catalano and Neckerman 127). Mark Moore of the Kennedy School at Harvard draws a similar conclusion, "there is almost no evidence yet indicating that community policing programs can be successful in preventing or reducing crime and criminal victimization" (B 295).

Juvenile Targeted Police Programs

Most police programs targeted at juvenile crime have focused on gangs and most anti-gang programs have aimed at suppressing the gang through a vigorous lock them up and throw away the key approach, similar to that which is used against organized crime (B Spergel 206). Unfortunately, "there is little evidence that the various specialized suppression programs and tactics have been effective in reducing the gang problem in either large or small cities" (B 206–207).

A better solution is to move to incorporate an anti-gang component in community policing, This approach focuses on involving the community, identifying the causes of gang membership and violence, establishing police relationships with members of the community, and so forth (see B Spergel, chapter 12).

Irving Spergel of the University of Chicago describes a targeted anti-gang program that could be included within a community policing program:

> Police, outreach youth workers, some former gang members, probation , and pretrial court service workers are in contact with each other share information about targeted gangs and gang youth, and collaborate closely in control and supervision, as well as providing social support, training, and job opportunities. The gang violence reduction team is on the street from 4:00 p.m to 12:00 midnight or 1:00 a.m., or later as needed, weekdays and weekends to control gang outbreaks, counsel gang youths, protect the community from gang violent activity, and facilitate a greater involvement of targeted gang youth with conventional institutions. (D *The Gang Problem* 73)

Such a program could be quite effective. Spergel's pilot program, "The Gang Violence Reduction Program in Little Village," led to the formation of a local neighborhood organization in which a number of community organizations and businesses assisted in confronting the gang problem. The program has had impressive results, including a 50% reduction in gang homicide and reductions in both aggravated assaults and aggravated battery (D The *Gang Problem* 73–74). Similarly, a program in Philadelphia led to a "sharp reduction in gang homicides" that was maintained over a decade (B Spergel 234). Thus, there would seem to be a strong case for a Federal program modelled after Spergel's various pilot studies. That Federal program either would set standards for the states to meet in conducting anti-gang activities or use a grant system to produce a similar result.

While Spergel's results in fighting gang activity are impressive, there are also major potential problems with expanding an anti-gang program nationwide. Initially, it is important to remember that much juvenile violence occurs outside of the context of gang conflict. A decrease in gang crime does not necessarily imply a similar decrease in overall juvenile crime.

Second, anti-gang programs are notoriously difficult to implement. While Spergel cites several effective programs, there have been many many anti-gang programs applied across the country and few have produced the same level of results as in the examples cited by Spergel. The failure of many previous experiments with anti-gang programs is understandable. For one thing, anti-gang programs are difficult to implement because the gang culture is so strong. Luis Rodriguez has chronicled how the culture pushes even "good" kids to violence (P 605). Moreover, gangs serve strong functions for man youths. Rodriguez writes that "For many, a gang embraces who they are, gives them the initiatory community they seek and the incipient authority they need to eventually control their own lives. These are things other institutions, including schools and families, often fail to provide" (P 605).

In addition, there are good reasons to suspect that a nationwide program will not be as effective as a pilot study. As I have explained previously, national programs are inevitably bureaucracies and bureaucracies are not as effective as dedicated people. For one thing, a national program would not have the advantage of someone like Irving Spergel providing his expertise in running each individual project. Thus, there is a high likelihood that an expanded program would not be nearly as effective as the pilot projects and there is even some risk that the program could be counterproductive. Spergel himself cites a program in Los Angeles, in which there was higher recidivism in the probation group than in the comparison group (B234).

Third, anti-gang programs are costly. The brief descriptions of Spergel's police program emphasized the extensive resources that would need to be committed to it. I will discuss cost issues in the final chapter.

Fourth, anti-gang programs easily could be used to widen the net of youths brought into the system. Local police will not necessarily be committed to using such programs to foster a preventive approach. Instead, they may use the program as a means of catching more gang members. There is also a danger that the program could be implemented in a racist fashion, since a high percentage of gang members are either African-American or Hispanic.

On balance, there is good evidence supporting targeted anti-gang programs. At the same time, there is strong evidence on the other side. One key to defending an anti-gang approach to juvenile violence is to be able to model a particular proposal after a pilot program and argue both that the pilot program is easily translated into a national program and that negative evidence must be applied specifically to the pilot program to be considered relevant.

Violence Against Women

There are horrendous statistics indicating a terrible problem of violence against women. Senator Mikulski explains the magnitude of the problem:

> We learned that one-fifth of all aggravated assaults in the United States occurred in the home; 3 to 4 million American women a year are victims of family violence; one-third of all American women who are murdered die at the hands of a husband or boyfriend; one third of all women who go to emergency rooms in this country are there because of family violence; an estimated 700,000 American women are raped each year; children in violent homes are 1,500 times more likely to be abused or neglected; over the last 10 years, crimes against women have risen nearly three times as fast as the total crime rate… (CR "Department of Commerce" 28 September 1995 S14509).

This data explains why Senator Biden says that "The No. 1 threat to the health of America's women is a violent attack at the hands of a man" (CR "Department of Commerce" 28 September 1995 S14506).

What does this have to do with juvenile crime? One answer is that many of the women who are attacked are also teens. Thus, a program to expand protection for women would also result in a reduction in violence against youths. And since many of the attackers are young men, such a program also could reduce juvenile violence by preventing them from beating their wives and girl friends.

Moreover, violence begets violence. Adele Harrell of The Urban Institute, explains that there is "Strong evidence that patterns of violence persist from one generation of a family to the next . . . " (D *Youth Violence Prevention* 117). Ms. Harrell concludes that roughly 25 to 35% of juveniles who live in an abusive household will become abusers themselves (D *Youth Violence Prevention* 117).

For all of these reasons, it seems likely that a program which substantially reduced spouse and child abuse would over time have a major effect on juvenile crime. What can be done about those problems? The Urban Institute advocates a four-part program to deal with violence against women. It includes tough law enforcement, training for those in the justice system relating to spousal violence, provision of safe housing for battered spouses and children, and violence prevention education (testimony of Harrell in D *Youth Violence Prevention* 119). Once again, such a program could be implemented either through Federal standards that would be tied to loss of funding in the justice area or through targeted grant programs.

Despite the clear data indicating a major problem in relation to violence against women, an anti-violence against women program has some significant problems, when evaluated as a means of reducing juvenile crime. Initially, there seems to be a strong argument that the Violence Against Women Act and similar programs are not aimed at reducing juvenile crime. I am not denying that a reduction in juvenile crime might be a side effect of such legislation, but that is not its primary or even secondary purpose. The authors of the act were not concerned with juvenile crime, except to the extent that juveniles were attacking women. In the Congressional debate on the issue, for instance, full funding of the law is justified based on what it can do to help women, not what the law will do about juvenile crime.

Second, Congress passed the Violence Against Women Act in 1994. Admittedly, there are questions concerning the level of funding for this legislation, but surely it makes sense to give the present system time to implement the provisions of that act, before implementing a new policy.

Third, a program aimed at cutting violence against women faces major implementation problems. No one (except for a few nuts) is for violence against women. The violence occurs because some men are violent and think it is ok to harm a woman. They get away with it because in some instances the woman is not anxious to prosecute. In others, the police or prosecutor doubts the existence of a strong case. Sometimes law enforcement backs off from what they think is a "family matter." These barriers to effective law enforcement will be difficult to overcome.

Fourth, the negative could argue that providing further resources in this area, when the Congress recently has passed legislation dealing with the same problem, would be counterproductive. The argument here is that the resources could be spent more effectively elsewhere. Alternatively, the negative might focus on the costs of the plan.

Police Program Summary

Of the law enforcement approaches to curtailing juvenile violence, probably the strongest is a targeted anti-gang program. Such a proposal is the most easily defended, because of past successes of pilot studies in the area.

Drug Enforcement

The final criminal justice solution to juvenile crime is improved drug enforcement. In this section, I will consider three possible options: strengthened enforcement; threatening Mexico with loss of loan guarantees to ensure Mexican assistance in fighting drug sales, and increased support for drug treatment.

Stricter Enforcement

The rationale for a strengthened drug enforcement program is simple: present drug enforcement is failing. The 1995 Executive Branch report on a national drug strategy noted that "Drugs are readily available to anyone who wants to buy them. By historical standards, cocaine and heroin street prices are low and purity is high, making their use by any mode of administration both more feasible and affordable than ever before" (D *President's Drug Control* 11). Moreover, "Fewer youth report a clear understanding of the risks associated with drug use" (D *President's Drug Control* 11). This probably explains the increased juvenile use of drugs, which I cited in chapter two.

Stricter enforcement of drug laws could reduce juvenile crime in two ways. First, there are many juvenile drug dealers. Stricter enforcement could put them out of business. Second, drug crime is related to many other types of crime. This means that a program that successfully reduced drug use would have the effect of significantly cutting crime, including juvenile crime. For example, Solomon notes that "police chiefs across the United States believe that the number one way to reduce crime is to reduce drug use. The fact is that mandatory minimum drug penalties put in place in 1988 was followed by the Nation's largest decrease in drug use" (CR Solomon E2393).

Therefore, one solution to the drug use problem would be to drastically increase sentences for drug users. Solomon argues, for instance, that the average drug user convicted under Federal law serves only eight months and concludes that we need tougher sentencing laws (CR Solomon E2393). And the drug diversion program included in the 1994 crime bill should reduce drug sentences further. With harsher sentences, it could be argued that drug use will drop again.

While not denying that drug use is a problem in this nation, strengthening enforcement of anti-drug laws is probably not a good way of reducing juvenile crime. First, there is no certainty that strengthened drug enforcement will reduce juvenile crime at all. Initially, despite what Solomon says, current drug laws are not exactly weak. On the contrary many think that they are too strict. One result of current laws is that small-time drug users sometimes get sent to prison for extended periods of time, a result that often forces the state to release a more dangerous offender. Thus, stricter laws might increase juvenile crime.

Support for the view that stricter drug enforcement could increase crime is found in the literature on drug legalization, which I will discuss in the next chapter. That literature emphasizes that high drug prices produce large amounts of crime, because the addict must steal more goods to pay for his/her habit. This means that, paradoxically, tougher sentences or more effective police control of crime, may have the effect of increasing criminal activity.

Additionally, strict drug enforcement makes it very difficult for people to find steady work. The result, according to Hagedorn, is that "Incarceration for drug charges undercut their efforts to find steady work and led them almost inevitably back to the drug economy" (P 216).

The conclusion that stricter enforcement will not work and could be counter-productive is strongly supported by the literature. Many sources argue that we already have tried a severe drug policy and that it has failed. Beginning with the 1986 Anti-Drug Abuse Act and continuing with an even tougher 1988 act, Congress passed extremely harsh laws dealing with crack, laws that established penalties that were significantly stricter than for powder cocaine (P Johnson, Golub, and Fagan 288). The result was a vast increase in the number imprisoned for drug crimes, a situation that will persist into the future because of the harsh sentences meted out to drug offenders (P Johnson, Golub, and Fagan 289). Moreover, tough imprisonment policies have not been effective. According to Johnson, Golub, and Fagan, the lowest recidivism rates were in the group of persons sentenced to probation, with higher rates for those who actually went to prison (P 289).

It is not just that stricter enforcement is unlikely to work, but also that these problems cast doubt on whether a proposal to increase drug enforcement even falls into the resolution. If the policy is unlikely to be effective, then can it reasonably be thought of a "program to substantially reduce juvenile violence"? Moreover, anti-drug enforcement is a good example of a policy that conceivably might have the effect of reducing juvenile crime, but that no one would think of as an anti-juvenile crime issue.

Aside from solvency and topicality, there are other problems as well. The Clinton administration has a four prong policy calling for the following actions to control drugs:

> (1) reducing the demand for illicit drugs; (2) reducing crime, violence, and drug availability; (3) enhancing domestic drug program flexibility and efficiency at the community level; (4) strengthening interdiction and international efforts aimed at disrupting the production and flow of drugs into the United States. (D *President's Drug Control* 11–12)

Again, it makes little sense to implement a new policy, before giving the current one a little time to work.

In addition, anti-drug policies often impact civil liberties. In order to reduce drug use, the police must use intensive surveillance, wire taps, and so forth. Such actions threaten individual liberty. And an anti-drug enforcement policy could be quite expensive. To make a major improvement on the present system will require more police, judges, social workers and so forth. And imprisoning low-level drug users is also immensely expensive. On balance, stricter drug enforcement is not a sensible way to attempt to reduce juvenile crime.

Mexico and Drug Enforcement

An alternative means of cutting drug crime would be to limit the supply of drugs in the United States. Earlier this year, a bill was introduced that would cut off extensions of loan guarantees to Mexico unless that country more strongly acts to "eradicate drug activities" (Representative Miller CR "Mexico" H1204).

The threat to cut the loan guarantees is justified by the claim that Mexico has not assisted the United States in fighting the drug war, especially in the area of dealing with extradition requests (CR "Mexico Must" H1204).

In response to that problem, the Feinstein/Damato/Miller proposal calls for ten specific actions to be taken by the Mexican government including "adoption of a comprehensive program for drug enforcement" (CR "Mexico Legislation" S556).

Such an approach could have a significant impact on drug supplies in the United States. Representative Miller notes that:

> The Drug Enforcement Agency estimates that 75 percent of all cocaine available in the United States travels through Mexico, up to 80 percent of all foreign-grown marijuana in the United States originates in Mexico, and 90 percent of the chemical used to make the drug speed flows through Mexico before infecting our neighborhoods. (CR "Mexico Must" H1204)

More broadly, Senator Feinstein notes the estimate of the Drug Enforcement Agency that of all illegal drugs, 60–70% come from Mexico (CR "Mexico Legislation" S555).

While a high percentage of drugs do enter the United States from Mexico, the threat to cut off loan guarantees is not a wise policy option. First, such a proposal can be considered a program to cut juvenile crime in only the most general sense. A strong argument could be made that it is not sensible to define a threat to cut off loan guarantees as a program aimed at cutting juvenile violence. If you accept such a definition then any crime control program can be considered to be topical.

Second, the Clinton administration implemented an anti-trafficking program in 1993. The Presidential directive "called for a three-pronged international drug control strategy that emphasizes (1) providing assistance to those nations that show the political will to combat narcotrafficking through institution building, (2) conducting efforts to destroy narcotrafficking organizations, and (3) interdicting narcotics trafficking in both source countries and transit zones" (D *President's Drug Control* 44). As part of the policy, the Clinton administration is also strengthening efforts to stop drugs at or before the U.S. border, including adding 700 Border Patrol agents (D *President's Drug Control* 74). Given the recent evolution in policy, it makes sense to not act until we are certain that the policy has failed.

Third, the administration believes that there have been positive developments in Mexico, including official statements expressing commitment to fight drugs and continuing efforts to develop an antidrug police force (D *President's Drug Control* 101–102). Nor is it clear that Mexico could do a lot more than it is doing now.

Finally, it is probably not a good idea to threaten to cut off loan guarantees, unless we really want to go ahead and take that action. The loan guarantees were provided to prevent an economic catastrophe from occurring in Mexico. If the Mexican economy went into a depression, the effects upon the United States could be severe. Not only would illegal immigration increase dramatically, but those sectors of our economy that are dependent upon exports to Mexico could be devastated. That devastation could ripple through our economy, perhaps causing a severe recession.

It is important to understand that an economic recession in the United States produces substantial harms. In a recession, many people lose their jobs, their homes, and so forth. A recession also drastically increases the budget deficit, both because tax revenues fall as people lose their jobs and because social service outflows increase at the same time. Of course, we are on the verge of having a plan to balance the budget; now would be a very bad time to have a recession.

There are also more speculative potential impacts of a recession. Given the importance of the U.S. economy to the world economy, there is a significant danger that a U.S. recession might cause a global recession, or even a depression. There is literature that indicates that the chance of war increases in times of economic stress. Certainly, that was the case with the Second World War. Moreover, economic instability often leads to political instability. And political instability can lead to tyranny, fascism, and also war.

I am not saying that threatening to cut off Mexico's loan guarantees is certain or even very likely to produce such effects. But I am saying that such a result is both possible and plausible. The arguments that I have mentioned are relatively low probability, but low probability and no probability are very different things. As a country, we should avoid policies that could produce such enormous problems.

Increased Treatment

The final criminal justice means of decreasing juvenile crime would be to put more emphasis on drug treatment. A treatment-oriented approach to drug crime would be based on two principles: increased and improved education about drug use and diversion of drug offenders into appropriate treatment programs.

Advocates of treatment argue that we need both more drug education to prevent people from using drugs and expanded treatment for drug users. In relation to education, the U.S. National Drug Control strategy endorses the need for an expanded program: "The recent increase in marijuana use among adolescents, as well as changes in their attitudes about the dangers of drug use, is alarming and underscores the need for educating each generation about the consequences of drug involvement" (D President's Drug Control 12). In Congressional debate, Senator Hatch argued that music in general, and rap in particular, often glorifies drug use (CR "Drug-Related" S361). He also noted that media coverage of the drug issue has decreased and that anti-drug organizations, such as the Partnership for a Drug Free America, have been having difficulty getting access to the media (CR "Drug-Related" S362).

The second need is for more drug treatment programs for drug users. Unfortunately, there are about 1 million people who need drug treatment, but find it unavailable (D *President's Drug Control* 38).

Expanded programs in these two areas might be quite effective in minimizing drug-related crime. First, expanded education programs could reduce the number of juveniles choosing to use drugs. Any number of sources argue that the anti-drug education programs of the 1980s and early 1990s were quite effective. While the Reagan "Just Say No" program was ridiculed at the time, it now appears to have been quite successful. In a recent *Wall Street Journal Editorial,* Nancy Reagan herself called for a revitalization of that program (the editorial is included in CR Rangel E180).

In regard to drug education, research suggests that interactive drug education programs in which the students make an active commitment to avoid drug use are more effective than more passive programs, such as Drug Abuse Resistance Education (DARE) (P Glazer "Preventing" 662). Students in a Life Skills Training program were substantially less likely to take drugs than other students. For example, in one program, those receiving the drug education were 44% less likely to use marijuana than those in the control group (P Glazer "Preventing" 664). Unfortunately, few schools are using such an approach (P Glazer "Preventing" 664). A Federal program could either require the use of an interactive program through the threat to cut off Federal funding or provide grants to encourage its use.

Second, expanded clinical treatment programs also could reduce drug-related crime. A program might both provide more support for such treatment programs and divert low level drug users from the criminal courts into treatment. The shift toward treatment might produce major benefits. A study of the Wisconsin Treatment Alternative Program, which is modelled after the national Treatment Alternatives to Street Crime program, found sizable benefits from the TAP approach in comparison to imprisonment. The Wisconsin study discovered a significant decline in the number of arrests following completion of the program (P Mauser, Van Stelle, and Moberg 586). Similarly, a study of California drug treatment found that in 1992 alone, drug treatment for 150,000 drug abusers cost $209 million, but saved an estimated $1.5 billion, most of which was "in the form of reductions in drug-related crime" (D *President's Drug Control* 38). A Rand corporation study confirms the value of treatment, which according to one estimate produces a seven to one cost-benefit ratio (D *President's Drug Control* 55). Thus, the evidence clearly suggests that money spent on expanded drug treatment programs is more productive than money spent on prosecuting drug offenders.

While there is strong support for an education/treatment oriented approach to drug crime, there are problems with such a perspective. First, the present system strongly supports both education and treatment. The Clinton administration already has launched a national anti-drug campaign "to deglamorize drug use in the mind of every child in America" (D *President's Drug Control* 12). This is designed to compliment existing private anti-drug campaigns (D *President's Drug Control* 12). Moreover the Federal Office of National Drug Control Policy is serving as the agency in charge of coordinating state, local and Federal anti-drug use initiatives (D *President's Drug Control* 65).

In addition, given the prevalence of anti-drug messages in the media, it is hard to see that many kids would be uninformed about the problem. Of course, peer pressure may cause them to ignore the current anti-drug message, but a Federal education program cannot solve that problem.

The Clinton administration is also committed to providing adequate clinical treatment (D *President's Drug Control* 38–39). In particular, the "Drug Courts Initiative" in the recent Crime act exemplifies a treatment-oriented diversion approach:

> The Drug Courts Initiative within the Crime Control Act establishes drug courts and similar offender management programs at the State and local levels. Existing drug court programs have been tested and proven effective in jurisdictions across the Nation. They ensure certainty and immediacy of punishment for nonviolent arrestees with substance abuse problems who might otherwise go unpunished or receive only unsupervised probation or a minimal sentence. Such programs free up jail and prison space for violent, predatory criminals. (D *President's Drug Control* 56)

The drug courts are designed to sentence many defendants to a treatment program, rather than prison. Given the Clinton administration's commitment to treatment, the advocate of change would have to show the residual benefits of adding additional treatment resources to the present system.

Second, once again, the argument could be made that expanded drug education and treatment is really a drug program, rather than a program to substantially reduce juvenile crime. The negative clearly should argue that if this program is accepted as resolutional then any crime control program would have to be accepted as fitting within the topic.

Third, there is a strong argument that additional dollars spent on education and treatment will not be as productive as in earlier programs. The reason for this is that those who most want to be educated about the issue or receive treatment for their addiction already have done so. Expanded programs would be aimed at reaching people who have been excluded so far. There is, therefore, good reason to doubt if new programs would be nearly as productive as previous programs.

Fourth, a commitment to drug treatment might be circumvented by state and local criminal officials, many of whom favor putting drug criminals in prison, rather than in treatment. These officials could circumvent the proposal simply by accusing the defendant of possessing enough of the drug to qualify as a drug dealer. In general, diversion programs deal with ordinary users, not drug dealers.

Finally, an expanded treatment/education program would be quite expensive. Simply providing funds to treat one million users would be extraordinarily expensive and link to the cost disadvantages that will be discussed in the final chapter.

Conclusion

In this chapter, I have discussed a wide variety of potential means of dealing with juvenile crime with new or expanded programs from within the criminal justice system. One general conclusion emerged from this discussion. While lock-em up and throw away the key proposals are popular with the public, they are not backed up by the literature.On the contrary, it is programs of graduated sanction or treatment that are supported by the strongest evidence.

4 Social Reform as Means of Controlling Juvenile Crime

The focus of this chapter is on social reform as a method of reducing youth crime. I begin by discussing social service alternatives for reducing juvenile crime, including targeted juvenile programs, employment based alternatives, and general social service programs. I then consider welfare reform issues as they relate to juvenile crime and proposals for massively increasing economic growth and job creation. In the third main section I consider education-based means of dealing with juvenile crime. In the last section on societal reform, I consider a number of public policies that might be used to improve social conditions and reduce juvenile crime. I focus on proposals for drug legalization, media regulation, and gun control.

Social Service Programs and Juvenile Crime

There are two basic ways of dealing with juvenile crime. You can try to deter crime and catch criminals after the fact. Or you can try to prevent kids from becoming criminals. Social service programs are designed to fulfill the prevention function.

Targeted Juvenile Programs

One approach to juvenile crime would be for the United States to target an array of social service programs on children living in poverty in order to prevent them from becoming criminals. For example, Richard Lerner believes that this country should create a comprehensive youth policy aimed at dealing with the host of problems afflicting America's young, including crime. He argues that we need broad systemic change, because the various problems confronting the young are interrelated. Thus, "an integrated, community-wide effort is necessary to foster positive youth development" (B 120). This program would develop "community-based youth organizations" to deal with issues relating to education, employment, juvenile justice and health (B Lerner 120).

A comprehensive approach to prevention, such as that described by Lerner, is based on the following premises. First, advocates of prevention argue that current programs are inadequate, both because they are not supported adequately and, because they are poorly organized. In regard to both of these problems, Senator Dodd observed in May 1994 that:

All and all, there are 266 different and distinct Federal programs cutting across seven departments that focus on delinquent at-risk youth. That is a maze, long and complicated enough to discourage even the most intrepid local group from finding the resources that they need. We need to boost funding for these programs, but more importantly or just as importantly, we need to boost local groups ability to find them in the first place. (D *Before Dreams* 3)

Dodd is undoubtedly correct about the need for organizational simplification, but he may be underestimating the funding shortfall. According to the GAO, only about $28 million "directly targets youth violence prevention" (D *Youth Violence Prevention* 82).

Second, advocates of a comprehensive prevention program argue that the only long-term solution to juvenile crime is prevention. For example, one of the foremost conservative criminologists (and a former national collegiate debate champion), James Q. Wilson of UCLA, writes that "Maybe we know how to make them better when they're 3 years old and in preschool, but we don't know how when they're 15 or 17" (qtd. in P Glazer "Juvenile" 177). Representative Ross makes the same point, noting that:

we know how to prevent crime. There have been studies for decades, almost centuries that tell us how to reduce crime and it involves a continuum of services and attention to children starting even before they are born with teen pregnancy prevention, prenatal care, early childhood education, relevant educational opportunities; recreational opportunities in the afternoons so that they have something to do with their time; summer jobs, job training and jobs; drug rehabilitation; and the kinds of thing that can get people in the right path, keep them in the right path; guaranteed college scholarships. All of those will actually reduce crime. (in D *Hearing on Juvenile* 5)

On this same subject, attorney General Janet Reno has testified that sheriffs from across the nation have told her that "unless we start preventing it [juvenile crime] we are not going to win this battle" (in D *Hope For Tomorrow* 15). A good summary of the prevention literature is found in Hawkins, Catalano and Brewer, "The evidence is clear: Prevention approaches applied from conception through age 6 that seek to reduce risk and enhance protection can be effective in preventing crime, violence and substance abuse in adolescent and young adulthood" (B 48).

Third, a prevention program should be comprehensive. That is, it should deal with all aspects of the child's social environment in order to create a situation in which he or she can thrive. For example, Hawkins, Catalano and Brewer argue for an approach which assesses the individual and societal risk factors that face kids in order to target programs at those most in need of help. For those in need, they argue for providing pre- and perinatal medical care, health education for the mother, immunizations, parent training, social services that assist in parent-child bonding, pre-school and Head Start programs, and educational daycare programs, which include a focus on "social competence" (B Hawkins, Catalano and Brewer 52–56).

In other words, the most successful prevention program will deal with a variety of social problems facing the child.

Fourth, advocates of prevention argue for using community-based anti-crime programs to target their assistance on kids. In reporting on analyses of more than

130 studies, Welsh, Harris, and Jenkins conclude that community-based programs may have much higher cost effectiveness and produce lower recidivism than institutional programs, if properly designed (P 77-78). They summarize such programs as involving "efforts to strengthen families, support core social institutions, promote prevention strategies, intervene immediately when delinquent behavior first occurs, and establish a broad range of graduated sanctions" (P 78).

A selection of community-based programs in an area would, in combination, offer the comprehensive services mentioned previously. Philip Coltoff, Executive Director of the Children's Aid Society of New York, explains that an effective prevention program:

> is not any single program in isolation. It is comprehensive programs that are there for children day in and day out, where they can have fun and grow with people they trust; programs that are woven into the fabric of their communities. (D *Youth Development* 10)

Such community programs can change the lives of disadvantaged children. For example, Coltoff notes that "youth in Boys and Girls Clubs or Campfire or 4-H programs are happier, more likely to finish school, less likely to be involved in juvenile delinquency, and more likely to be good community citizens" (D *Youth Development* 12). Such programs are also cost-effective. According to Coltoff, community programs cost about $500 per child per year, as opposed to more than $25,000 a year to put a child in a prison (D *Youth Development* 11).

Fifth, advocates of comprehensive prevention often favor combining the approach with graduated sanctions. When prevention programs are combined with graduated sanctions, the result could be a substantial reduction in crime. According to the Office of Juvenile Justice and Delinquency Prevention, "The combined effects of delinquency prevention and increased juvenile justice system effectiveness in intervening immediately and effectively in the lives of delinquent offenders should result in measurable decreases in delinquency" (in D *Hearing Regarding* 33).

In sum, in advocating targeted prevention programs, the affirmative will argue that current programs are too bureaucratic and not adequately funded and that expanded community programs could provide comprehensive services in order to prevent children from becoming criminals. There are several specific types of community programs that the affirmative could advocate.

Community Clubs Some argue that support for community clubs such as the Boys and Girls Clubs, could make an enormous difference in preventing juvenile delinquency. For example, Anthony P. Conza, a member of the Board of Boys and Girls Clubs of America argues that

> community-based youth programs have helped millions of Americans grow into responsible, productive, adults—but millions of today's youth lack access to these programs. Millions of Americans can testify from their own experience to the

effectiveness of community-based youth development programs. Community-based youth development organizations need Government's help in mobilizing resources to reach out to millions of young people who cannot afford or cannot find the supports which are available. (in D *Youth Development* 29)

Conza concludes that a $2 billion Federal program could have a "multiplier effect" (D *Youth Development* 41).

School Building Programs A second approach is to place community programs in existing school buildings, but keep them open for much longer periods. The building becomes a site for recreation, education, and specialized programs. Such an approach already has been tried. Senator Danforth testified that 675 schools in Missouri have been kept open for community use (in D *Hope For Tomorrow* 32). Gregory McDonald of the General Accounting Office, endorses such an approach, citing as example a successful comprehensive program built around use of school services at Ensley High School in Birmingham, CA.

Comprehensive programs in schools can serve a number of functions in addition to delinquency prevention. For example, Senator Dodd argues that school programs might substantially reduce illegitimate births, since "70 percent of the teenage mothers become pregnant between three and five in the afternoon" (D *Before Dreams* 32). Such programs also could be used for drug, alcohol and tobacco education. In a program in San Antonio, tobacco use dropped 25% and cocaine use fell 17% (testimony of Beverly Davids in D *Youth Development* 61).

Early Intervention A third alternative form of prevention is called early intervention, for it is based on providing services to very young children. In some cases, early intervention programs go so far as to provide pre-natal care. The idea behind early intervention programs is that kids are heavily influenced by their environment early on. If that environment can be changed, then we can prevent them from becoming criminals. Gregory McDonald of the GAO defends the value of early intervention programs providing "preventive health, social support or educational services directly to pre-school-aged children and families in their homes" (D *Youth Violence Prevention* 11). Examples of such programs can be found in the state of Hawaii and also in Ypsilanti, Michigan. In the Ypsilanti example, a rigorous study showed that such intervention reduced by 40% the number of kids who would be arrested by age 19. It also reduced the likelihood of serious or violent crime (Mcdonald in D *Youth Violence Prevention* 11). McDonald concludes that the program was beneficial. "As a result of the savings from reduced crime and welfare and increased employment, evaluators estimated that the program returned $3 to $6 for every $1 invested in it" (D *Youth Violence Prevention* 12).

Recreation Programs The type of prevention approach that has received the most treatment in the media is use of recreation programs. Recreation programs can take a variety of forms. Some areas have set up midnight basketball leagues to give young men something to do late at night. Other localities have opened recreation centers or established a variety of sports leagues. Ronald Stephens explains the basic rationale behind recreation programs: "Offering sports, drama, music, and other programs will provide recreational activity as well as develop a sense of self-worth and self-respect in young people. Youths involved in worthwhile extracurricular programs are less likely to seek reassurance from gang membership" (P 32).

Moreover, simply by keeping kids occupied, recreation programs could make a big difference. Bob Herbert notes:

> The National Center for Juvenile Justice released a study last fall showing that the peak hours for juvenile crime are between 3 and 6 P.M., the period immediately after school. If adults saw to it that youngsters were constructively engaged in that period, crime would go down. Instead, for a variety of reasons, including relentless budget cuts, we are giving youngsters less and less to do after school. (P "Trouble" A15)

In this way, recreation programs serve a purpose similar to the incapacitation function of prisons. They keep the kids so involved in activities that they don't have time to commit crimes. Senator Bumpers put the rationale for such programs quite clearly, "you get them on the basketball courts, and keep them out of the criminal courts" (D *Miscellaneous National* 16).

It is important to note that recreation programs "need not be limited to sports—basketball or football, but should also include anything that will interest and excite young minds—a neighborhood glee club, a neighborhood debate center, a neighborhood discussion group about insects" (Senator Bradley D *Before Dreams* 39). Bradley's point about providing a variety of recreational alternatives (including debate) is a good one.

Unfortunately, recreation programs are sorely lacking in the present system. In this regard, Representative Vento has argued for the importance of additional funding, because recreation centers have fallen into disrepair. He concludes "these programs are chronically underfunded and often do not reach millions of at-risk youth" (D *Urban Recreation* 10).

What kind of effectiveness has characterized prior recreation programs? In general, the literature strongly supports the efficacy of recreation programs. For example a midnight basketball program in Washington led to a substantial drop in crime (P Gest and Friedman 28) and recreation programs offered by Boys & Girls Clubs of America are reported to have helped cut crime by 13% (P Gest and Friedman 28). In Cincinnati, a program provided midnight basketball to thousands at a cost of "pennies per person" and helped produce a 24% decrease in crime in a particularly dangerous neighborhood (P Wall 1035). In Glenarden, Maryland, juvenile crime dropped by 60% following the establishment of recreation programs (testimony of Michael Standifer in D *Urban Recreation* 138).

One of the strongest pieces of evidence for the recreational alternative can be found in reviews of a program established in the 1930s, the Chicago Area Project, which relied heavily on establishing athletic leagues as a means of strengthening the social structure of the community and providing youths with recreational outlets. Reviews of the program have concluded that it was quite successful. An analysis conducted twenty-five years after the fact found that "While delinquency was certainly not eradicated in the targeted neighborhoods of Chicago, it was apparently substantially reduced" (B Bynum and Thompson 437).

Overall, the literature strongly supports the value of recreational programs for reducing youth crime. A comprehensive review of recreation programs concluded very favorably about the potential of recreation programs, labeling them a "promising intervention for preventing delinquency and violence" (B Brewer, Hawkins Catalano and Neckerman 100). That review cited one program in which there was a 75% decrease in juvenile arrests, for those participating in a recreation program, while in the comparison program there was a 67% increase (B Brewer, Hawkins Catalano and Neckerman 100). That is a more than 100% difference in effectiveness.

Anti-gang   Another type of community prevention program focuses on gangs as a major cause of youth violence and targets gang members and potential gang members for assistance. Such programs are similar to, but slightly different from the anti-gang programs mentioned in the previous chapter. Those programs focussed on law enforcement interaction with gang members. Gang prevention programs focus on dealing with the social conditions that lead to gang membership and gang violence. For example, Rodriguez describes a cooperative community anti-gang program, which he organized in Chicago. In the program, he worked with young people, both in and out of gangs, to find solutions to the violence problem (P 608, 609).

Prevention-oriented gang programs have been successful in the past. For example, "Police in Dallas recorded a 26% drop in juvenile arrests after a gang-intervention program, sponsored by 17 civic organizations, began reaching out to 3,000 youths in 1989 with education, recreation and job-training programs" (P Smolowe "Going Soft" 64). A similar program in Fort Myers, Florida led to a drop in juvenile crime of 27% and a vast improvement in academic performance by those involved (P Smolowe 64).

Implementing a Prevention Program

Up to this point, I have described the premises upon which targeted prevention programs are built and a number of specific types of prevention programs. It is now appropriate to consider how a prevention-oriented strategy for decreasing juvenile crime could be implemented.

An expanded prevention program could be implemented either through application of Federal standards to the states or through a Federal grant program. If the standards approach is utilized, then an appropriate Federal agency would draft standards specifying the types of services for juveniles that must be provided. Every community would be required to provide those services or risk losing Federal aid. That type of enforcement procedure commonly has been used to require states and localities to implement Federal mandates, in such areas as highway safety and many others.

Under the grant approach, the Federal government either would provide grants to support particular prevention programs or what is called a block grant. Senator Kassebaum defends a block grant program that provides funding to the states to distribute to local organizations, many of them non-profit. Under this approach, the Federal Government would provide money under very general guidelines to states, which would in turn give it to the best local organizations. These local organizations could spend that money, largely free of Federal regulations (see D *Youth Development*).

There are two essential strategic choices that the affirmative must make in constructing a prevention program. The first choice relates to the funding source and method of implementation. Block grants give discretion to the states to choose the best local prevention program. With a block grant approach, a funding system might be established which would allocate funds based on two factors: the current juvenile crime rate and the trend in that rate. Under that approach, communities with greater crime problems would get more resources. It should be noted that this plan has the unfortunate effect of punishing communities that have been doing a good job and rewarding those that haven't. Another problem with a block grant program is that the approach makes it more difficult for the affirmative to advocate a particular prevention strategy, since there is no guarantee that the states would choose programs using that strategy.

On the other hand, setting standards for prevention that the states must reach may be completely unrealistic, given financial problems in many regions. Probably the best approach is to construct a program in which the Federal government provides grants to local providers in order to implement a specific prevention strategy.

The second choice is between advocating a comprehensive prevention program or a specific program such as expanded recreational alternatives. Clearly, the experts in the field support the value of a comprehensive approach. On the other hand comprehensive programs are expensive and by limiting themselves to a particular program the affirmative also can limit the kinds of arguments that the negative can present against them.

While there is strong evidence favoring prevention, there are a number of powerful positions that can be developed against that approach. First, the opponent of expanded prevention programs should argue that the present system provides an appropriate level of prevention support. There are a large number of locally supported prevention programs, many of them run by charities. Moreover, community-based treatment is at the core of the Strategy issued by the Office of Juvenile Justice Delinquency and Prevention in March 1994 (P Welsh, Harris, and Jenkins 78 citing the *Federal Register,* 31 March 1994, p. 15273). In this effort, the Federal Government continues to aid states and localities in developing prevention programs. For example, in October 1994, Health and Human Services awarded $2 million in planning grants to assist localities in developing plans to deal with juvenile crime and delinquency (P "Planning Grants" 2-3). Thus, the existence of a host of successful community programs arguably proves that there is no need for an expanded Federal effort.

Second, the opponent of expanded prevention should combine a defense of current prevention programs with the argument that the addition of new programs under a Federal mandate will not be effective. There are two important positions that back up this judgment. Present prevention programs are developed at the local level and run by people who are committed to them. Such programs cannot be duplicated nationally, precisely because they respond to local conditions.

In addition, any new Federal program would be so bureaucratic that the benefits of prevention would be lost. According to Representative Ballenger, "what has happened to our youth programs, [is] that even though there is money available at the Federal level, we have put so many strings and various and sundry ways of restricting the usage that we aren't providing anything except jobs for people here in Washington" (D *Joint Hearing* 146). Marc Wilkins, of the executive committee of the Police Chief's Youth Task Force, emphasizes this point, "You have so many programs, like you say now, but you have people that are not really doing their job or taking their job seriously in these programs. You can have 100,000 programs, but if you have somebody that is just sitting at a desk saying, 'yes, I have a program,' you are not doing anything" (D *Youth Violence Prevention* 27).

A third argument against expanding prevention programs is that even well-designed programs don't work very well. In this regard, advocates of community-based treatment admit that many previous programs have been poorly designed and yielded uneven results (P Welsh, Harris, and Jenkins 78-79). In a systematic review of prevention programs, Bynum and Thompson come to a similar judgment. They cite failed programs in Boston, New York City, New Jersey and Minnesota (B 437–440). Overall, prevention programs have produced disappointing results.

A review of various types of prevention programs highlighted many different failures (B Brewer, Hawkins Catalano and Neckerman). For example, research indicates that mentoring programs are not effective in changing child behavior (B Brewer, Hawkins Catalano and Neckerman 99–100). Anti-gang programs also have failed: "programs that seek to redirect existing gangs and gang members toward more prosocial activities through the efforts of street workers appear to be counterproductive" (B Brewer, Hawkins Catalano and Neckerman 104). Spergel agrees, noting that street work anti-gang programs generally have failed and that in some cases, the gang took over the program and used it as a cover for criminal acts (B 252).

At minimum the failure of many current efforts indicates that the need for full research prior to implementing a large scale program (P Welsh, Harris, and Jenkins 79). That would seem to argue for continuing the current approach.

Moreover, there is a danger that expanded programs actually could make things worse. For example, recreation programs might help gangs recruit. According to Irving Spergel, of the University of Chicago, "Recreation, midnight basketball, traditional youth services, especially group activities, simple and occasional mentoring may not be sufficient, and under certain circumstances may serve to cohere gang youth and even increase delinquent gang activity" (D *The Gang Problem* 72).

Fourth, prevention programs will be quite costly. In order to provide the kind of supervision and treatment needed to help disadvantaged kids, a large commitment of resources will be needed. Disadvantaged kids need health care, drug, sex, alcohol, tobacco, and violence education, mentoring, recreation opportunities, access to cultural institutions, and so forth. A full-scale prevention program would cost the proverbial bundle.

Finally, prevention programs could be perceived as racist. Advocates of prevention suggest that the programs should be targeted on youths who suffer from the most societal conditions that are correlated with crime and violence. That means the program will be targeted almost exclusively on disadvantaged youths in the urban underclass, most of whom are members of minority groups. It, therefore, is quite possible that the program could be perceived as racist. There is also a substantial risk of parental backlash, given that several components of the prevention model require parental education efforts. And successful implementation of programs might require actions that would substantially impact civil liberties.

In sum, there is very strong evidence supporting a comprehensive approach to prevention. On the other hand, there is reason to believe that a Federally organized prevention program would have only a modest effect on juvenile crime and might produce community backlash. Moreover, given the current climate in Washington, expanded support for prevention could produce a strong political backlash, making it impossible to achieve a long-term budget deal, or leading to cuts in other programs.

Post-conviction Prevention

A second form of prevention focuses on helping offenders after they have been released. These post-conviction prevention programs provide counseling, job training and placement, and other services to the offender in order to reduce the recidivism rate.

Some programs have been quite successful. As a general rule, the most effective programs have focussed on providing skills and changing behavioral responses, including teaching how to avoid anti-social behavior (P Glazer "Juvenile" 175). These effective programs also tend to be run by private charities, as opposed to government agencies. For example, a group of Christian organizations have put together the "Christian Peacemaker Corp." This organization is "networking with other peacemaking groups, escorting people threatened by violence, and training individuals in conflict mediation and nonviolent principles" (P Tapia 47).

Well designed post-conviction programs can be effective in reducing offender recidivism. For example, juveniles who go through the Southwest Key post-release treatment program have a 65% lower re-arrest rate than kids who are just released from institutions (testimony of Juan Jose Sanchez in D *Hope For Tomorrow* 83).

Another model for post-conviction treatment is found in the VJO (Violent Juvenile Offender) program which "combines secure care with community reintegration strategies for each young person" (Michael Saucier in D *Hearing on Juvenile Crime* 38). The VJO program include:

> (1) early reintegration efforts that begin in the secure setting and follow the youth into the community upon release, (2) intensive supervision in the community to provide support upon reentry; and (3) life skills and social skills training. "Tough" legislation becomes "smart" with community care. (testimony of Michael Saucier in D *Hearing on Juvenile Crime* 38)

A post conviction treatment program could be implemented in exactly the same way as the community prevention programs that I discussed earlier.

While there are a number of successful post-conviction treatment programs, it is obvious that such an approach has far less potential to reduce juvenile crime than a pre-conviction treatment program. The reason is simple. It is a lot easier to prevent a person from becoming a delinquent and then a criminal then it is to rehabilitate someone once they have become a criminal. Rusell Eisenman supports this conclusion, arguing that treatment is often too late by the time the juvenile is fifteen or sixteen, because he/she "may be dedicated to an anti-social lifestyle" (P 28).

The most important argument against post-conviction treatment programs is that they don't work. Mark Lipsey of Vanderbilt University has reviewed more than 400 studies of small-scale rehabilitation programs and found "that rehabilitation programs reduce recidivism only by about 10%" (P Glazer "Juvenile" 175).

And, as I have argued at several points previously in this chapter, a Federally mandated post-conviction program is unlikely to be as effective as programs found in the present system. A report by the Rand Corporation backs up this judgment. A Rand review of rehabilitation concluded that small programs do not have a large enough sample to produce data that is useful (P Glazer "Juvenile" 175).

In addition to attacking the effectiveness of such programs, the negative ought to argue that adequate programs are out there for any offender who is willing to make the effort to find them. Those who are unwilling to make that effort are unlikely to be helped in any case.

Post-conviction programs are also subject to the same cost arguments as pre-conviction programs. Given the vast number of juveniles in prison currently, the cost of providing a full range of services to released felons could be quite high.

Job Training and Creation Programs

A third type of social policy that could be used to fight juvenile crime is a job training and/or creation program. The basic argument for job training and creation programs is simple: give a delinquent a good job and suddenly you have a good citizen.

Some research supports the efficacy of job training and placement programs. A recent study of gang members in Milwaukee suggests that many gang members would move to full-time employment if it were available (P Hagedorn 197). It is therefore plausible that a successful job program might have a significant effect on juvenile crime. Krisberg and his colleagues conclude: "The importance of 'real' work as a strategy for preventing serious and violent juvenile offending and deeper penetration into the justice system clearly fits with what we know about adolescent development and about protective factors against a variety of problematic behavior as youths move toward young adulthood" (B 167). Senator Simon agrees with the judgment that providing work is one key to reducing crime. Consequently, he argues strongly for both job training and job creation programs. He says that we should "Start jobs programs that put people of limited skills to work. Show me an area of high unemployment, and I will show you an area of high crime, whether it is African-American, Hispanic, or white" (CR "Crime Is Down" S19271).

Results of previous programs in the area back up these judgments. A program developed by Milton Shore and Joseph Massimo in Massachusetts illustrates the importance of work. In their program, low-income high school dropouts were placed in jobs and provided other services via the job placement process. The program was extremely successful, although it served only a few youths (see B Krisberg et al 166-167). Similarly, the Federal Job Corp program, which serves "a rather similar [to juvenile criminals] population of high-risk youths," "has been shown to prevent a substantial amount of later serious violent crime" (B Krisberg et al 167). Spergel also emphasizes the proven success of Job Corp programs in helping people "decide to 'move away from the gang'" (B 275).

Based on the experience with job training programs, and research suggesting that lack of jobs was a major factor in pushing kids into crime, some conclude that job training programs are the key to controlling juvenile crime. Others go much farther and argue for massive job creation programs. For example, Spergel writes in relation to the gang problem:

> Some policy analysts and legislators have suggested the development of a new-style Works Progress Administration or National Youth Service, e.g., AmeriCorps, that would include gang members, with appropriate social support and social control arrangements for them. There is ample evidence that gang youths would like to become employed, and in fact most find employment in due course. The lack of decent jobs and gang member access to them, and the lack of appropriate gang member academic and vocational skills and social attitudes, are problems that have to be resolved at both national and local levels for a reduction of the gang problem. (B 280)

On balance, there is strong evidence that providing employment opportunities could play an important role in reducing juvenile crime.

On the other hand, there is also strong evidence that employment-related programs will not be successful in reducing juvenile crime. Initially, it is important to recognize that it could be argued that job creation programs do not meet the resolution, because they are not designed "to" reduce juvenile crime. If "to" means "for the purpose of" it could be argued that the job creation programs are for the purpose of getting youths employed and that the crime reduction is only a side effect. For example, Krisberg, who I cited above, refers to the Job Corp program as "not specifically aimed at offenders." Therefore, the opponent of change should argue that such employment and training programs are not aimed at juvenile crime at all and thus do not fall within the confines of the resolution.

On the other hand, the fact that previous programs did not have as their primary purpose reduction of youth crime, does not necessarily mean that a new program would not have that purpose. For example, after reviewing studies on various means of reducing youth crime, Krisberg and his colleagues conclude "We believe that preparation for stable employment and placement in solid jobs should have a prominent place in programming for older adolescents" (B 167). Moreover, it seems clear that one purpose of job training programs always has been to create good citizens, and, therefore, prevent kids from becoming criminals. The fact that job creation programs serve other purposes is not relevant. A job creation program would be designed "to" substantially reduce juvenile crime, as well as serve other needs. Thus, the stronger argument would seem to be that such programs do meet the demands of the resolution.

A second argument against employment alternatives for reducing juvenile crime is there is no clear relationship between jobs and crime. Opponents of job training for juveniles note that many of the criminal acts are committed by 11, 12, and 13 year olds and that these children are not eligible to work in our society. Moreover, there was no significant youth crime problem at earlier periods in American history when jobs were in short supply, such as during the Great Depression. And if jobs were the crucial issue, then one would have expected youth crime to peak in the recessions of 1982 and 1992 and decline in periods of growth. Of course, youth crime continually has increased since about 1980.

Third, the negative should argue that job training and creation programs are generally ineffective. According to Charles Murray, the Job Corp program produced only "modest gains in average earnings—a matter of a few hundred dollars per year" (B 103). Mead agrees, noting that the income gains were "not enough to solve the war on poverty problem" (B "Reducing" 264). And the best that can be said for the massive CETA training program, which was funded with as much as $19 billion per year, is it produced "some positive impact on women, but not on men" (B Mead 103). Of course, since most crime is committed by males, it is crucial to help them get jobs.

Not only have general job training and creation efforts not been very effective, but a program that was targeted at juveniles, the Neighborhood Youth Corps program of 1960s, apparently had little effect. Studies found that "participation in the Neighborhood Youth Corps program was unrelated to delinquency prevention or reduction" (B Bynum and Thompson 439). A recent review of local project backs up the judgement that employment and training programs are not very useful. Of nine programs, six "showed no significant program effects," and in one case crime increased (B Brewer, Hawkins Catalano and Neckerman 113).

Fourth, the opponent of Federal action should argue that training programs can do nothing in the long term, without creation of new jobs. As Christopher Jencks notes, "Training schemes can rearrange the queue for jobs, but they cannot eliminate it" (P 43). To accomplish anything, individuals must be trained for jobs that exist. And of course job creation programs are extremely expensive.

Minimum Wage

Another alternative for reducing youth violence would be to increase the minimum wage. The argument here is that one cause of crime is that people living in the inner city cannot earn a decent income. Gueron has observed that in the early 1970s, a full-time minimum wage job was enough to lift a family of three out of poverty. By 1990, such a job left the family of three "27% below the poverty line" (B 240). Moreover, wages for unskilled workers have fallen rapidly over the last decade (B Gueron 240).

To deal with this problem, the minimum wage could be substantially increased, perhaps to $ 6.50 an hour. Another alternative would be to guarantee what is called a "working wage." Several localities have taken steps in this direction. For example, Baltimore, Milwaukee and Santa Clara County, California all have enacted living wage regulations that require that companies which do business on public land or in some way benefit from the public must pay their employees at least $6 an hour (P Uchitelle A1). Mayor Kurt Schmore of Baltimore is quoted as justifying the living wage as necessary to prevent having to pay "out more in food stamps and welfare" (qtd. in P Uchitelle A1).

While there are strong arguments for increasing the minimum wage, I don't think those arguments are necessarily linked to a program aimed at reducing juvenile crime. First, the negative should argue that the goal of an increase in the minimum wage is to help workers earn more and not to cut juvenile crime. Once again, they should note that acceptance of this affirmative topicality position has the effect of making virtually all social and economic programs topical.

Second, the negative should argue that juveniles do not turn to crime because of a relatively small shortfall in income, such as that which would be solved by an increase in the minimum wage to roughly $6.00. No one says, "Gosh, if I could earn $2.00 an hour more, I wouldn't have to sell drugs."

An increase in the minimum wage primarily would help the parents of potential juvenile criminals, but the data on the relationship between poverty and juvenile crime is iffy, as I explained in chapter two. Mead notes in this regard that "the vast majority of poor workers actually earn above the minimum wage; they are poor mainly because of low working hours" (B "Reducing" 258). He also notes that most minimum-wage workers are "secondary workers" and that "the minimum wage actually has little connection to poverty" (B "Reducing" 258). Increasing the minimum wage will not significantly reduce poverty, "because few poor adults are employed" (B Mead "Reducing" 263).

Third, the negative should use sources from the business community to argue that they cannot remain competitive while paying a much higher minimum wage (P Uchitelle C9). Therefore, the net result of a minimum wage hike, according to conservative economists, would be loss of jobs. Mead writes that "A higher minimum wage probably reduces work levels because it eliminates some jobs, and this causes some youths to withdraw from the labor force" (B "Reducing" 263).

Fourth, the negative should argue that increasing the minimum wage is inflationary, since it raises wage costs and that the Federal Reserve will react to any hint of inflation by raising interest rates. The potential impact of such a raise is to cause a recession. I will discuss this argument in more depth in the final chapter.

Increased Social Spending in General

Some commentators argue that the real cause of much juvenile crime is the terrible conditions in which poor children live. A recent study of eighteen industrialized nations found that poor kids in the United States were worse off than children in fifteen of the other seventeen industrialized nations, including countries like Italy that in overall terms are much poorer than the United States. The study noted that the United States is much less generous than most European nations in guaranteeing basic services to poor kids and that income inequality in the United States is the greatest in the world (P Bradsher A7). The authors of the study were quite critical of attempts to cut social programs and clearly favored expanding such support (P Bradsher A7). Therefore, an advocate might argue for massive increases in social programs across the board as a means of confronting youth crime. Eitzen puts it simply: "The link between poverty and street crime is indisputable. In the long run, reducing poverty will be the most effective crime fighting tool. Thus, as a society, we need to intensify our efforts to break the cycle of poverty. This means providing a universal and comprehensive health care system, low-cost housing, job training and decent compensation for work" (P 472). Eitzen also defends education improvement programs and job programs as essential means of reducing crime in the long term (P 472).

Another alternative would be to launch a program to decrease the impact of child abuse. By improving the family situation facing many children, such a program might substantially reduce juvenile crime. According to Dr. Russell Eisenman of McNeese State, "Early intervention with parents may help prevent crimes from happening by deterring the abuse before it occurs" (P 27).

Greater support for public health also might be part of the increased social spending strategy. Terrie Moffitt, a psychologist at the University of Wisconsin, notes, "I'd put my money on public health programs to improve infant health and prenatal care as the best ways to prevent delinquency" (qtd. in P Bower 233).

Another option might be to implement a comprehensive housing policy aimed at getting poor people into better housing. The idea would be that if the poor could be removed from ghetto conditions, they would be less subject to crime and, therefore, juvenile crime would decrease. One approach would be to rely on a variety of incentive programs in which housing assistance grants would be linked to tenant income. In such a program, increased work would not lead to a one for one reduction in housing subsidy. Thus, the tenant would have an incentive to work more in order to raise his/her income. Home ownership incentive programs also might be utilized.

Many of the possible housing programs were championed by Jack Kemp when he served as Secretary of HUD in the Reagan and Bush administrations (for a summary of the ideas of Kemp see B Weicher).

The social program strategy also might include additional funds for an expanded and improved Head Start program. Head Start provides pre-school education and services for poor children. Currently, only a small proportion of those eligible for Head Start are able to participate in the program, due to funding limitations. And current programs are for a half day during the school year only, dramatically limiting the number who can participate. Zigler and Styfco of Yale argue that Head Start should be fully funded for all children and should be a two year program supplied year round, in a full day model (B 317-319). They also propose expanding early childhood efforts to include a "parent-child" program that would cover the child until three, and a kindergarten to third grade program that would pick up after Head Start (B 330).

In sum, liberals argue for expanding a wide variety of social service programs as a way of confronting the terrible conditions in which many poor kids live. They claim that such programs substantially would reduce juvenile crime over time, by eliminating the causes of that crime.

While strong arguments can be made for increased support for social spending, there are also reasons to doubt whether such a program could be very effective in reducing juvenile crime. First, the negative should argue that increased social spending programs are not "for the purpose of" decreasing juvenile crime and that if you accept such a loose standard than virtually any social program could be considered to be topical. Against this, the affirmative will argue that social programs serve precisely the purpose of reducing juvenile crime (along with a host of other purposes as well). In response the negative should claim that specific affirmative evidence linking public health, or child abuse, or some other specific social program to juvenile crime actually proves their point, that acceptance of such a standard essentially removes meaningful limits from the resolution.

Second, the negative should argue that, while it is terrible that so many people live in bad conditions, those conditions are not the causal factors behind increased juvenile crime. I have cited several sources on this point already. Fagan supports the view that poverty is not the cause of crime quite clearly, when he says, "if it were true, there would have been more crime in the past, when more people were poorer" (P 157). He concludes, that "History defies the assumption that deteriorating economic circumstances breed crime and that improving conditions reduce it" (P 157).

Third, the opponent of Federal action should argue that social programs don't work. Many conservatives (and some moderates) agree that social spending fails.

Leslie Lenkowski of the Hudson Institute summarizes the research on a number of social service program that were designed to assist the poor in leaving poverty. Her conclusion is that social service programs make only a modest difference for the poor (B 300-302). And, perhaps more importantly, she argues that this situation is inherent. Social programs cannot be expected to make much difference for the poor because the basic problems of the poor are not tied to lack of services. She writes: "Recent surveys suggest that although families in poverty are more troubled and disadvantaged than those not, the differences are relatively small" (B 302). Noted conservative theorist Charles Murray agrees with Lenkowski that social programs don't make much difference. He points out that even Head Start has produced only small effects (B 101-102).

Murray goes on to argue that the underclass will be very hard to help, because people do not change readily after adolescence. He writes that "everything we know from social interventions indicates that by adolescence, the personality and cognitive traits in question are for practical purposes hard-wired" (B 104). Murray's ultimate conclusion is that we don't know how to implement a successful social program (B 104).

Conservatives also deny that social spending impacts crime rates. Recently, Patrick Fagan of the Heritage Foundation observed that, "Since 1965, welfare spending has increased 800 percent in real terms, while the number of major felonies per capita today is roughly three times the rate prior to 1960" (P 157). His conclusion is that crime is not related to social spending. If it were, crime should have plummeted.

Similar arguments could be made about any of the particular social spending programs that are touted as means of reducing juvenile crime. For example, in relation to housing programs, the opponent of action could argue that the theory that improved housing, by itself, will lead to a significant improvement in social conditions is questionable. John Weicher, former assistant secretary for policy development and research at HUD, writes "Decent housing by itself proved to have limited value as a vehicle for improving the social and economic positions of poor persons" (B 201).

Fourth, the negative should argue that it is not possible to reason from small pilot programs cited by the affirmative to how a major national program would work. I have explained this argument previously, but the basic point is that pilot programs often are much more effective than a large-scale national effort.

Fifth, the negative should argue that the public is totally opposed to expanded social programs and that passage of such a proposal will lead to a massive outpouring of public backlash and repeal of the plan. The argument is not that the plan could not be passed, but that after passage, public anger will force repeal. Alternatively, the negative might suggest that passage of such a plan would cause backlash that would aid extreme conservatives in taking over the country and eventually producing social conditions that are much worse than in the present system.

Sixth, the negative should argue that a program of increased social spending would be quite expensive. That seems obvious. For example, Lenkowski concludes in relation to cost, that "implementing the new services strategy on a scale (and over the time) necessary to have a significant effect on poverty would be extremely expensive" (B 304). Such expense could have major economic effects, a point that I will take up in the final chapter.

Negative Income Tax

Charles Murray has proposed eliminating all Federal social programs and replacing them with a Negative Income Tax (NIT) that would guarantee everyone of age 18 or older an income of $7500. He assumes that some form of universal health care also will be guaranteed. For those below the $7500 level, the Federal Government would provide money to raise them to the base. People over the base would pay taxes on their income as in the present system. The effect, Murray argues, would be to give every person the revenue necessary to live. No one would be forced into crime, because of poverty. He also believes that the program would eliminate perverse incentives for welfare recipients to have children, since a child would only decrease their spendable income. The program would create incentives for people to improve their lives and therefore, in the long term, might decrease juvenile crime (B 82-109).

While Murray's radical proposal is interesting, it probably is not a good one to defend as a means of reducing juvenile crime. First, Murray would never view his proposal as a policy for the purpose of reducing juvenile crime. Murray and other social conservatives do not believe that poverty is a primary cause of crime. Therefore, there are good reasons to doubt both the topicality and the solvency of such a proposal.

Second, there are obviously enormous risks associated with eliminating all current social programs. On a risk level, Murray's proposal seems a foolish alternative. If Murray is wrong about how his program would work, many people could be harmed.

Third, Murray assumes the passage of some kind of universal health care system. That has not happened and any national program would be quite expensive. Of course, the issues related to health care were covered in depth in a previous version of this book.

Finally, the negative would be on strong ground in arguing the political backlash position that I discussed earlier, although with a different link. Murray's proposal depends for funding on elimination of Social Security and other programs for the elderly. Public backlash against such an idea would be enormous.

Welfare Reform

Many believe that the current welfare system plays a causal role in creating conditions that lead juveniles to become criminals. Conservatives argue that welfare has created a culture of dependence and that current programs must be tightened. On the other hand, a diverse group of principled conservatives, neo-liberals, and moderates argue that requiring welfare recipients to work is an appropriate way of dealing with poverty. I will consider these two major proposals in turn.

Tighten Requirements

The view that access to welfare should be limited is based on the idea that continued reliance on welfare creates dependence. In the present system, not quite ten million children receive AFDC benefits (P "Current Programs" 167). Some argue that families remaining on welfare for extended periods of time are harmed by the system. According to Representative Bill Archer of Texas, "The current welfare system destroys families and undermines the work ethic. It traps people in a hopeless cycle of dependency." (in P "Should the House Pass" 174). UCLA physician Norman Brill concurs, "The welfare system that was developed out of humane and altruistic motives has had an unfortunate result of fostering a degree of dependency (along with an attitude of entitlement) that is said to have destroyed the fabric of the Black ghetto society" (B 19).

If welfare causes dependence, the obvious solution is to limit access to it. The result of enacting such limitation would be to help, not hurt, poor Americans. James Dorn, of the Cato Institute, argues that previous to the welfare state, poor Americans were able to build strong families. Even communities of poor immigrants, possessed a "moral order" (P 10). Welfare, however, has created an "inner-city landscape" which is "cluttered with crime-infested public housing and public schools that are mostly dreadful, dangerous, and amoral" (P 11). In the view of conservatives, there is a clear relationship between a failed welfare system and societal conditions that lead to juvenile crime. Charles Murray notes:

> Federal welfare policy has been a disaster. In black inner-city areas, upward of 80 percent of children are born without fathers. In many poor white communities, the figure is nearing 50 percent. Children in these neighborhoods suffer from neglect and abuse at rates that dwarf those for other Americans. Lacking parents who are prepared to take on the responsibilities of parenthood, millions of children face futures stunted in ways that no amount of money for schools or services can remedy. (P A11)

The answer, in the view of Murray and others, is to tighten the current welfare system in order to push people away from a life of dependency.

A more restrictive welfare system might be produced, either by simply tightening Federal regulations or by turning welfare over to the states. Under the Republican proposal, welfare would be returned to the states and current programs would no longer maintain their status as entitlements. Aid would be denied to teen mothers and to new children of mothers on welfare. There also would be a lifetime limit of five years for the receipt of welfare (P Polakow 591). In addition, adults would be required to work in order to receive benefits after an initial two-year period (P "Bill Summary" 168).

According to conservatives, one benefit that could be achieved from the Republican proposal is experimentation by the states in order to discover the optimal system. Representative Archer refers to the states as "laboratories of democracy" (in P "Should the House Pass" 176).

There is evidence indicating that restrictions on welfare can lead to improvements in the system. When New Jersey prohibited increased welfare payments to recipients who had another child, the birthrate dropped 10% (P Samuelson 45). And Wisconsin has cut its roles by 27%, in part by increasing funds for training, job placement and child care (P McCormick 32). Governor John Engler of Michigan cites the experience of his state in cutting 60,000 cases from the welfare roles as proof that the states can do a better job than the Federal Government of implementing welfare reform (P 38). He also argues that the states will be more efficient than the Federal Government has been, both because competition from other states will push toward efficiency and because the states may develop "public/private partnerships" with organizations such as the Salvation Army (P 40).

The advocates of welfare tightening also strongly attack liberals who predict disastrous results from welfare reform. Charles Murray notes in this regard, "The reality is that, for 35 years, liberal predictions about welfare have been consistently wrong and conservative predictions have been consistently right" (P A11).

While it is clear that the current welfare system is failing in important ways, there are very good reasons to believe that neither tightening the eligibility requirements nor simply handing the program off to the states would be a good idea. First, it is not clear that welfare is a cause of juvenile crime at all. It is widely believe that social spending programs have failed, but many experts disagree with that conclusion. Susan Mayer, a professor at the University of Chicago, and Christopher Jencks, a professor and famed social theorist at Northwestern, argue that social programs have been quite effective in achieving their aims (P A15).

Nor is it clear that welfare benefits have acted as an incentive for people not to work. Welfare hardly provides a substantial income. Judith Gueron has observed that "Between 1972 and 1991, AFDC benefits eroded by a dramatic 41% in real terms (B 238). Mayer and Jencks also note that increased out of wedlock births do not seem to be tied to spending on poverty programs (P A15). In recent debate, Senator Moynihan identified what he believes to be the amount of evidence indicating that welfare benefits are encouraging additional illegitimate births as "None" (CR "Family" 14 September 1995 S13560). Additionally, there is strong evidence that welfare is not addictive. Christopher Jencks writes that "If welfare were addictive, we would expect a large fraction of those who get benefits to stay on the rolls as long as they legally can. That is not the case. Most people who go on welfare get off in less than 2 years" (B "Can We" 71).

Thus, there is strong evidence that the welfare system is not the cause of personal dependency. If that is the case, then welfare is not a cause of juvenile crime. This argument both undercuts the benefit of welfare tightening and casts doubt on whether such a program is resolutional.

Second, there are a number of reasons to believe that a pro-tightening proposal would fail. Initially, it is important to recognize that the states already have considerable latitude to experiment with welfare reform. In recent debate, Senator Dole explained that twelve states have received waivers to experiment with some type of family cap (CR "Family" 13 September 1995 S13487). This undercuts the need for the Republican proposal, at least in reference to the need for experimentation.

In addition, there is considerable question about whether the states would do a better job than the Federal government of administering a welfare system. Recently, Forrest Chisman, President of the Southport Institute for Policy Analysis, noted that states and localities do not receive high marks for their work in the areas of education and law enforcement (P 600). Many believe that placing the states in charge of welfare reform would be a disaster. Recently, Valerie Polakow chronicled the problems that welfare recipients face in Michigan. She described how inadequate resources may force them into homelessness and how there is not nearly enough support to live a decent life. The point of her essay was to indict the idea of welfare reform that merely cuts back on current programs. And of course Michigan has been cited as a model for how the states might take over the national welfare program (P Polakow 590-592). Even conservatives doubt whether state programs can be very effective. Writing in the National Review, Marvin Olasky argued that state reform efforts have not been very effective in placing welfare recipients in jobs (P 44–46).

Moreover, many argue that the Republican program would create a "race to the bottom" in which states would compete for business by creating the lowest possible support for welfare (P "Work Fear" 7). Over time, this problem could get worse. "As the states compete through low taxes to attract industry and well-off residents, state-controlled programs helping poor people will get still more stingy" (P Bergmann and Hartmann 592).

Third, the result of the Republican proposal, in the view of many, would be to harm poor people. To some, it seems inevitable that the Republican program would result in people being cut off from government assistance. Representative Brown cites data from his district in California indicating that while there are 64,000 potential workers receiving AFDC benefits, there are a maximum of about 5300 available jobs (in P "Should the House Pass" 181). The obvious implication is that only a small percentage of welfare recipients will be able to find work. At the end of the five year period, the result will be that people will have no job and will be ineligible for government support. They could starve to death.

Even if they get jobs this may not be enough to provide them with a minimally adequate income. Christopher Jencks argues that most welfare recipients will not be able to earn enough money to live on and that the only viable option is, therefore, continued government support in one form or another (B "Can We" 77–78).

The legislation also might endanger children. Barbara Bergmann of American University and Heidi Hartmann of the Institute for Women's Policy Research argue simply, "The fact is that the welfare system, dysfunctional as it currently is, was invented to take care of a real problem: There are single mothers who need help because they cannot earn enough to cover the minimal needs of their families" (P 592). Senator Moynihan agrees with this view and quotes conservative columnist George Will, who says simply "The bill is reckless because it could endanger the well-being of the poorest children in society in the name of a series of untested theories about how people may respond to some new incentives" (CR "Family" 14 September 1995 S13558). We should not, in Moynihan's view, "deny benefits to children because of the mistakes" of their parents (CR "Family" 13 September 1995 S13488). An estimate produced by the Department of Health and Human Services indicates that the Senate welfare bill would put 1.2 million additional children into poverty (P Pollit 777), possibly creating a large group of "street families" (P DeParle 64).

Fourth, the Republican welfare proposal in fact might produce exactly the opposite effect demanded by the resolution. In this view, cutting off welfare recipients could push them into crime. Representative George Brown of California recently argued that "if we simply throw people off welfare and provide no job or safety net income, which is what the Republican plan would do after two years, then I think we can be assured that crime will rise" (in P "Should the House Pass" 177, 179).

Fifth, some argue that an unintended consequence of the Republican reform effort would be increased abortion. The so-called family cap prevents women from receiving additional benefits if they have more children. This could encourage abortion. After New Jersey instituted a family cap, there was a decrease in the rate of births to women on welfare, but also a 4% increase in abortions (P "Right Questions" 4).

A review of the literature on welfare reform makes it quite clear that the balance of expert opinion is that further tightening is not needed and probably would be counterproductive. In any case, welfare reform should not be understood as a means of reducing juvenile crime.

Workfare

In response to the conservative approach, many argue that the real issue is jobs. For example, Representative Brown says simply that "The real problem is unemployment, and the culture of despondency and poverty that it creates" (in P "Should the House Pass" 179). If the real problem is jobs, then the appropriate solution is to link receipt of welfare benefits to work.

Work is a powerful means of getting people out of poverty. According to Lawrence Mead of New York University:

> The effect of employment is tremendous. Nonworkers suffer poverty at two and three quarters to six times the rate occurring among workers. More than 80% of female family heads with children are poor if they do not work; only 12%—below the average for the population—are poor if they work full-year and full-time. (B "Raising" 256)

Mead also notes that work requirement programs at the state level have been effective in the past and could be expanded (B "Reducing" 266-268).

Therefore, in order to reduce welfare dependency and help people out of poverty, some argue for workfare, in which, with some exceptions, people receiving welfare benefits would be required to work in either a private or public sector job. Mickey Kaus, a long-time editor at *The New Republic,* proposes offering every American over 18 a job "performing a useful public service at a wage slightly below the minimum wage, then let's subsidize the wages of all low-wage workers, whether in public jobs or in private jobs, so that they can raise reasonable-size families in dignity, out of poverty" (D *Rethinking* 18). He also supports providing day care for single mothers (D *Rethinking* 18).

Another alternative would be to guarantee health care and child care to women on welfare who got jobs. Under that circumstance, some argue that even a minimum wage job, when combined with food stamps and the earned income tax credit would be enough for a family to live. According to Barbara Bergmann and Heidi Hartmann, such a system "would powerfully increase the incentive to leave welfare for a job, and many current welfare recipients would try to do so" (P 594). They note that a similar program in France results in a situation in which "only 6 percent of French children are poor, compared with 23 percent" in the United States (P 595). On the other hand, they also admit that their program would cost about $90 billion in new spending per year (P 595).

Workfare could reduce juvenile crime in two ways. First, workfare encourages work and as noted earlier gainful employment is a key to getting out of poverty. Second, workfare could cut welfare dependency and give people a sense of self-esteem. In so doing, it also might help restore the urban family. Mead claims that only restoration of the family can rebuild culture in the ghetto. He argues that mandatory work requirements would make a big difference in that regard. "Above all, it [government] can require that poor parents work, because employment failures are the greatest cause of family failures" (B "Reducing" 274).

While a strong case can be made for workfare, there are problems with such a proposal. First, once again, it is not clear that workfare should be thought of as a program to decrease juvenile crime, as opposed to a program aimed at reducing welfare dependence that might have a side effect on the juvenile crime rate.

Second, there are strong arguments denying that a workfare program would reduce crime. While work is a key to earning a good income, it is not at all certain that mandatory work for the government would produce the same benefits as work in the private sector. Crucially, previous experiments with workfare incentive and requirement programs indicate that they "did little to reduce poverty" (B Gueron 239). If that is the case, then there is little reason to believe that they would reduce juvenile crime.

Nor is it certain that a workfare program could change the values of the underclass or help save the family. In fact, because work would take parents out of the home and, therefore, reduce supervision, it is arguable that a mandatory workfare program might increase juvenile crime.

Third, administering a workfare program will be complex. Government will need to find jobs for people and rigorously require that people work, but at the same time make appropriate exceptions for the disabled, mothers who recently have given birth, and so forth. Government also will need to administer child-care and other programs necessary for the work program to succeed. Many doubt that government could administer an effective program in this area. Even some conservatives argue that workfare is unlikely to succeed. George Gilder has argued recently that workfare programs likely would fail, because they would require an enormous expansion in government (P 25).

Fourth, a workfare program would be quite expensive. "Simply to guarantee work to all recipients still on the rolls after 2 years of aid might require 1.5 million positions and cost $40 billion a year" (B Mead "Reducing" 272; also see B Patterson 239). In addition to paying for the job, the Congressional Budget Office estimates that each recipient would cost "about $6,000 for supervisors and child care" (cited in P "Work Fear" 7). All told the cost could be quite high. Earlier, I cited an estimate that one proposal might cost $90 billion additional dollars a year. Others put the cost at between $30 and $50 billion more than in the present system (B Jencks "Can We" 80).

A strong case can be made for workfare. Political leaders from Ronald Reagan to Bill Clinton have argued for such a program. Yet, the relationship of workfare to juvenile crime control is small and the costs of such a plan are very high.

Reducing Juvenile Crime Through Economic Growth

There are some who argue that the only way to deal with the underclass problem in this country is to massively increase economic growth, thus creating so many jobs that anyone who wants to work can earn a decent living. Such a program could significantly reduce juvenile crime, by cutting poverty. Moreover, many argue that more good jobs equals less crime (P Eitzen 470).

In addition, there is evidence that economic inequality leads to crime. Stanley Eitzen writes, "The greater the inequality in a neighborhood, city, region, or society, the higher the crime rate. In other words, the greater the disparities between rich and poor, the greater the probability of crime" (P 470). A massive program to create growth could decrease the inequality.

Thus, the advocate of change might argue for a program to increase growth and create jobs. One way of producing this result would be to increase investment in infra-structure including roads, bridges, airports, public buildings and so forth. According to Federal Reserve System Chair, Alan Greenspan, "Our current capital stock is becoming obsolete far more rapidly than in past years" (P 80). The U.S. Advisory Commission on Intergovernmental Relations agrees and cites the conclusion of the National Council on Public Works Improvement that "America's infrastructure is barely adequate to fulfill current requirements, and insufficient to meet the demands of future economic growth and development" (D iii).

Increased investment in infrastructure would dramatically increase growth. Recently, famed MIT economist Lester Thurow testified about the importance of investing in infrastructure. He noted that "if you look at American economic history, we had big bursts of economic growth after we would have a big infrastructure development" (D *Rebuilding America* 16). Levy makes a similar point, noting that spending on infrastructure would be "extraordinarily effective in creating jobs" (D *Rebuilding America* 20). In fact, according to Representative Hamburg of California, $1 billion spent on infrastructure pays off with between 25,000 to 60,000 jobs (D *Rebuilding America* 41). Robert Eisner, an economist from Northwestern, puts the job creation capacity of infrastructure spending into perspective. Recently, he testified that "if you got $10 billion to accelerate spending, you might reduce unemployment by 200,000" (testimony in D *Anti-Recession* 64).

A program to rebuild infrastructure could be implemented simply by increasing Federal investment in the area. Thirty or forty billion dollars of increased spending each year would go a very long way to improving the job prospects of poor Americans. Another possibility is for the Federal Government to "commit to reimbursing State and local governments for the interest they pay on bonds they use to finance infrastructure construction projects. Under this approach, the Federal share of the spending would be spread over the lifetime of the new investment projects" (testimony of Dr. David Levy of Bad College in D *Rebuilding America* 20). In this way, the infrastructure investment would not have a major impact on the deficit. Moreover, since a one percent decrease in the unemployment rate cuts the Federal deficit by $50 billion, such a program might not be as expensive as it first seems (testimony of Lane Kirkland of the AFL-CIO in D *Anti-Recession* 13).

The advocate of change also might be able to claim benefits from specific types of infrastructure development. For example, spending money on water pollution clean up could both create jobs and decrease juvenile crime and save lives by reducing environmental pollution.

There is no question that the United States needs greater investment in infrastructure. But as a means of reducing juvenile crime such an approach has problems. First, in order to consider investment in infrastructure a juvenile crime control program one must use an extremely broad definition of such programs. That is problematic for all of the reasons I have explained previously.

Second, many doubt that the problems of the underclass are tied exclusively to lack of access to a good job. For example, Mead argues that "about a third of the work problem among the seriously poor might be attributable to limits to opportunity in all forms" (B "Reducing" 262). The remainder, he attributes to "the culture of poverty" (B "Reducing" 262).

Third, job creation programs have not been very effective in the past. Mead cites the CETA job creation program of the 1970s, which funded 750,000 jobs a year, but "gains in earnings were marginal at best, and after CETA most clients did not go on to employment in the private sector" (B "Reducing" 264).

Fourth, any additional benefit from infrastructure spending easily could be achieved without the resolution. Take the water pollution control example I mentioned earlier. The negative could argue for a program of spending money on water pollution control, but cutting money from elsewhere in the investment portion of the Federal budget. This counterplan would achieve the affirmative advantage in relation to pollution, but not create any additional jobs and thus not be topical.

Fifth, the high costs of infrastructure spending create major problems. Clearly, Congress would have difficulty funding $30 or $40 billion dollars of additional spending. Therefore, the result of such a mandate might be to derail a budget agreement or cause the Federal Reserve to clamp down on interest rates. Both issues will be discussed in the final chapter.

Education and Juvenile Crime

There are a number of approaches for reducing juvenile crime that are located within the educational system. These methods can be grouped in the categories of educational reform, violence education, anti-gang education, and a safe schools initiative.

Educational Reform

It could be argued that the key to reducing juvenile violence is educational reform. For example, Douglas Besharov of the American Enterprise Institute argues that one of the best ways to increase the income of poor people is to improve the educational system. He notes that income is highly correlated with education (B 41). Thus, a successful education reform initiative could decrease poverty, which in turn would lead to a decrease in juvenile crime.

Some experts say that improved educational performance directly leads to crime reduction. Terrie Moffitt of the University of Wisconsin argues that programs aimed at improving the academic performance and personal involvement of potential delinquents "may also cut down on law-breaking" (views cited in P Bower 233).

Although any number of different methods of reforming education could be tried, the current literature focuses on utilization of a voucher plan. Under a voucher plan, public school students would not be assigned to a school. Instead, their parents would be given a voucher worth so much money, which they could apply to pay for their child's education at a public or private school of their choice.

A voucher proposal is built on the ideas that parents know best about how to educate their children and that the competitive marketplace, which a voucher plan would generate, is the best means of improving schools. Chubb and Moe write:

> Markets appear better suited than institutions of direct democratic control to promoting educational quality. Markets seem to encourage the more equitable treatment of students within schools and the more equal distribution of quality from across different schools. (B 152)

Thus, market based reform might lead to a reduction of juvenile crime.

On-balance, however, the arguments clearly do not favor a voucher approach to juvenile crime control. Initially, it seems clear that the primary aim of a voucher program is not to reduce juvenile crime, but to improve educational quality and guarantee school choice. Thus, a strong case can be made that the proposal does not fall within the resolution. Moreover, a recent consideration of the effects of alternative schooling proposals on delinquency found that they produced no effect (P Cox, Davidson, and Bynum 219). If vouchers (or some other educational reform program) fall within the topic then there are virtually no limits on the resolution.

There are also good reasons to doubt whether a voucher plan would be a good alternative for the nation. Initially, it is not clear that a shift to reliance on private schooling would improve education. According to Albert Shanker, a national assessment of performance in private and public schools reveals "virtually no difference in the performance of public and parochial and other private schools" (B 155). Shanker admits that private school students perform slightly better than public school students, but goes on to observe that when the much lower social economic status of the average public school student (in comparison to the average private school student) is considered "what is surprising is not that private school students, on average, performed slightly better than public school students but that they did not leave public school students behind in the dust" (B 158).

Moreover, a voucher experiment carried out in Milwaukee apparently has been a failure. Data indicates that "there were certainly no dramatic gains in achievement made by the voucher students in private schools, either in absolute terms or relative to the Milwaukee public school (MPS) students" (B Shanker 167). Based on all the available data, one researcher concluded that *"there is no systematic evidence that choice students do either better or worse than MPS students once we have controlled for gender, race income, grade and prior achievement"* (research conclusion of J.F. Witte cited in B Shanker 167, italics added by Shanker).

Vouchers also could exacerbate the educational problems facing America. Wallace Peterson notes that a voucher system "could easily lead to a further polarization of American society, along lines of income and class, rather than improve the quality of education" (B 235).

Additionally, there is an argument that voucher plans unfairly punish students of uncaring or uneducated parents. A voucher plan works only if parents actively seek information on the best schools. If the parent doesn't care or cannot process the information, then the child may be punished with a bad education. On balance, it does not seem that a voucher proposal is a good means for reducing juvenile crime.

Anti-violence Education

Another means of reducing juvenile violence would be to include a program of anti-violence education within the public school curriculum. Some argue that a program emphasizing the importance of walking away from violence might significantly reduce the impact of youth crime. The Institute of Mental Health has developed models and programs to help young people recognize the alternatives to violence (see P "Alternatives to Violence" 14–15). One program uses the phrase "Squash It," to emphasize that kids should walk away from violence (P Stevens "A Media Campaign" 28).

Based on the success of anti-drunk driving advocacy programs, such as the designated driver program, Stevens argues that the "Squash It" program might have a significant effect on juvenile violence (P "A Media Campaign" 28).

While anti-violence education may be a good idea, it hardly seems that such a proposal can be a centerpiece of a juvenile anti-crime program. First, the negative should argue that it is not credible that such a program ever could substantially reduce juvenile crime. They also should claim that no advocate of anti-violence education program would ever claim that a truly substantial decrease was a likely result of implementation of their program. Thus, the negative could say that the program was not "for the purpose of substantially reducing juvenile crime."

Second, the negative should back up their topicality position by attacking the solvency of the proposal. In a review of studies, Brewer, Hawkins, Catalano and Neckerman found that data on conflict resolution and violence prevention programs did not strongly demonstrate the effectiveness of such programs. They note, "in addition to the specific methodological problems in each evaluation and the lack of random assignment to study groups, these limitations suggest that the few positive results should be interpreted very carefully" (B 83).

Once again, the success of pilot programs proves little in the context of what a national program could do. There is also an argument that anti-violence education cannot work in the areas where it is most needed. Children in violence-prone areas know that violence is dangerous; they see its effects daily. Is it really credible that telling them to "Squash It" is going to make much difference?

Third, there is a strong argument that the Federal government should not be establishing school curriculum guides at such a detailed level. Is it sensible for the Federal Government to mandate a specific violence curriculum when we don't do the same thing for English, speech, or history? Historically, public schools have been the province of states and localities. There is a strong argument that curriculum regulation mandating anti-violence education violates the principle of federalism that I will consider in the final chapter.

Fourth, requiring an anti-violence program inevitably means curtailing other programs. You can teach only one subject at a time. Moreover, it does not seem sensible to enforce such a requirement nationally, when many schools have no violence problem.

Anti-gang Education

Another alternative would be to include an anti-gang education program in the curriculum of schools threatened by gang activity. That program could be required by the Federal Government under a threat of loss of Federal funding or it could be supported via a grant program. One review found that a gang prevention curriculum, when combined with recreational opportunities, "may hold promise for preventing at-risk youths from joining gangs and perhaps associating with delinquent and violent peers more generally" (B Brewer, Hawkins Catalano and Neckerman 104). Goldstein and Glick provide a detailed overview of an anti-gang violence program, which they label "Aggression Replacement Training Curriculum" (B 61-63). They cite several studies indicating the effectiveness of the approach (B chapters 5 and 7).

Many of the same arguments can be made against an anti-gang education program as against violence education in general, although such an effort does seem to be oriented toward substantially reducing juvenile violence.

There are good reasons, however, to doubt the effectiveness of an anti-gang program. The foremost expert on the subject, Irving Spergel, emphasizes that research studies do not clearly support the claim that anti-gang education programs are effective in reducing gang activities (B 272). Spergel's conclusion makes sense. Kids join gangs because the gang serves a strong function for them in confronting life in their community. No one says, "Gosh, I'll join a gang because I want to be a vicious criminal." Therefore, anti-gang education programs face an uphill battle, because they cannot change the social conditions that lead to gang membership. In addition, the success of a few pilot programs is virtually meaningless. Remember, pilot programs are almost always more effective than large-scale implementation.

Safe Schools

The final educational program that I will consider is an initiative to create "Safe Schools." Senator Kerry of Massachusetts notes that "about 11 percent of all our crimes in this country occur each year in our 85,000 public schools" (CR "Department of Commerce" 7 December 1995: S18153). That adds up to three million crimes a year (Senator Kerry in CR "Department of Commerce" 7 December 1995: S18153).

Therefore, one means of reducing juvenile crime would be to create a safe schools program. Ronald Stephens has described a number of steps that schools could take to reduce the threat of juvenile crime (P 29-31). An affirmative might use his program as a model for what should be done nationally.

While a safe school program may be sensible, it is unclear that a Federal effort is necessary. Many of the steps needed to improve school safety relate to dealing with staff in the school, establishing emergency policies, and so forth. While such initiatives are undeniably important, it is hard to see how a Federal initiative is needed.

There is even an argument that a Federal program could be counterproductive by encouraging a "one size fits all" mindset. A school in Dodge City, Kansas and a school in the Bronx face different problems. It also seems clear that imposing a Federal approach nationally risks violating the Federalism principle which I mentioned earlier.

In addition, some of the possible ways to improve schools seem impractical. For example, Ronald Stephens argues that students should be allowed only mesh or clear plastic book bags (P 31). This may seem reasonable in certain urban environments, but not in the rest of the country. He also endorses providing students with two sets of books, so that they can have one at home and one at school. This idea seems excessively costly.

Drug Legalization

One of the most important (and most radical) means of reducing youth crime would be to legalize some or all drugs. There is no doubt that legalizing drugs dramatically would reduce juvenile crime; for one thing juvenile drug use would no longer be criminal (depending upon how the legislation was written). Stanley Eitzen summarizes the many ways in which drug legalization substantially could reduce crime:

> If drugs were legalized or decriminalized, crimes would be reduced in several ways: (a) By eliminating drug use as a criminal problem, we would have 1.12 million fewer arrests each year. (b) There would be many fewer prisoners (currently about 60 percent of all federal prisoners and 25 percent of all state prisoners are incarcerated for drug offenses). (c) Money now spent on the drug war ($31 billion annually, not counting prison construction) could be spent for other crime control programs such as police patrols, treatment of drug users, and jobs programs. (d) Drugs could be regulated and taxed generating revenues of about $5 billion a year. (e) It would end the illicit drug trade that provides tremendous profits to organized crime, violent gangs, and other traffickers. (f) It would eliminate considerable corruption of the police and other authorities. (g) There would be many fewer homicides. Somewhere between one-fourth and one-half of the killings in the inner cities are drug related. (h) The lower cost of purchasing drugs reduces the need to commit crimes to pay for drug habits. (P 472)

Moreover, putting juveniles in prison for drug crimes may have the effect of "giving these kids a criminal identity," (Joseph D. McNamara, former Police Chief in San Jose, Calif in P "End the War" A11). Drug legalization also would decrease crimes against juveniles, since oftentimes "small children are incidental victims of the street battles that result [from conflict produced by drug sales]. By one estimate, we have 10,000 drug-related homicides a year" (P Lewis "End the War" A11).

Thus, the advocate of drug legalization could claim that crime would be reduced in numerous ways if drugs were legalized. It is important to remember that after legalization, organized crime could no longer market drugs, because other businesses would be able to produce the product at a much lower price.

In addition to the crime advantage, advocates of drug legalization argue that current laws send many innocent people to prison. According to *New York Times* columnist Anthony Lewis, there are 100,000 nonviolent drug offenders in prison (P "First" A15). Overall, a high percentage of the one million in prison are there

because of drug laws (P Anthony Lewis "Ending the War" A11). The imprisonment problem is especially serious in the black community, where one-third of
young black men are in prison (or under supervision), many for drug offenses (P
Anthony Lewis "End the War" A11).

How would drug legalization work? Ethan Nadelmann of Princeton describes
a program in which "government makes most of the substances that are now
banned legally available to competent adults, exercises strong regulatory powers
over all large-scale production and sale of drugs, makes drug-treatment programs
available to all who need them and offers honest drug-education programs to
children" (B "The Case" 19). Under this approach, one or more currently illegal
drugs would be legalized for sale in a regulated fashion.

It is important to note that in order to maximally reduce juvenile crime, the
advocate of change must legalize the sale of drugs to at least some juveniles. A
program that legalizes drugs for adults only would reduce juvenile crime, because
the market for drugs would decrease, leading to a decline in drug sales by
juveniles. However, the crime reduction of an adults only program would be much
less than if drugs were legalized for all.

It is also important to note that the advantages of drug legalization depend
upon the scope of that legalization. A program that legalizes marijuana, cocaine,
and even heroin will have a much greater effect than one that merely legalizes
marijuana.

One approach that might be included in the program is to allow for the sales of
drugs in a mild form. In the present system, for example, pure alcohol is not sold;
rather, even hard liquor is only a certain percentage alcohol. A similar approach
might be taken with cocaine and heroin (see B Alexander 299). There is some
strong evidence that beverages containing coca could be used, without producing
the harmful effects associated with cocaine and crack. In fact, President William
McKinley apparently consumed such a a coca containing wine (B Karel 81).

What would be the effects of drug legalization? First, as I already have noted,
proponents of legalization argue that crime would drop for several reasons.
Second, they argue that legalization might help reduce the spread of AIDS, since it
would make it much easier for addicts to get sterile needles (B Karel 99).

Proponents of legalization also claim that drug use would not increase substantially. First, legalization would allow a much more effective program of drug
treatment. Karel notes that "publicly available drugs would be taxed and revenues
turned to administer and expand drug treatment and distribution centers and drug
education programs" (B 86). Second, they argue that drug prohibition clearly has
failed. Certainly, all of the antidrug efforts have not made crack unavailable or
priced marijuana out of the market (P D'Angelo 30). Anthony Lewis puts it
simply: "Prohibition of drugs began in 1915. The experiment has been going for
80 years now, and by every rational test it is a ghastly failure" (P "End the War"
A11).

Third, they argue that research indicates that legalization would not result in an
increase in use. Alexander emphasizes that policies that have moved toward

legalization have been successful: "Marijuana legalization for personal use in Alaska, decriminalization in several other American states, and de facto legalization in the Netherlands continue to seem reasonable to the people directly involved and have done no visible harm to bordering states and provinces" (B 295). Nadelman backs up this point, noting that "the decriminalization of marijuana by about a dozen states during the 1970s did not lead to increases in marijuana consumption" (B "The Case" 41). Fourth, it can be argued that people who do turn to drugs rarely move into ever more serious drugs. For example, about 80% of high school marijuana users do not move on to other drugs (P Glazer "Preventing" 668).

Fifth, legalization advocates argue that it makes no sense to allow sales of alcohol and tobacco, but ban drugs (B Nadelmann 25). They also claim that it is easy to over-estimate the harmful effects of drugs. In fact, there is strong evidence that drugs are not nearly as dangerous as alcohol. Nadelmann argues that "the vast majority of Americans who have used illicit drugs have done so in moderation . . . [and] relatively few have suffered negative short term consequences. . . [and] few are likely to suffer long-term harm" (B "The Case" 38). He claims that even heroin "causes relatively little physical harm to the body" (B Nadelman "The Case" 40). Richard Karel notes that "The primary medical problem attributable to long-term opiate addiction is chronic constipation" (B 84). And numerous experts deny that there are any serious long-term effects from marijuana consumption (P Glazer "Preventing" 666).

The harms of drugs are easily overstated. Ed D'Angelo notes that there are no known deaths from marijuana and only a few thousand from crack, which he says is on-par with the number killed by aspirin (P 3).

In sum, a strong case can be made for legalizing some or all of the drugs I have mentioned. Such a proposal, especially if it were extended to cover 17 and 18 year old juveniles, would have massive effects on crime. And there are good reasons to prefer drug legalization on moral grounds. With this said, it is important to recognize that the bulk of evidence supports the continuation of current drug policies.

First, there are good reasons to doubt whether a program that legalizes drugs only for adults is in fact topical. Such a program could fit the resolution only because of the indirect effects of the plan. And strong arguments can be made for the illegitimacy of this standard.

Moreover, solid research suggests that legalization would not reduce juvenile crime. James Fox and Glenn Pierce argue that drug use is a "symptom, not a cause" of crime (P 25). They conclude that "If the U.S. somehow were to eliminate drug use, it would not necessarily reduce crime" (P 25). In that regard, some argue that without social change, drug legalization will have little overall effect on crime. In this view, in the absence of drug use, some other pathology would develop in poor areas that would lead to crime. From this perspective, it is the lack of economic opportunities and an unfair social structure that causes most urban crime.

Second, the negative should argue that current drug law has been effective. Overall drug use is way down from historic highs. As Lee Brown, Director of the

National Drug Control Policy, noted, "data from the nation's household's and secondary schools show substantial declines in overall drug use over the past decade: In 1989, more than 23 million Americans used some illicit drug. By 1992 the number had dropped to 11.4 million" (P 578). Brown, the nation's chief drug enforcement officer, strongly believes that enforcement has played a major role in the decline in use. He notes that

> effective enforcement serves to reduce drug supply, drive up prices, reduce the number of users and decrease the effects of chronic hard-core use. There is a demonstrable inverse relationship between the price of cocaine and the number of individuals seeking emergency room treatment. The criminal justice system, moreover, provides means to remand drug offenders to effective treatment. (P 579)

Similarly, Senator Grassley notes that the efficacy of drug enforcement can be seen in the 50% decline in overall usage (70% for cocaine) from the highs reached in the 1960s (CR "Drug Legalization" S328).

Third, the weight of evidence suggests that drugs should not be legalized. For example, the consensus of opinion at an in-depth, two-volume House of Representatives Hearing in 1988 was that "There is no data to support the theory that legalizing illicit drugs would result in less crime, more affordable narcotics or decreased drug experimentation, abuse or addiction" (D *House Report Legalization of Illicit Drugs: Impact and Feasibility* 4). In general, the societal consensus is overwhelmingly against legalization (see D *Legalization of Illicit Drugs,* parts 1 and 2).

Fourth, Senator Grassley makes the point that "legalization will not end black markets for drugs, unless we are prepared to legalize drug use for all ages down to the age of 6 or 7" (CR "Drug Legalization" 328). This is a crucial point. For legalization to be effective, it must be thoroughgoing. If drugs are not legalized across the board, then the black market will still exist. This places the affirmative in a really awkward situation. They either must exempt juveniles and undercut their topicality or go ahead and legalize for juveniles, an act that almost no one favors.

Fifth, there are good reasons to believe that legalization drastically would increase drug use. One commentator notes that after the repeal of prohibition, alcohol consumption shot up and concludes that "repeal of drug control laws would, likewise, result in an immediate, sustained rise in the use of drugs—and a concomitant rise in the casualties of the use of drugs" (P Brown 579). Brown also argues that legalization led to a doubling of the number of heroin addicts "every sixteen months" when it was tried in Great Britain (P 579). One estimate is that legalization would lead to a tripling of drug abuse (views of Lee Brown in CR Solomon E2392). Use might increase still farther, if advertising for drugs were allowed (B Inciardi and McBride 57).

The view that drug use might triple is supported by the experience in the Netherlands, where the "number of heroin addicts tripled or quadrupled since 1977" (B Brill 63).

Opponents of drug legalization then argue that any increase in drug use is unacceptable, since drugs are extremely dangerous. Dr. Mitchell Rosenthal, President of the Phoenix House in New York, puts the risks into perspective:

> Projections that drug use would double or even triple under legalization should be taken seriously. The greatest increase would come from those between the ages of 12 and 21 years old. Projections of drug-related deaths post-legalization range from 100,000 to 500,000. (D House Report *Legalization of Illicit Drugs: Impact and Feasibility* 19)

Nor can even marijuana be thought of as a "riskless" drug. Many experts emphasize the harms associated with marijuana and other drugs (see B Inciardi and McBride 50-54) and claim that marijuana is a gateway drug that leads to greater future drug use (P Glazer "Preventing" 666). Of course, almost no one disputes the harmful effect of cocaine, and especially, crack.

Sixth, some argue that legalization of drugs could harm the black community in America. Wilson Goode, then Mayor of Philadelphia, testified in Congressional Hearings: *Drug Legalization—Catastrophe for Black Americans:*

> The end result [of legalization] is, in fact, poverty, economic dependency, and family deterioration. There would be no incentive to do anything but apply enforcement on the criminal element in whatever way that would then be defined. But, above all, there would be no incentive for this group to seek prevention, treatment, or training. The result could be a destruction or social genocide of the lower class, the underbelly of society, which America has historically tried to ignore. (D 6)

In the views of some, drug legalization would have an almost genocidal effect on the black community. According to former drug czar Lee Brown, "I do not think it is an exaggeration to say that legalizing drugs would be the moral equivalent of genocide" (qtd. in CR Solomon E2392).

Seventh, there is also a significant chance that any drug legalization program would produce so much public backlash that it immediately would be repealed. Senator Grassley observed in early 1996 that "there is no public support for the idea of legalization, and none in the Congress" (CR "Drug Legalization" S327). Again, the negative would not argue that the plan could not be implemented, but only that backlash after implementation would both force repeal of the proposal and then lead to still tighter drug enforcement.

Finally, it is important to recognize that the case for drug legalization assumes that a relatively complete scheme of legalization is put in place. If it were not, then the "harms" of the criminalization of drugs would continue (for a description of some of the issues involved in drafting a legalization proposal see B Inciardi and McBride 47-49). For example, in order to get the claimed benefits of legalization, drugs must be sold in stores at relatively low prices. If that does not occur, then the drug sellers will continue to sell their product. However, it seems very unlikely that society would allow a pure system of drug legalization to be put in place. General public opposition to drugs is so high that it seems likely that public pressure would force modification of the proposal. The result could be the worst of all possible worlds. The new proposal would produce the harms associated with drug legalization, but would not achieve any of the benefits of such an approach.

In sum, there are powerful arguments against drug legalization. The combination of the increased use, black genocide, and political backlash arguments (among others) is quite overwhelming. This situation led a committee of the House of Representatives to conclude: "The burden of proof regarding the benefits of drug legalization must be placed on the advocates of such a policy. Until the proponents of drug legalization can demonstrate that the benefits of such a policy outweigh the risks to health and drug-related violence, drug legalization should be rejected" (D House Report *Legalization of Illicit Drugs: Impact and Feasibility* 4).

The Media and Juvenile Violence

Some argue that to be effective a program aiming at producing a substantial decrease in juvenile crime must focus upon the causes of that crime. In relation to cause, a number of commentators believe that violence on television, in film, in music, and pornography on the internet are primary causes of youth violence. In each case, they argue for regulation to deal with the problem.

Television and Film

The case for regulation of television and/or film in relation to violent and/or sexual content is based on the following premises. First, critics claim that the media is crammed with inappropriate material. According to the American Psychological Association, an average child will see 100,000 acts of violence on television before he/she finishes grade school (P Clark 1021).

Moreover, the trend is now not just toward violent acts, but toward gratuitous meaningless violence (P Silver 66). One expert says that more "than 90 percent of programs during children's prime viewing hours are violent. Every year, the average American child watches more than 1,000 rapes, murders, armed robberies and assaults. . . " (P Hundt 674). In the view of some critics, the problem is getting worse year by year (see Senator Lieberman in CR "Prime Time" S13813). One study found that material that is generally considered inappropriate for children rose 94% between 1990 and 1994 (P Clark 1019).

The problem is not limited to violence, but also includes portrayals of sexuality. In an article reviewing the fall 1995 television season, Marc Silver described, what he labelled as "the rise of sex" in prime time (P 62). An advocacy group for children, "Children Now," polled 750 kids between the ages of 10 and 16. Of this group, "Six out of 10 say sex on TV sways kids to have sex at too young an age" (P Silver 65).

Second, some argue that violence and sexuality in the media produce violence and an excessive concern with sex in real life. Suzanne Levine writes simply that "Any parent can tell you that there is a connection between these numbers [murders in the media and 247,000 violent crimes committed by kids every year], regardless of the ongoing debate among experts" (P 23; also see D *Implementation of the Television*). Leonard Eron, Chair, American Psychological Association Commission on Violence and Youth, puts it very simply, "There can no longer be any doubt that heavy exposure to televised violence is one of the causes of aggressive behavior, crime and violence in society" (D *Youth Violence Prevention* 32). According to Carl Cannon, only one out of 85 major studies of TV violence, denied that there was a link to societal violence, and that study was paid for by NBC (P 96).

The consensus of experts seems to be that television is the root cause of a great deal of violence. According to Reed Hundt, chairman of the FCC, "Some studies have concluded that TV accounts for an increase in the level of violence in our society by between 5 and 15 percent" (P 674). Aletha Huston, of the University of Kansas, suggests that 4-6% of crime can be linked to media violence (P Clark 1021). George Comstock of Syracuse University, puts the figure slightly higher. He estimates that about 10% of antisocial acts are linked to television (P Silver 67). Some sources say the effect is much greater. According to Brandon Centerwall "the introduction of television in the late 1950s caused a subsequent doubling of the homicide rate" (B 188).

In addition to causing violence, some argue that the media is a factor that helps create irresponsible sexual practices. According to former judge Robert Bork, there is enough evidence to "give a qualified 'yes' to the questions whether the sexual messages being sent promote irresponsible sexual behavior, encourage unwanted pregnancies, and lead to teenagers having sex earlier, more frequently, and outside of marriage" (in CR "Some Second Thoughts" S16105).

Third, advocates of some form of regulation argue that current efforts to control the media are inadequate. For example, they criticize the so-called V-chip agreement that President Clinton extracted from the media. Under the V-chip accord, television must rate every show for violence and make the rating available to parents. At the same time, new televisions will be produced containing the so-called V (for violence) chip, which will allow parents to program the television to prevent their kids from watching violent programming. Not everyone agrees that the V-chip agreement is likely to be successful. For example, Senator Dole noted in August 1995 that the V-chip is untried, really undeveloped technology (CR "The Mysterious" S12208). Moreover, the efficacy of the V-chip may be diminished by the vagueness of any rating system. Hollywood player Barry Diller recently observed sarcastically that a rating could be very easy to create: "Comedies all have sex, so be advised; dramas all have some violence, so be advised" (qtd in P Rich A13).

In fact, the V-chip might actually be counterproductive. According to Suzanne Levine, editor of the Columbia Journalism Review, the V-chip could "give parents the false confidence that by pushing a button, they have fulfilled their responsibility to articulate and 'sell' their values to their children" (P 24). Moreover, children who are forbidden to see a show may seek it out in another location and then pay close attention to it (P Levine 24).

If the V-chip agreement is inadequate, what is to be done about violence in the media? Newton Minow argues that some form of regulation is justified by the broadcast license law, which grants a license under the requirement that broadcasters "serve the 'public interest'" (P Minow and Lamay 70). In his view, broadcasters might be required either to provide a certain amount of educational television each week for kids, or lose free use of the spectrum and pay as much as 3% of annual revenues into a pool to provide education for kids (P Minow and Lamay 70, 72).

Some go so far as to call for censorship. Former Judge, and rejected Supreme Court nominee, Robert Bork, says that we should first encourage the industry to implement self-regulation (CR "Some Second Thoughts" S16105). If that fails, the next step would be direct regulation. He argues, "We had censorship for 300 years on this continent, and for 175 years as a nation, and we had a far healthier culture." He goes on "We either allow some censorship (perhaps starting by restoring some form of the old Hays Code that used to govern movies) or resign ourselves to a dangerously ugly society" (qtd. in P Clark 1026).

While there is strong evidence indicating that television violence may cause some violence in society, there isn't much that is feasible that we can do about this problem, beyond actions that the present system is taking.

First, the opponent of further action should argue that violence has been common in entertainment and literature throughout civilization. There is, after all, a great deal of violence in the Bible and Shakespeare and that material did not necessarily cause kids to react in a violent way.

And cross-cultural research seems to deny that television is a major cause of juvenile crime. For example, Leonard notes that there is far more violent media material available in Japan, but the Japanese also have a much lower crime rate than in this country (P 92). Similarly, filmmaker Lionel Chetwynd notes that essentially the same media are available in Canada, "And yet, Canada appears virtually free of the enervating social pathologies that erode American society" (qtd. in P Clark 1033). Todd Gitlin concludes that "Violence on the screens, however loathsome, does not make a significant contribution to violence on the streets" (P 92).

Second, some broadcasters argue that the marketplace is capable of dealing with the problems of excessive violence or sex in the media. After a summit of leaders of the soap opera industry and those concerned with violence and sex, a number of soap opera producers changed storylines to produce "more responsible portrayals of sex" (P Clark 1023). One result of past pressure concerning violence on television is that "there is less violence on network television than there used to be" (P Leonard 91).

Third, some argue that controlling television violence is the responsibility of the parent. In this regard, the V-chip agreement may give parents adequate means of controlling the amount of violence to which their children are exposed (P

Bellafante 64). Ted Turner has commented that because of the V-chip and the voluntary rating "parents should be able to push one button and knock gratuitous violence out of their homes" (P Bellafante 64). His view is supported by experience with a pilot program using the V-chip in Canada. The families in the area where the pilot program has been tried have been quite favorable about how the program allows them to screen out inappropriate material from their children's viewing (P Farnsworth A1, A2).

In addition, the voluntary rating system may be used by advertisers to press television executives to produce more family-friendly shows. The argument is that companies will not want to advertise on shows that receive a high rating for violence or sex. Ted Turner has predicted that a ratings system would "change the face of television. 'I think it's going to result in more Brady Bunch-type programming'" (qtd. in P Mitchell "TV Executives" A7).

Fourth, if parents are aware of the material to which their kids have been exposed, they can deal with the problem themselves. An expert from Kansas State University, Tom Grimes, has done research which has led him to conclude that "if parents take the time, they can undo any inappropriate messages sent by TV." Based on this conclusion, he opposes efforts to legislate against TV violence (P Garron D1, D2).

Fifth, some argue that regulation of television would be counterproductive, because of all the valuable material it presents. John Leonard notes how much people can learn from television, even violent television. He cites an episode of the NBC series, *Homicide,* from which he says that he "learned more about the behavior of fearful men in small rooms than from any number of better known movies, plays, and novels on the topic" (P 93). Regulation could eliminate much of value on television.

Fifth, there are strong reasons to doubt that regulation of television or film would be effective. Put simply, regulation often fails. After Congress passed The Children's Television Act of 1990 requiring broadcasters to provide educational programs for kids, broadcasters responded by creatively claiming that reruns like *Leave It to Beaver* or *The Jetsons* met the standard in the act (P Minow and Lamay 70). And certain types of television would be very difficult to regulate. For example, some say that television talkshows contain a great deal of in appropriate material (see P Clark 1022–1023), but they would be almost impossible to regulate because of the constitutional guarantee of free expression.

Finally, except for Judge Bork, almost no one is for outright censorship. Even social conservatives value free expression. Nothing less than outright censorship can solve the problem of television violence and no one (except for a few extremists) favors that censorship.

Music

Some sources make almost precisely the same arguments about the effect of music on America's youth as are made about television. For example, Senator

Carol Moseley-Braun refers to "the substantial and growing body of scientific research indicating a clear link between exposure to violent music and a corresponding increase in violent attitudes and behavior" (Moseley-Braun in D *Shaping Our Response* 5). Robert Phillips of the American Psychiatric Association emphasizes that research studies have established a linkage between violence in music and violence in life (D *Shaping Our Response* 16).

The problem is that rock and rap, in particular, contain "extremely brutal, vulgar and misogynistic music" (testimony of Senator Moseley-Braun in D *Shaping Our Response* 5). C. Delores Tucker, Chair, National Political Congress of Black Women, cites the views of Coretta Scott King that "young people often look to performing artists for moral guidance and inspiration, as well as entertainment, but when these artists glorify guns and beatings, they are injecting poison into the veins of America's future" (in D *Shaping Our Response* 11–12).

Possible solutions to this problem include outright censorship (see Tucker in D *Shaping Our Response* 14-15) or required warning labels (D *Shaping Our Response*) on music.

The arguments against music censorship are similar to those against regulation of television and film. First, some deny that music causes violent acts by youths. Michael Dyson argues that vulgarity found in music is a part of much literature, including Chaucer's *Canterbury Tales* (D *Shaping Our Response* 23). He also argues that "gangster rap represents a cry and a scream against the invisibility" of a "white racist America" (D *Shaping Our Response* 23).

Second, the opponents of regulation note that record companies currently use a voluntary label to warn people about offensive language or themes (testimony of Hilary Rosen, Recording Industry Association of America in D *Shaping Our Response* 60). Rosen notes that "virtually every recording that has been the target of public controversy has a Parental Advisory sticker on its cover" (D *Shaping Our Response* 63).

Third, a number of commentators claim that regulation is dangerous and that music acts as an active voice for social reform. For example, Darryl James, founding editor of *Rap Sheet,* observes that "any solution aimed at the reshaping of the hip-hop community must come from within" (D *Shaping Our Response* 52). He concludes that "The answer will not come from the stifling of voices of a few vocal musicians, but from viewing these voices as pleas for help" (D *Shaping Our Response* 53). Quincy Jones makes a similar point, noting that "The hip-hop culture has tremendous energy and it has become the medium through which young people are voicing a whole range of problems and solutions. Rap is really the language that addresses those solutions, and as a cultural force it holds hope that there are alternatives to gangs, drugs and dying at 23" (D *Shaping Our Response* 60).

Finally, as in the cases of television and film, almost no one favors censorship. In recent Congressional Hearings, even Senator Moseley-Braun opposed censorship and called for voluntary action (D *Shaping Our Response* 77, 80). And representatives of the ACLU testified that government mandated labels would violate the First Amendment (testimony of Lee and Peck in D *Shaping Our Response* 93).

Internet and Pornography

The final area of the media that is discussed in relation to youth crime is the internet. Some people argue that both kids and adults are being exposed to pornography on the internet, that this pornography causes some to commit violent sexual acts, and that greater regulation of the internet is needed. These arguments are quite similar to those made about television and music.

In the view of the advocates of regulation, the proper action is to ban pornography on the internet. Recently Representative Dornan cited the views of the former Director of the Child Exploitation and Obscenity Office of the Department of Justice, Patrick Trueman, that such a ban should be implemented and could be effective (CR Dornan E153–E154). The means of implementing the ban would be to make access providers liable for allowing access to pornographic material. Such a regulation would force Compuserve, American On-Line, and so forth to clean up the pornography problem on sites of which they had some direct control (CR Dornan 154). According to Trueman, a tough German law proved its effectiveness in forcing Compuserve to block a pornographic site (CR Dornan E154). A similar law could work in this nation. Trueman also argued that current law allows the Department of Justice to prosecute for computer pornography (in CR Dornan 154).

The arguments against regulating pornography on the internet are quite similar to those made against regulation of television or music. In this case, however, the negative clearly should argue that it is not credible to believe that regulation of the internet could be thought of as a program aimed at substantially reducing juvenile crime. Juvenile crime was skyrocketing before there was any significant internet.

Second, the negative should deny that there is a clear link between pornography and violence. Nadine Strossen of the ACLU writes, based on a review of the literature, that "A causal connection between exposure to pornography and the commission of sexual violence has never been established" (P 8). She continues:

> If anything, studies suggest an inverse relationship: a greater availability of sexually explicit material seems to correlate not with higher rates of sexual violence but, rather, with higher indices of gender quality. For example, Singapore with its tight restrictions on pornography, has experienced a much greater increase in rape rates than has Sweden, with its liberalized obscenity laws. (P 9)

Thus, even effective regulation would not have much effect on juvenile crime and could increase it.

Third, the negative should argue that adequate laws already exist to deny kids access to pornographic material on the internet. For example, Senator Hollings notes that under current law, "We already have crimes on the books that apply to the Internet, by banning obscenity, child pornography, and threats from being distributed over computers" (CR "Unanimous Consent" S694). And the legislation regulating the internet that was passed recently also banned pornography (and other speech as well), although it is not being enforced by the Clinton administration.

Fourth, the negative should argue that regulation cannot be effective, because pornography is quite difficult to define, as is indicated in the famous statement of former Supreme Court Justice Potter Stewart, "I shall not today attempt further to define; and perhaps I could never succeed in intelligibly doing so. But I know it when I see it" (qtd. in P Strossen 7). In the context of the internet, where there are millions of users, regulation will be nearly impossible.

Finally, the negative should argue that censorship could chill legitimate speech. Senator Hollings cites several instances in which valuable material, such as E-mail among breast cancer survivors, has been censored. It is easy to see that a ban on indecent materials could lead to a significant restriction on free address (CR "Unanimous Consent" S694).

Gun Control

The final major area of the topic to be considered is gun control. There is no question that children have access to guns. Bob Herbert, a columnist for the *New York Times,* reports on a panel on teen violence in which a student said that for $40, he could procure a gun in about 20 minutes (P "Trouble" A15). One result of this access to weapons is that many juveniles commit gun crimes and many juveniles are shot. Herbert notes that in 1992 5,379 kids under the age of 19 were killed with firearms (in CR "Kids Pay " S16686). Between 1979 and 1991, there were about 50,000 kids killed by guns (testimony of Marian Wright Edelman in D *Caught in the Crossfire* 34).

According to the American Psychological Association, "There is considerable evidence that the alarming rise in youth homicides is related to the availability of firearms" (qtd. in P Gitlin 93). Howell, Krisberg and Jones explain that "During the past 10 years, the single most important impact on youth violence, in general, and juvenile homicide specifically has been the availability of firearms" (B 5). They conclude, "There is little question that the availability and increasing lethality of firearms is contributing to this violence" (B 7). Statistics seem to back up this judgment. Approximately three quarters of all murders by juveniles are committed with guns (see P Glazer" Juvenile" 171).

Given the magnitude of juvenile gun violence, what is to be done about it? In testimony titled, "The Prevention of Youth Violence," Ronald Slaby of Harvard University, advocates strict gun control, gun education, and technological innovation as means of reducing violence (D *Youth Violence Prevention* 159). Similarly, based on the dangers of gun violence, sociologist Stanley Eitzen argues that "We must make a special effort to get guns out of the hands of juveniles" (P 471).

The advocate of change could support either a general gun control law or a law banning juvenile access to guns. I will focus on the second alternative, because public support for gun access is so strong that an outright ban on gun ownership clearly could not be enforced at the present time. In all likelihood an effort to ban handguns would produce immediate public backlash, repeal of the proposal and other unfortunate results. By contrast, a ban on juvenile access to guns is feasible.

Any number of sources have argued for a ban on handgun possession by juveniles (see a statement by Senator Herb Kohn qtd. in P Glazer "Juvenile" 185; Representative Conyers in D *Caught in the Crossfire* 6–7). And there is strong evidence that such a ban might be effective. Mayor Payne of Chandler, Arizona, reports that after a ban on kids carrying guns in Chandler, "Violent crimes as far as firearms are concerned have diminished somewhat since we enacted that ordinance" (D *Youth Violence: A Community* 14).

It is also important to note that many of the normal arguments against gun control are not applicable to a law limiting juvenile access to guns. For example, Joseph M. Arpaio, Sheriff of Marciopa County (Phoenix) explains: "I see no damage to the second amendment by a law that would prohibit children from carrying guns willy-nilly. After all, the right to bear arms is linked by the Constitution to the citizen's obligation to militia" (D *Youth Violence: A Community* 75).

Against a proposal to limit juvenile access to handguns, the negative might argue that crime rates are not related to gun ownership. In an analysis of the data available on the health effects of guns, Don B. Kates and his colleagues concluded that gun availability is not linked to murder rates (P Kates et al 572–573). The negative also should note that there is no reason for the Federal Government to act on this problem, since a number of states already have banned juvenile possession of a firearm (see P Glazer "Juvenile" 184).

In addition, the negative should argue that given the number of guns available in society, no ban on juvenile possession is likely to be effective. Kids who currently carry guns, either for self protection or for use in crimes, are not going to be deterred by a law banning possession. Remember, that it is illegal almost everywhere to carry a concealed weapon. Apparently those laws are not preventing people from carrying weapons.

Fourth, the negative should argue that a law banning juvenile use of guns should not be accepted, because there are many legitimate reasons for juveniles to use guns, including sports, hunting, and self-defense. Moreover, limiting juvenile access to guns arguably would reduce the degree to which gun ownership could deter crime.

Finally, the negative could argue that a ban on juvenile access to guns has the potential to snowball into more general regulation of weapons. They would argue that such regulation would be counterproductive.

The evidence is mixed on whether a proposal to limit juvenile access to handguns could be effective. Clearly, such a proposal is not going to have a very large effect, since it will not influence those who currently are using weapons illegally. But it does have the potential to reduce juvenile crime to some degree.

Conclusion

This chapter has discussed a host of alternative means of reducing juvenile crime. The wide variety of proposals considered here (from prevention programs to job creation to drug legalization to regulation of entertainment to gun control) is indicative of the breadth of the resolution. It also indicates that the opponent of change will face major problems in preparing to debate all aspects of the resolution. It is to general questions of affirmative and negative strategy that I turn in the final chapter.

5 Strategic Dimensions in Debating About Juvenile Crime Policy

The focus of this chapter is on the strategic dimensions of debating about U.S. juvenile crime policy. I briefly will comment about general affirmative strategy in the first section. I then will lay out principles of an effective negative strategy. The chapter concludes with outlines of sample arguments.

Before discussing affirmative and negative strategy, however, it is important to note one major difference between the juvenile crime resolution and other topics. The juvenile crime resolution is extremely broad, including within it a host of very different public policy initiatives. As a result, there are fewer truly generic negative positions than on other resolutions. As a consequence, the discussion of generic arguments is somewhat briefer than in the past.

Affirmative Strategy

A wise affirmative team will develop a specific strategy dealing with juvenile crime, keeping the following principles in mind. First, it makes sense to choose a particular case that fits in the middle of the resolution. Given a variety of very strong proposals for decreasing juvenile crime, there is little reason to pick a proposal on the edges of the resolution. Second, always look for a proposal where the balance of evidence supports the affirmative position. It should be self-evident that it is easier to defend a position where the evidence is overwhelmingly on your side.

Third, it makes sense to emphasize real-world arguments. I am sure that one could argue that juvenile criminals could threaten the nation via nuclear terrorism, but such a position lacks credibility. Why would potential nuclear terrorists hire juveniles instead of people with more expertise? I am not saying that all arguments need to be conservative, but it makes sense to emphasize arguments on which a clear causal explanation can be developed.

Fourth, it makes sense to choose a proposal with potential negative arguments in mind. For instance, the graduated sanctions program is designed to be both more lenient and harsher than the present system, but for different classes of juveniles. That plan takes into account possible negative arguments. Finally, it is wise to limit negative ground by focussing the affirmative proposal. So, for instance, prevention could be included with a graduated sanctions program. But to do so would be to broaden the case unnecessarily. It makes more sense to limit graduated sanctions to punishment options only.

Based on the above principles, I have the following suggestions for developing an affirmative proposal dealing with juvenile crime. In relation to drafting a plan, it makes sense to model the proposal after a particular proposal in the literature or a pilot program. By taking this step, the advocate of action can both make the proposed policy seem more realistic and claim that general negative evidence is inapplicable to the particular proposal. Second, I think that it makes sense to implement the proposal with some combination of Federal guidelines and grants. In so doing, the affirmative can claim to include states and localities within the administration of the proposal, thus making Federalism less of an issue.

In relation to particular affirmative proposals, there are any number of defensible ideas, but I want to highlight four specific cases. First, I think that the graduated sanctions approach is well-designed to limit negative ground. If the affirmative can win the efficacy of their risk assessment program, then there are almost no available negative arguments for attacking the policy itself, although there are arguments that can be made against any particular method of implementation or funding.

Second, I think a strong case can be made for particular targeted prevention programs, especially the extended school model or recreation. The literature is overwhelming that such programs work. It also might be possible to fund those programs by taking money from other Federal programs in the area that are not effective.

Third, I think a good case can be made for a specific anti-gang program, either at the educational level or at the police level. Here the key is to defend a particular model for a program and argue that general negative evidence is inapplicable.

Finally, I think that a strong case can be made for banning juvenile gun ownership. That position is an example of a narrow case on which the balance of evidence is quite positive. There are negative arguments, but they only cut into the harm and do not outweigh it.

There is one additional case that I want to mention because of its potential for advantages from outside the juvenile crime subject area. Of all the proposals for decreasing juvenile crime through the application of indirect means, I think the strongest is a program creating massive economic growth. It is important to note that on such a case the advantages need not be limited to juvenile crime. The affirmative could claim major other benefits from growth.

Of course, with this case the affirmative would have to be prepared to defend economic growth as a good thing, but the real-world literature on that subject is overwhelmingly supportive. And on that case the affirmative legitimately could claim enormous additional advantages. The key problems with the economic growth case relate to topicality and the danger of FRB overreaction to growth leading to interest rate hikes and a recession.

Negative Strategy

In relation to negative strategy, similar principles to those I mentioned concerning affirmative strategy apply. As much as possible it makes sense to run real-world arguments that are supported by the balance of evidence. It makes sense for the negative to develop relatively few arguments, but in great depth, in order to maximize their chances of defeating the affirmative. It always makes sense to adapt strategies to the judge. With these constraints in mind, I want to discuss potential counterplans and then general dimensions of effective case and plan strategies.

Counterplans

There are a couple fairly obvious counterplans on this resolution. The negative could argue that rather than the Federal Government, the states should implement their program. Alternatively, the negative could argue that rather than action, further study of the problem is necessary, prior to acting.

I don't think either of these counterplans is an especially strong position. In relation to state action, it is important to remember that the resolution specifies action by the federal government. The presence of a small "f" in federal indicates that state action is acceptable under the resolution. The states in total and combination with the national government make up the "federal government."

Moreover, there is no easy way for the states to act in a unified fashion absent Federal control. In the real world, the states only act as a group if they have been coerced or encouraged to do so by the Federal Government. Thus, there is no means of mandating action by all the states, save Federal action. And there is no barrier to state action at the present time. Thus, a state counterplan is arguably topical and lacks any justifiable means of implementation.

A similar point can be made about the so-called study counterplan. Traditionally, the counterplan has called for conducting additional studies and disseminating that research, prior to action. In the context of juvenile crime, however, a host of studies have been conducted, thus undercutting the need for further research. Moreover, a study counterplan is either potentially topical or it does nothing. If the study counterplan results in action then it arguably implements the resolution, since it would be part of a federal program to substantially reduce juvenile crime. If it does not result in action, it has no impact.

Case Arguments

In relation to case arguments, the negative faces an odd situation. On most topics, the negative focuses case arguments upon developing general prepared arguments to minimize the affirmative harm. In relation to juvenile crime, however, there is no question about the growing threat posed by youth criminals. It, therefore, becomes almost impossible for the negative to succeed in denying the affirmative harm. What then can be done on the case?

There are five specific sorts of general case arguments that should be developed in depth. First, the negative should be well-prepared to debate topicality. It is especially important that the negative be able to make a cogent argument for limiting the resolution to proposals that directly aim at reducing juvenile crime. As I have noted on several occasions, to broaden the resolution to a consideration of policies that indirectly could result in decreases in juvenile crime is to broaden the resolution to include almost every contemporary domestic policy proposal. Thus, the negative needs to work very diligently to develop a strong position relating to the "to means for the purpose of" argument that I discussed in chapter one.

Second, the negative should be well-versed on the literature concerning the causes of juvenile crime. This material is important for two reasons. Literature on alternative causes might be used to undercut affirmative claims of solvency for a given proposal. More importantly, this literature can be used to deny claims that an affirmative proposal eliminates factors that cause juvenile crime. So, for instance, the well prepared negative debater will be able to refute the claim that poverty is a major cause of juvenile crime. The same point can be made about other potential causes, such as lack of jobs or the current welfare system.

Third, the negative should be prepared to indict the solvency of any program based on the general principle that pilot programs are always more effective than large expansions of those programs. In this regard, Charles Murray argues that local, especially voluntary, programs can be quite good, but that when the program is expanded it becomes bureaucratic and not nearly as effective (B 103). The negative should work on this argument because it is a key to attacking affirmatives that model their approach after a pilot program.

Fourth, the negative should be prepared to argue that reform efforts will fail because of the tendency of the system to counterbalance any attempted change. In other words, the system has a certain point of equilibrium and reform efforts will simply lead to counterbalancing actions elsewhere. Thus, attempts to change sentencing or prosecution standards ultimately may achieve little. In this regard, Feyerherm emphasizes that juvenile justice varies by state and locality and that those justice systems tend to remain at a point of balance. In other words, if the system is reformed in one direction, there is a built in tendency to move back toward the original resting point of the system. The result may be that reform has a transitory effect only (see B Feyerherm 6–7).

Fifth, the negative should be prepared to argue that absent larger social reform, there is nothing that we can do as a society to deal with the juvenile crime issue. In essence this argument says that causal factors in the larger society must be addressed in order to effectively decrease juvenile crime. This argument obviously is not applicable to proposals to reform those social conditions, but it is widely useful otherwise. On this point Carl Pope concludes:

> policy initiatives must not only address problems in the case processing of juvenile offenders. . . but also preexisting social conditions. Only by such a two-pronged attack can we have any chance of reducing crime among our youths . . . . (B 216)

Krisberg and his colleagues make much the same point:

> Put simply, the efforts of even a very good intervention program are bound to be weakened or nullified in many cases if youths are simply "dropped off" afterward into communities with shrinking opportunities for work, self-sufficiency, and social contribution. (B 166)

In other words, social conditions are the primary cause of juvenile crime and, absent change in those conditions, not much can be done to reduce that crime.

Disadvantages

I think that a much higher percentage of effective negative argumentation on the juvenile crime topic is plan specific than on many other topics, but there are several generic arguments that merit consideration.

First, the negative could consider developing a Federalism position. The Federalism argument says that certain policy areas are reserved to the states and criminal justice is one of those areas. Staff researchers for the House Committee on Natural Resources note "state and local governments have the primary responsibility for crime control" (D *Urban Recreation* 4). This point was echoed by Senator Ashcroft: "If the goal is to reduce juvenile crime, then fundamental changes must occur at the state level. This is because States and local governments handle the vast majority of juvenile offenders" (CR "The Violent" S13657).

The Federalism disadvantage also says that a "federal" solution is superior to a national governmental solution to a problem. No one thinks that a Federal one-size-fits-all program is appropriate in the juvenile area. According to John Wilson of the Office of Juvenile Justice and Delinquency Prevention, "We are not, as the Federal Government, going to go in and tell communities how to do prevention or what interventions to use. It is up to the communities and their leaders to come together and make these decisions" (D *Hearing Regarding* 11). Moreover, the states have been acting in creative ways in the area. Two commentators note that "at least a dozen states were involved in some stage of an effort to reform their juvenile correctional systems in the early 1990s" (B Guarino-Ghezzi and Loughran 38). It, therefore, makes no sense to undercut the fundamental creativity of the current federal system.

The disadvantage is also built on the claim that the recent trend in action has been to revitalize the general doctrine of Federalism. To turn away from that policy, therefore, could undercut the revitalization effort. What then is the impact of Federalism. Many have argued that Federalism is at the core of our constitutional system for protecting liberty and adding stability to the political system. I have discussed these issues in depth in earlier works from this series.

While the Federalism position has merit, it has important problems as well. First, the wording of the resolution arguably gives the affirmative the right to implement their plan at either the national government level or at the level of individual states. If the states are included, there would seem to be no violation of Federalism. Second, the states have not exactly been successful in the area of juvenile crime. In some cases, states have begun, but then retreated from the reform process. This has happened, for instance, in Georgia (B Guarino-Ghezzi and Loughran 39-40). And many state programs are the very antithesis of reform. For example, in Texas 70% of youth offenders are placed in training schools (B Guarino-Ghezzi and Loughran 43). This is actually better than in California, where 95% go to training schools (B Guarino-Ghezzi and Loughran 43). In fact, "most states continue to operate large institutions as their primary response to juvenile crime" (B Guarino-Ghezzi and Loughran 158). Thus, it is hard to see how the Federal government could do much worse.

Moreover, given the many Federal programs that have encroached on the states in the past, it could be argued that the disadvantage is both empirically denied and non-unique. In relation to these issues, it is important to note

> that beginning with the Juvenile Justice and Delinquency Control Act of 1974, Federal actors have been quite intrusive in applying standards to the states. It would seem that in the juvenile justice area, Federalism was all but dead for almost twenty years, without any great effects on American democracy.

The Federalism position is an important one, but clearly the best evidence supports the affirmative answers to the position.

Second, the negative should develop a disadvantage relating to Federal spending. The most sensible option is to say that by implementing a major new program, the affirmative will undercut the previously negotiated balanced budget agreement. The negative would argue that the balanced budget agreement is needed to prevent an eventual budget collapse. The affirmative, therefore, risks creating a depression with their support of the new program.

Clearly, there is risk that a major initiative in the area of juvenile crime could lead to collapse of any budget agreement. Testifying in support of infrastructure spending in 1992, Lane Kirkland of the AFL-CIO put it quite clearly, "Well, sir, we, of course, support the breaking of the firewall in the budget agreement" (D *Anti-Recession* 14). Kirkland meant that it was worth it to him to violate the budget agreement of the time.

I cannot discuss this disadvantage in any depth, however, because at this writing Congress has not finalized any particular balanced budget agreement. That makes it particularly important for debaters to research this issue in depth as the summer progresses and an agreement on the 1997 budget is reached.

Alternatively, the negative could argue that increased Federal support requires cuts in other programs. The affirmative mandated increase could cause crucial cuts in other areas. The same argument could be made in regard to increased costs for state and local programs. Georgia Judge Glenda Johnson has observed that both states and the Federal Government face a problem of "limited resources" (D *The State* 58–59).

As in the case of the budget agreement argument, the negative will need to gather up to date literature on the current status of Congressional or state spending plans. The key on this argument is to find specific evidence that increases in spending for juvenile justice will result in cuts in some other area of spending. Obviously, the negative wants to argue that the cuts will devastate some crucial program, so it makes sense to look for evidence that some sort of research or technology program would, in all likelihood, be cut. In the past, there has been evidence that increased spending could lead to cuts in NASA. And of course there is excellent evidence arguing that any cut in space exploration and development could be catastrophic.

There are, however, difficulties with this position. Once again, the Congressional budget process is in such a state of flux that it is difficult to know exactly what would happen if a major spending initiative were passed. In addition, under the current budget rules, spending programs are divided into categories. An increase for a program must be offset by a decrease in another program in the same category. Of course, juvenile programs fall into the justice category and the most likely cuts would be in funds for prison construction. And, as I made clear in chapter two, the evidence is quite clear that more prison cells are not needed. It is hard to see how the negative could argue that juvenile justice funding would produce a cut in NASA or another research program.

Third, the negative should develop a position in relation to the effects of the affirmative plan on economic growth. Here, the argument is simple. If the affirmative helps the economy in a substantive way, the effect could be to cause the Federal Reserve Board to slam on the monetary breaks and push the economy into recession.

It seems clear that the Federal Reserve Board (FRB) would not allow a major job creation program, or any other policy that either increases economic growth or increases inflation. Several times in recent weeks the stock market has fallen downward, because job creation in the economy was somewhat higher than expected (P Wyatt C1, C8). In one case, when double the expected number of new jobs were created in February 1996 (700,000 instead of 350,000), the market fell 171 points on the realization that the FRB would not cut interest rates further (P Whatt C8). The key point is that the Federal Reserve Board will not allow economic growth to reach levels that they perceive could cause inflation.

The Fed is very likely to perceive any major job creation program as posing a significant inflation risk. In response, they will step on the monetary economic breaks by raising interest rates. The result could be drastically reduced economic growth leading to a recession, or even a depression.

I think the FRB overreaction argument is the most important economic disadvantage available on the resolution. It is far more credible than other economic disadvantages, some of which are based on the principle that even small quantities of economic growth could produce major dislocation. Such arguments would be built on the claim that crime harms economic growth, because it takes money out of the economy. By preventing crime, therefore, the affirmative fuels faster growth, which is harmful because of the relationship between growth and pollution. Possible impacts include species destruction, increased risk of global warming, and so forth. There are four obvious problems with this position. First, no affirmative is going to free up so much money that a major effect on economic growth will occur. Second, money stolen in crimes is not taken out of the economy. It is spent by juvenile criminals. Thus, it is not clear that saving money by preventing crime would have more than a negligible effect on economic growth. Third, the reasons that some argue that growth is harmful are tied to massive economic growth, not tiny changes in U.S. economic patterns. Fourth, in the real world the overwhelming weight of evidence supports economic growth as a good thing. For all of these reasons it makes far more sense to develop the FRB disadvantage than an incremental growth is bad position.

The FRB position is tied to the perceptions of the Federal Reserve and there is strong real world evidence supporting its reasonability. Moreover, the impact of the FRB disadvantage is that a recession or depression would be a very bad thing for the United States and the world and the overwhelming weight of evidence supports that conclusion.

Fourth, the negative should prepare a net widening position. As I have explained at several points, one risk associated with efforts to reform the juvenile justice system is that programs aimed at helping the juvenile may result in greater social control of them. The idea is that local authorities will take a new program and apply it to youths who are not receiving anything more than a warning or probation in the present system. The authorities will not take the program and reduce the number of youths who are being sentenced to prison or state reform school. Krisberg et al describe this risk:

> This does not mean that every young person who is arrested, or runs afoul of school authorities, necessarily needs intensive, protracted intervention of a formal kind. Some clearly do not, and attempting to extend that kind of response to all of the 2 million-plus juveniles arrested each year for all kinds of offenses would not only strain resources to the breaking point but also amount to an excessive degree of "net widening." (B 154)

There is historical precedent to think that net-widening might be a likely result of a reform effort. The 1974 Juvenile Justice and Delinquency Prevention Act called for the creation of "community-based alternative" to incarceration (B Guarino-Ghezzi and Loughran 35). There is reason to believe, however, that vague Federal guidelines allowed states and localities to use these "community-based" programs to place more youths under sanction than had been in the system previously. "The vagueness of the federal legislation and its limited guidelines encouraged the practice of net-widening, or expanding the net of control to include low-risk offenders who previously might have only received probation, rather than using the programs for youths who previously would have been institutionalized" (B Guarino-Ghezzi and Loughran 35).

Finally, I want to discuss a series of political disadvantages as possible generic negative positions. One obvious disadvantage is to argue that passing an effective program of juvenile crime control will make President Clinton much more popular and either aid his reelection or make him more effective in his second term. The negative then would argue negative impacts from Clinton remaining in office.

While similar disadvantages have been popular in the past, I do not think that the Clinton position is very strong. First, it is not clear that passing a law on juvenile crime would have any effect on Cilnton's popularity at all. The American people seem to be far more attuned to other issues than the impact of juvenile crime legislation. Moreover, the Republicans could claim partial credit for any law that was passed. And passage of the 1994 crime bill certainly did not produce a major outpouring of support for the President. Moreover, the time frame is wrong for this disadvantage. A juvenile crime law is likely to decrease crime only in the long-term. Thus, there would be no link to a near-term political disadvantage. And a wise affirmative might write their proposal to be implemented on January 1, 1997, after the election, and claim that other issues will determine the President's popularity at that point.

Second, the discussion of impacts in a political disadvantage of this kind is entirely speculative. There are any number of factors that influence a President's ability to get things done and the impact of a policy, if it is passed. And it is hard to see that Clinton is doing anything that threatens the nation's security. For all of these reasons, I do not think a Clinton popularity argument should be at the core of a negative strategy.

On the other hand, I think there is more potential for a political backlash argument. This position would be run against any affirmative proposal that liberalized treatment of juveniles. The negative would claim that the proposal would give conservatives a new issue to take to frustrated voters. The impact would be to put the "Conservative Revolution" back on track. There is an argument, for example, that a program to replace imprisonment of kids with treatment would make many people quite angry.

The impact of such a disadvantage might be to gut our social service system, including welfare, which in turn could be linked to a greater chance of racial conflict, even race war. The last impact is speculative, but it is certainly not unreasonable to believe that major cuts in our already quite limited social service programs could result in increased racial antipathy and conflict.

Conclusion

In this chapter, I have discussed general issues relating to affirmative and negative strategy on juvenile crime and possible generic arguments. In the following section, I will outline some of the major arguments relating to the topic.

Outline of Selected Affirmative and Negative Arguments

Affirmative Positions

I. Juvenile Crime Threatens America

    A. Juvenile crime rates are high

    B. Juvenile murder has skyrocketed

    C. Juvenile crime is increasing

    D. Juvenile criminals are becoming more violent

II. Current Crime Control Programs Are Inadequate

    A. The present system is committed to incarceration of juveniles

    B. Imprisonment fails

        1. Imprisonment produces hardened criminals

        2. Prison serves as a school of crime

        3. Imprisonment fails to deter juvenile crime

    C. Treatment for juveniles is limited

III. Prevention Programs Are Inadequate

    A. Few resources are allocated to prevention

    B. Prevention programs are not oriented at the causes of juvenile crime

IV. Graduated Sanctions Solvency

    A. Accurate prediction of dangerousness is possible

    B. Graduated sanctions imprisons the most dangerous juveniles

    C. Graduated sanctions provides effective treatment for less dangerous juveniles

V.   Prevention Solvency

    A. Comprehensive prevention programs are effective

    B. School-based extended hour programs cut juvenile crime

    C. Expanded recreation programs curtail juvenile crime

VI. Drug Treatment Solvency

    A. Drug treatment programs are currently inadequate

    B. Expanded drug treatment programs reduce crime

VII. Ban Juvenile Handgun Possession

    A. Juveniles handgun possession is legal in many states

    B. Juveniles commit many crimes with handguns

    C. A ban on juvenile handgun possession would be effective

Negative Positions

I.   "To" Means For the Purpose Of

    A. To means for the purpose of

    B. The Affirmative proposal may impact juvenile crime, but it is not "for the purpose of" substantially reducing juvenile crime

    C. The affirmative definition should be rejected

        1. It denies reasonable ground to the negative

        2. It makes the topic impossibly broad

II.   Expanded Programs Fail

   A.   The affirmative models their proposal after a pilot
        program

   B.   Pilot programs are uniquely effective because they have the most
        motivated staff

   C.   Expanded national programs become bureaucratic and fail

III. Expanded Incarceration Fails

   A.   U.S. imprisonment policy has failed

   B.   Juveniles do not understand the law and can't be deterred
        by it

   C.   Failure of current laws denies juvenile deterrence

IV.   Prevention Programs Fail

   A.   Juvenile crime is caused by the decline of the family

   B.   Past prevention efforts have failed

V.   Anti-poverty and Pro-growth Programs Fail

   A.   Poverty is not the cause of juvenile crime

   B.   Crime rates were lower when growth was lower

   C.   Increased crime occurred when poverty was decreasing and
        economic growth increasing

VI.   Federalism

   A.   The affirmative implements a Federal program

   B.   Crime control is the responsibility of states and localities

   C.   Federalism has been reinvigorated

   D.   The affirmative threatens the trend toward reinvigorating
        Federalism

     E.   Destroying Federalism is harmful

         1.   Federalism is the key to effective government

         2.   Federalism protects liberty

VII.   Budget Collapse

     A.   The affirmative drastically increases spending

     B.   A budget agreement prevents a deficit crisis

         1.   A budget agreement exists

         2.   The budget agreement solves the deficit crisis

     C.   The affirmative violates the budget agreement

     D.   Deficit collapse will ensure

         1.   Other programs will be funded based on the affirmative precedent

         2.   The deficit will soar

         3.   A long-term deficit equals U.S. depression

VIII. FRB Overreaction

     A.   The affirmative increases economic growth (or inflation)

     B.   The FRB will raise interest rates

     C.   A raise in interest rates equals recession

     D.   Recession risks depression

     E.   Depression equals starvation and risk of war

IX.   Net Widening

     A.   Affirmative provides an additional juvenile crime control program

     B.   States and localities will use this program to expand the net of law enforcement to cover more juveniles

Bibliography

Books and Book Chapters

Ainsworth, Robert G., and Barbara B. Oakley. "The Eight Percent Set-Aside as a Coordination Incentive." *Welfare System Reform: Coordinating Federal, State, and Local Public Assistance Programs.* Eds. Edward T. Jennings Jr. and Neal S. Zank. Westport, CT: Greenwood, 1993. 111-122.

Alexander, Bruce K. *Peaceful Measures: Canada's Way Out of the 'War on Drugs.'* Toronto: University of Toronto Press, 1990.

Anderson, Elijah. "Neighborhood Effects on Teenage Pregnancy." *The Urban Underclass.* Eds. Christopher Jencks and Paul E. Peterson. Washington: Brookings, 1991. 375-398.

Allison, Kevin, Peter E. Leone, and Ellen Rowse Spero. "Drug and Alcohol Use Among Adolescents: Social Context and Competence." *Understanding Troubled and Troubling Youth.* Ed. Peter E. Leone. Newbury Park, CA: Sage, 1990. 173-193.

Anderson, James E., and Robert G. Schwartz. "Secure Detention in Pennsylvania, 1981-1990." *Reforming Juvenile Detention: No More Hidden Closets.* Eds. Ira M. Schwartz and William H. Barton. Columbus, OH: Ohio State University Press, 1994. 128-146.

Austin, James. "The Overrepresentation of Minority Youths in the California Juvenile Justice System: Perceptions and Realities." *Minorities in Juvenile Justice.* Eds. Kimberly Kempf Leonard, Carl E. Pope, and William H. Feyerherm. Thousand Oaks, CA: Sage, 1995. 153-178.

Ayoob, Massad F. *The Experts Speak Out: The Police View of Gun Control.* Bellevue, WA: Second Amendment Foundation, 1981.

Bailis, Lawrence Neil. "Coordination Among Administrative Agencies." *Welfare System Reform: Coordinating Federal, State, and Local Public Assistance Programs.* Eds. Edward T. Jennings Jr. and Neal S. Zank. Westport, CT: Greenwood, 1993. 43-54.

Bartelt, David W. "Housing the 'Underclass." *The 'Underclass' Debate: Views From History.* Ed. Michael B. Katz. Princeton: Princeton University Press, 1993. 118-157.

Barton, William H. "Implementing Detention Policy Changes." *Reforming Juvenile Detention: No More Hidden Closets.* Eds. Ira M. Schwartz and William H. Barton. Columbus, OH: Ohio State University Press, 1994. 147-161.

Barton, William H., and Ira M. Schwartz. "Reforming Juvenile Detention: No More Hidden Closets." *Reforming Juvenile Detention: No More Hidden Closets.* Eds. Ira M. Schwartz and William H. Barton. Columbus, OH: Ohio State University Press, 1994. 1-12.

Barton, William H., Ira M. Schwartz, and Franklin A. Orlando. "Reducing the Use of Secure Detention in Broward County, Florida." *Reforming Juvenile Detention: No More Hidden Closets.* Eds. Ira M. Schwartz and William H. Barton. Columbus, OH: Ohio State University Press, 1994. 69-96.

Bayes, Jane. "Labor Markets and the Feminization of Poverty." *Beyond Welfare: New Approaches to the Problem of Poverty in America.* Ed. Harrell R. Rodgers Jr. Armonk, NY: M.E. Sharpe, 1988. 86-113.

Bayley, David H. "International Differences in Community Policing." *The Challenge of Community Policy: Testing the Promises*. Ed. Dennis P. Rosenbaum. Thousand Oaks, CA: Sage, 1994. 278-281.

Bennett, Trevor. "Community Policing on the Ground: Developments in Britain." *The Challenge of Community Policy: Testing the Promises*. Ed. Dennis P. Rosenbaum. Thousand Oaks, CA: Sage, 1994. 224-246.

Berry, Jeffey M., Kent E. Portey, and Ken Thomson. "The Political Behavior of Poor People." *The Urban Underclass*. Eds. Christopher Jencks and Paul E. Peterson. Washington: Brookings, 1991. 357-372.

Besharov, Douglas J. "Poverty, Welfare Dependency, and the Underclass: Trends and Explanations." *Reducing Poverty in America: Views and Approaches*. Ed. Michael R. Darby. Thousand Oaks, CA: Sage, 1996. 13-56.

Besteman, Karst J. "War Is Not the Answer." *The Drug Legalization Debate*. Ed. James A. Inciardi. Newbury Park, CA: Sage, 1991. 130-134.

Blank, Rebecca M. "The Employment Strategy: Public Policies to Increase Work and Earnings." *Confronting Poverty: Prescriptions for Change*. Eds. Sheldon H. Danziger, Gary D. Sandefur, and Daniel Weinberg. New York: Harvard University Press, 1994. 168-204.

Bobo, Lawrence and Ryan A. Smith. "Antipoverty Policy, Affirmative Action, and Racial Attitudes." *Confronting Poverty: Prescriptions for Change*. Eds. Sheldon H. Danziger, Gary D. Sandefur, and Daniel Weinberg. New York: Harvard University Press, 1994. 365-395.

Brewer, Devon D., J. David Hawkins, Richard F. Catalano, and Holly J. Neckerman. "Preventing Serious, Violent, and Chronic Juvenile Offending: A Review of Evluations of Selected Strategies in Childhood, Adolescence, and the Community." *Serious, Violent, & Chronic Juvenile Offenders*. Eds. James C. Howell, Barry Krisberg, J. David Hawkins, and John J. Wilson. Thousand Oaks, CA: Sage, 1995. 61-141.

Bridges, George S., Darlene J. Conley, Rodney L. Engen, and Towsand Price-Spratlen. "Racial Disparities in the Confinement of Juveniles: Effects of Crime and Community Social Structure on Punishment." *Minorities in Juvenile Justice*. Eds. Kimberly Kempf Leonard, Carl E. Pope, and William H. Feyerherm. Thousand Oaks, CA: Sage, 1995. 128-152.

Brill, Norman Q. *America's Psychic Malignancy: The Problem of Crime, Substance Abuse, Poverty and Welfare—Identifying Causes With Possible Remedies*. Springfield, IL: Charles C. Thomas, 1993.

Brown, Richard Maxwell. "American Violence, American Values, and Childhood Games." *Children and Violence*. Eds. Colette Chiland and J. Gerald Young. Northvale, NJ: Jason Aronson, 1994. 171-177.

Buerger, Michael E. "The Limits of Community." *The Challenge of Community Policy: Testing the Promises*. Ed. Dennis P. Rosenbaum. Thousand Oaks, CA: Sage, 1994. 270-273.

Burgess, Ann Wolbert, ed. *Child Trauma: Issues & Research*. New York: Garland, 1992.

Burtless, Gary. "Public Spending on the Poor: Historical Trends and Economic Limits." *Confronting Poverty: Prescriptions for Change*. Eds. Sheldon H. Danziger, Gary D. Sandefur, and Daniel Weinberg. New York: Harvard University Press, 1994. 51-84.

Bynum, Jack E., and William E. Thompson. *Juvenile Delinquency: A Sociological Approach*. 2nd ed. Boston: Allyn and Bacon, 1992.

Campbell, Anne. "Female Participation in Gangs." *Gangs in America.* Ed. C. Ronald Huff. Newbury Park, CA: Sage, 1990. 163-182.

Capowich, George E., and Janice A. Roehl. "Problem-Oriented Policing: Actions and Effectiveness in San Diego." *The Challenge of Community Policy: Testing the Promises.* Ed. Dennis P. Rosenbaum. Thousand Oaks, CA: Sage, 1994. 127-146.

Casey, Pamela and Ingo Keilitz. "Estimating the Prevalence of Learning Disabled and Mentally Retarded Juvenile Offenders: A Meta-Analysis." *Understanding Troubled and Troubling Youth.* Ed. Peter E. Leone. Newbury Park, CA: Sage, 1990. 82-101.

Centerwall, Brandon S. "Television and the Development of the Superego." *Children and Violence.* Eds. Colette Chiland and J. Gerald Young. Northvale, NJ: Jason Aronson, 1994. 178-197.

Chiland, Colette. "Human Violence." *Children and Violence.* Eds. Colette Chiland and J. Gerald Young. Northvale, NJ: Jason Aronson, 1994. 3-12

Chiland, Colette and J. Gerald Young, eds. *Children and Violence.* Northvale, NJ: Jason Aronson, 1994.

Chin, Ko-lin. "Chinese Gangs and Extortion." *Gangs in America.* Ed. C. Ronald Huff. Newbury Park, CA: Sage, 1990. 129-145.

Christy, Joseph T. "Toward a Model Secure Detention Program: Lessons from Shuman Center." *Reforming Juvenile Detention: No More Hidden Closets.* Eds. Ira M. Schwartz and William H. Barton. Columbus, OH: Ohio State University Press, 1994. 108-128.

Chubb, John E., and Terry M. Moe. "Politics, Markets, and Equality in Schools." *Reducing Poverty in America: Views and Approaches.* Ed. Michael R. Darby. Thousand Oaks, CA: Sage, 1996. 121-153.

Clarke, Kildare. "Legalization of Drugs and Beyond Legalization." *Searching for Alternatives: Drug-Control Policy in the United States.* Eds. Melvyn B. Krauss and Edward P. Lazear. Stanford, CA: Hoover Institution Press, 1991. 424-434.

Cohen, Yecheskiel. "Treating Aggressive Children Through Residential Treatment." *Children and Violence.* Eds. Colette Chiland and J. Gerald Young. Northvale, NJ: Jason Aronson, 1994. 91-105.

Conte, Jon R., and Linda Fogarty. "Sexual Abuse Prevention Programs for Children." *Child Trauma: Issues & Research.* Ed. Ann Wolbert Burgess. New York: Garland, 1992. 335-360.

Cordner, Gary W. "Foot Patrol Without Community Policing: Law and Order in Public Housing." *The Challenge of Community Policy: Testing the Promises.* Ed. Dennis P. Rosenbaum. Thousand Oaks, CA: Sage, 1994. 182-191.

Corman, Hope, Theoore Joyce, and Naci Mocan. "Homicide and Crack in New York City." *Searching for Alternatives: Drug-Control Policy in the United States.* Eds. Melvyn B. Krauss and Edward P. Lazear. Stanford, CA: Hoover Institution Press, 1991. 112-137.

Corsica, Joanne Y. "Employment Training Interventions." *The Gang Intervention Handbook.* Eds. Arnold P. Goldstein and C. Ronald Huff. Chamapign, IL: Research Press, 1993. 301-318.

Cortes, Ernesto, Jr. "Reweaving the Fabric: The Iron Rule and the IAF Strategy for Power and Politics." *Reducing Poverty in America: Views and Approaches.* Ed. Michael R. Darby. Thousand Oaks, CA: Sage, 1996. 175-198.

Covey, Herbert C., Scott Menard, and Robert J. Franzese. *Juvenile Gangs.* Springfield, IL: Charles C. Thomas, 1992.

Crane, Jonathan. "Efects of Neighborhoods on Dropping Out of School and Teenage Childbearing." *The Urban Underclass*. Eds. Christopher Jencks and Paul E. Peterson. Washington: Brookings, 1991. 299-320.

Curran, Thomas F. "Developing a Child Sexual Abuse Curriculum." *Child Trauma: Issues & Research*. Ed. Ann Wolbert Burgess. New York: Garland, 1992. 361-379.

Danziger, Sheldon. "The Economy, Public Policy, and the Poor." *Beyond Welfare: New Approaches to the Problem of Poverty in America*. Ed. Harrell R. Rodgers Jr. Armonk, NY: M.E. Sharpe, 1988. 3-13.

Danziger, Sheldon and Peter Gottschalk. *America Unequal*. Cambridge: Harvard University Press, 1995.

Danziger, Sheldon H., and Daniel H. Weinberg. "The Historical Record: Trends in Family Income, Inequality, and Poverty." *Confronting Poverty: Prescriptions for Change*. Eds. Sheldon H. Danziger, Gary D. Sandefur, and Daniel Weinberg. New York: Harvard University Press, 1994. 18-50.

Danziger, Sheldon H., Gary D. Sandefur, and Daniel H. Weinberg. "Introduction." *Confronting Poverty: Prescriptions for Change*. Eds. Sheldon H. Danziger, Gary D. Sandefur, and Daniel Weinberg. New York: Harvard University Press, 1994. 1-17.

Danziger, Sheldon H, Gary D. Sandefur, and Daniel Weinberg, eds. *Confronting Poverty: Prescriptions for Change*. New York: Harvard University Press, 1994.

Darby, Michael R. "Facing and Reducing Poverty." *Reducing Poverty in America: Views and Approaches*. Ed. Michael R. Darby. Thousand Oaks, CA: Sage, 1996. 3-12.

Darby, Michael R., ed. *Reducing Poverty in America: Views and Approaches*. Thousand Oaks, CA: Sage, 1996.

Dishion, Thomas J. "The Peer Context of Troublesome Child and Adolelscent Behavior." *Understanding Troubled and Troubling Youth*. Ed. Peter E. Leone. Newbury Park, CA: Sage, 1990. 128-153.

Dowdell, Elizabeth Burges and John B. Rabun, Jr. "Newborn Infant Abductions from Hospitals." *Child Trauma: Issues & Research*. Ed. Ann Wolbert Burgess. New York: Garland, 1992. 49-60.

Dunbar, Leslie W. *The Common Interest: How Our Social Welfare Policies Don't Work and What We Can Do About Them*. New York: Pantheon, 1988.

Duncan, Greg J., and Saul D. Hoffman. "Teenage Underclass Behavior and Subsequent Poverty: Have the Rules Changed?" *The Urban Underclass*. Eds. Christopher Jencks and Paul E. Peterson. Washington: Brookings, 1991. 155-174.

Duxbury, Elaine B. "Correctional Interventions." *The Gang Intervention Handbook*. Eds. Arnold P. Goldstein and C. Ronald Huff. Chamapign, IL: Research Press, 1993. 427-437.

Eck, John E., and Dennis P. Rosenbaum. "The New Police Order: Effectiveness, Equity, and Efficiency in Community Policing." *The Challenge of Community Policy: Testing the Promises*. Ed. Dennis P. Rosenbaum. Thousand Oaks, CA: Sage, 1994. 3-23.

Engelsman, Eddy L. "Drug Policy in the Netherlands From a Public Health Perspective." *Searching for Alternatives: Drug-Control Policy in the United States*. Eds. Melvyn B. Krauss and Edward P. Lazear. Stanford, CA: Hoover Institution Press, 1991. 169-174.

Everhart, Robert B. "Disruptive Behavior in Organizational Context." *Understanding Troubled and Troubling Youth*. Ed. Peter E. Leone. Newbury Park, CA: Sage, 1990. 272-289.

Fagan, Jeffrey, "Separating the Men From the Boys: The Comparative Advantage of Juvenile Versus Criminal Court Sanctions on Recidivism Among Adolescent Felony Offenders." *Serious, Violent, & Chronic Juvenile Offenders.* Eds. James C. Howell, Barry Krisberg, J. David Hawkins, and John J. Wilson. Thousand Oaks, CA: Sage, 1995. 238-260.

―――. "Social Processes of Delinquency and Drug Use Among Urban Gangs." *Gangs in America.* Ed. C. Ronald Huff. Newbury Park, CA: Sage, 1990. 183-219.

Farley, Reynolds. "Residential Segregation of Social and Economic Groups among Blacks, 1970-1980." *The Urban Underclass.* Eds. Christopher Jencks and Paul E. Peterson. Washington: Brookings, 1991. 274-298.

Farley, David and Barbara King Misechok. "JOBS and JTPA: Single Point of Contact in Pennsylvania." *Welfare System Reform: Coordinating Federal, State, and Local Public Assistance Programs.* Eds. Edward T. Jennings Jr. and Neal S. Zank. Westport, CT: Greenwood, 1993. 175-184.

Feld, Barry C. "The Social Context of Juvenile Justice Administration: Racial Disparities in an Urban Juvenile Court." *Minorities in Juvenile Justice.* Eds. Kimberly Kempf Leonard, Carl E. Pope, and William H. Feyerherm. Thousand Oaks, CA: Sage, 1995. 66-97.

Feyerherm, William H. "The DMC Initiative: The Convergence of Policy and Research Themes." *Minorities in Juvenile Justice.* Eds. Kimberly Kempf Leonard, Carl E. Pope, and William H. Feyerherm. Thousand Oaks, CA: Sage, 1995. 1-15.

Fink, Carolyn Molden. "Special Education Students at Risk: A Comparative Study of Delinquency." *Understanding Troubled and Troubling Youth.* Ed. Peter E. Leone. Newbury Park, CA: Sage, 1990. 61-81.

Frazier, Charles E., and Donna M. Bishop. "Reflections on Race Effects in Juvenile Justice." *Minorities in Juvenile Justice.* Eds. Kimberly Kempf Leonard, Carl E. Pope, and William H. Feyerherm. Thousand Oaks, CA: Sage, 1995. 16-46.

Freeman, Richard B. "Employment and Earnings of Disadvantaged Young Men in a Labor Shortage Economy." *The Urban Underclass.* Eds. Christopher Jencks and Paul E. Peterson. Washington: Brookings, 1991. 103-121.

Friedman, Warren. "The Community Role in Community Policing." *The Challenge of Community Policy: Testing the Promises.* Ed. Dennis P. Rosenbaum. Thousand Oaks, CA: Sage, 1994. 263-269.

Friedmann, Robert R. *Community Policing: Comparative Perspectives and Prospects.* New York: St. Martin's Press, 1992.

Funiciello, Theresa. *Tyranny of Kindness: Dismantling the Welfare System to End Poverty in America.* New York: Atlantic Monthly Press, 1993.

Garfinkel, Irwin and Sara McLanahan. "Single-Mother Families, Economic Insecurity, and Government Policy." *Confronting Poverty: Prescriptions for Change.* Eds. Sheldon H. Danziger, Gary D. Sandefur, and Daniel Weinberg. New York: Harvard University Press, 1994. 205-225.

Garfinkel, Irwin, Sara McLanahan, and Patrick Wong. "Child Support and Dependency." *Beyond Welfare: New Approaches to the Problem of Poverty in America.* Ed. Harrell R. Rodgers Jr. Armonk, NY: M.E. Sharpe, 1988. 66-85.

Garr, Robin. *Reinvesting in America: The Grassroots Movements That Are Feeding the Hungry, Housing the Homeless, and Putting Americans Back to Work.* Reading, MA: Addison-Wesley, 1995.

Genelin, Michael. "Gang Prosecutions: The Hardest Game in Town." *The Gang Intervention Handbook.* Eds. Arnold P. Goldstein and C. Ronald Huff. Chamapign, IL: Research Press, 1993. 417-426.

Gibbs, John C. "Moral-Cognitive Interventions." *The Gang Intervention Handbook.* Eds. Arnold P. Goldstein and C. Ronald Huff. Chamapign, IL: Research Press, 1993. 159-185.

Gilbert, Neil and Barbara Gilbert. *The Enabling State: Modern Welfare Capitalism in America.* New York: Oxford University Press, 1989.

Gimpel, James. "Congress and the Coordination of Public Assistance." *Welfare System Reform: Coordinating Federal, State, and Local Public Assistance Programs.* Eds. Edward T. Jennings Jr. and Neal S. Zank. Westport, CT: Greenwood, 1993. 33-42.

Giobbe, Evilina. "Juvenile Prostitution: Profile of Recruitment." *Child Trauma: Issues & Research.* Ed. Ann Wolbert Burgess. New York: Garland, 1992. 117-130.

Glasser, Ira. "Drug Prohibition: An Engine for Crime." *Searching for Alternatives: Drug-Control Policy in the United States.* Eds. Melvyn B. Krauss and Edward P. Lazear. Stanford, CA: Hoover Institution Press, 1991. 271-282.

Goldstein, Arnold P. *Delinquent Gangs: A Psychological Perspective.* Champaign, IL: Research Press, 1991.

———. "Gang Intervention: A Historical Review." *The Gang Intervention Handbook.* Eds. Arnold P. Goldstein and C. Ronald Huff. Chamapign, IL: Research Press, 1993. 21-51.

———. "Gang Intervention: Issues and Opportunities." *The Gang Intervention Handbook.* Eds. Arnold P. Goldstein and C. Ronald Huff. Chamapign, IL: Research Press, 1993. 477-489.

———. "Interpersonal Skills Training Interventions." *The Gang Intervention Handbook.* Eds. Arnold P. Goldstein and C. Ronald Huff. Chamapign, IL: Research Press, 1993. 87-158.

Goldstein, Arnold P., Barry Glick, with Wilm Carthan and Douglas A. Blancero. *The Prosocial Gang: Implement Aggression Replacement Training.* Thousand Oaks, CA: Sage, 1994.

Goldstein, Arnold P., and C. Ronald Huff, eds. *The Gang Intervention Handbook.* Chamapign, IL: Research Press, 1993.

Goldstein, Avram. "Drug Policy: Some Thoughts About Striking the Right Balance." *Searching for Alternatives: Drug-Control Policy in the United States.* Eds. Melvyn B. Krauss and Edward P. Lazear. Stanford, CA: Hoover Institution Press, 1991. 398-404.

Gottfredson, Denise C. "Changing School Structures to Benefit High-Risk Youths." *Understanding Troubled and Troubling Youth.* Ed. Peter E. Leone. Newbury Park, CA: Sage, 1990. 246-271.

Gottschalk, Peter, Sara McLanahan, and Gary D. Sandefur. "The Dynamics and Intergenerational Transmission of Poverty and Welfare Participation." *Confronting Poverty: Prescriptions for Change.* Eds. Sheldon H. Danziger, Gary D. Sandefur, and Daniel Weinberg. New York: Harvard University Press, 1994. 85-108.

Greene, Jack R., William T. Bergman, and Edward J. McLaughlin. "Implementing Community Policing: Cultural and Structural Change in Police Organizations." *The Challenge of Community Policy: Testing the Promises.* Ed. Dennis P. Rosenbaum. Thousand Oaks, CA: Sage, 1994. 92-109.

Greenstein, Robert. "Universal and Targeted Aproaches to Relieving Poverty: An Alternative View." *The Urban Underclass.* Eds. Christopher Jencks and Paul E. Peterson. Washington: Brookings, 1991. 437-459.

Greenstone, J. David. "Culture, Rationality, and the Underclass." *The Urban Underclass.* Eds. Christopher Jencks and Paul E. Peterson. Washington: Brookings, 1991. 399-408.

Greer, William C. "Aftercare: Community Integration Following Institutional Treatment." *Juvenile Sexual Offending: Causes, Consequences, and Correction.* Eds. Gail D. Ryan and Sandy L. Lane. Lexington, MA: Lexington Books, 1991. 377-390.

Grinspoon, Lester. "Marijuana in a Time of Psychopharmacological McCarthyism." *Searching for Alternatives: Drug-Control Policy in the United States.* Eds. Melvyn B. Krauss and Edward P. Lazear. Stanford, CA: Hoover Institution Press, 1991. 379-389.

Grissom, Grant R., and Wm. L. Dubnov. *Without Locks and Bars: Reforming Our Reform Schools.* New York: Praeger, 1989.

Grossman, Michael, Gary S. Becker, and Kevin M. Murphy. "Rational Addiction and the Effect of Price on Consumption." *Searching for Alternatives: Drug-Control Policy in the United States.* Eds. Melvyn B. Krauss and Edward P. Lazear. Stanford, CA: Hoover Institution Press, 1991. 77-86.

Guarino-Ghezzi, Susan and Edward J. Loughran. *Balancing Juvenile Justice.* New Brunswick, NJ: Transaction, 1996.

Gueron, Judith M. "Welfare and Poverty: Strategies to Increase Work." *Reducing Poverty in America: Views and Approaches.* Ed. Michael R. Darby. Thousand Oaks, CA: Sage, 1996. 235-250.

Hagedorn, John M. "Back in the Field Again: Gang Research in the 1990s." *Gangs in America.* Ed. C. Ronald Huff. Newbury Park, CA: Sage, 1990. 240-259.

Hagedorn, John and Perry Macon. *People and Folks: Gangs, Crime and the Underclass in a Rustbelt City.* Chicago: Lake View Press, 1988.

Harris, Linda A. "Lafayette Court Family Development Center: Bringing Social Services and Housing Programs Together." Welfare System Reform: Coordinating Federal, State, and Local Public Assistance Programs. Eds. Edward T. Jennings Jr. and Neal S. Zank. Westport, CT: Greenwood, 1993. 185-198.

Harris, Mary G. *Cholas: Latino Girls and Gangs.* New York: AMS Press, 1988.

Haveman, Robert. "The Nature, Causes, and Cures of Poverty: Accomplishments from Three Decades of Poverty Research and Policy." *Confronting Poverty: Prescriptions for Change.* Eds. Sheldon H. Danziger, Gary D. Sandefur, and Daniel Weinberg. New York: Harvard University Press, 1994. 438-448.

Hawkins, J. David, Richard F. Catalano, and Devon D. Brewer. "Preventing Serious, Violent, and Chronic Juvenile Offending: Effective Strategies From Conception to Age 6." *Serious, Violent, & Chronic Juvenile Offenders.* Eds. James C. Howell, Barry Krisberg, J. David Hawkins, and John J. Wilson. Thousand Oaks, CA: Sage, 1995. 47-60.

Hay, Joel W. "The Harm They Do to Others: A Primer on the External Costs of Drug Abuse." *Searching for Alternatives: Drug-Control Policy in the United States.* Eds. Melvyn B. Krauss and Edward P. Lazear. Stanford, CA: Hoover Institution Press, 1991. 200-225.

Hayes-Bautista, David. "Poverty and the Underclass: Some Latino Crosscurrents." *Reducing Poverty in America: Views and Approaches.* Ed. Michael R. Darby. Thousand Oaks, CA: Sage, 1996. 56-66.

Heclo, Hugh. "Poverty Politics." *Confronting Poverty: Prescriptions for Change.* Eds. Sheldon H. Danziger, Gary D. Sandefur, and Daniel Weinberg. New York: Harvard University Press, 1994. 396-437.

Heinz, Joseph, Gail Ryan, and Steven Bengis. "The System's Response to Juvenile Sex Offenders." *Juvenile Sexual Offending: Causes, Consequences, and Correction.* Eds. Gail D. Ryan and Sandy L. Lane. Lexington, MA: Lexington Books, 1991. 185-198.

Hochschild, Jennifer L. "Equal Opportunity and the Estranged Poor." *The Ghetto Underclass: Social Science Perspectives.* Updated edition. Ed. William Julius Wilson. Newbury Park, CA: Sage, 1993. 160-172.

Hollin, Clive R. "Cognitive-Behavioral Interventions." *The Gang Intervention Handbook.* Eds. Arnold P. Goldstein and C. Ronald Huff. Chamapign, IL: Research Press, 1993. 55-86.

Hopkins, Kevin. R. "The Presidency and the Coordination of Public Assistance." *Welfare System Reform: Coordinating Federal, State, and Local Public Assistance Programs.* Eds. Edward T. Jennings Jr. and Neal S. Zank. Westport, CT: Greenwood, 1993. 25-32.

Horne, Arthur M. "Family-Based Interventions." *The Gang Intervention Handbook.* Eds. Arnold P. Goldstein and C. Ronald Huff. Chamapign, IL: Research Press, 1993. 189-218.

Horowitz, Ruth. "Sociological Perspectives on Gangs: Conflicting Definitions and Concepts." *Gangs in America.* Ed. C. Ronald Huff. Newbury Park, CA: Sage, 1990. 37-54.

Howell, James C. "Gangs and Youth Violence: Recent Research." *Serious, Violent, & Chronic Juvenile Offenders.* Eds. James C. Howell, Barry Krisberg, J. David Hawkins, and John J. Wilson. Thousand Oaks, CA: Sage, 1995. 261-274.

Howell, James C., and Barry Krisberg. "Conclusion." *Serious, Violent, & Chronic Juvenile Offenders.* Eds. James C. Howell, Barry Krisberg, J. David Hawkins, and John J. Wilson. Thousand Oaks, CA: Sage, 1995. 275-278.

Howell, James C., Barry Krisberg and Michael Jones. "Trends in Juvenile Crime and Youth Violence." *Serious, Violent, & Chronic Juvenile Offenders.* Eds. James C. Howell, Barry Krisberg, J. David Hawkins, and John J. Wilson. Thousand Oaks, CA: Sage, 1995. 1-35.

Howell, James C., Barry Krisberg, J. David Hawkins, and John J. Wilson eds. *Serious, Violent, & Chronic Juvenile Offenders.* Thousand Oaks, CA: Sage, 1995.

Huff, C. Ronald. "Denial, Overreaction, and Misidentification: A Postscript on Public Policy." Gangs in America. Ed. C. Ronald Huff. Newbury Park, CA: Sage, 1990. 310-317.

———. "Gangs and Public Policy: Macrolevel Interventions." *The Gang Intervention Handbook.* Eds. Arnold P. Goldstein and C. Ronald Huff. Chamapign, IL: Research Press, 1993. 463-476.

———. "Gangs in the United States." *The Gang Intervention Handbook.* Eds. Arnold P. Goldstein and C. Ronald Huff. Chamapign, IL: Research Press, 1993. 3-20.

———. "Two Generations of Gang Research." *Gangs in America.* Ed. C. Ronald Huff. Newbury Park, CA: Sage, 1990. 24-34.

Huff, C. Ronald, ed. *Gangs in America.* Newbury Park, CA: Sage, 1990.

Huff, C. Ronald, and Wesley D. McBride. "Gangs and the Police." *The Gang Intervention Handbook.* Eds. Arnold P. Goldstein and C. Ronald Huff. Chamapign, IL: Research Press, 1993. 401-416.

Inciardi, James A. "American Drug Policy and the Legalization Debate." *The Drug Legalization Debate.* Ed. James A. Inciardi. Newbury Park, CA: Sage, 1991. 7-15.

Inciardi, James A., ed. *The Drug Legalization Debate.* Newbury Park, CA: Sage, 1991.

Inciardi, James A., and Duane C. McBride. "The Case Against Legalization." *The Drug Legalization Debate.* Ed. James A. Inciardi. Newbury Park, CA: Sage, 1991. 45-79.

Jackson, Thomas F. "The State, the Movement, and the Urban Poor: The War on Poverty and Political Mobilization in the 1960s." *The 'Underclass' Debate: Views From History.* Ed. Michael B. Katz. Princeton: Princeton University Press, 1993. 403-439.

Jankwoski, Martin Sanchez. *Islands in the Street: Gangs and American Urban Society.* Berkeley, CA: University of California Press, 1991.

Jargowsky, Paul A., and Mary Jo Bane. "Ghetto Poverty in the United States, 1970-1980." *The Urban Underclass.* Eds. Christopher Jencks and Paul E. Peterson. Washington: Brookings, 1991. 235-273.

Jencks, Christopher. "Can We Replace Welfare With Work?" *Reducing Poverty in America: Views and Approaches.* Ed. Michael R. Darby. Thousand Oaks, CA: Sage, 1996. 69-81.

———. "Is the American Underclass Growing." *The Urban Underclass.* Eds. Christopher Jencks and Paul E. Peterson. Washington: Brookings, 1991. 28-100.

Jencks, Christopher and Paul E. Peterson, eds. *The Urban Underclass.* Washington: Brookings, 1991.

Jennings, Edward T. Jr. "Patterns and Perceptions of Employment and Training Coordination in the States." *Welfare System Reform: Coordinating Federal, State, and Local Public Assistance Programs.* Eds. Edward T. Jennings Jr. and Neal S. Zank. Westport, CT: Greenwood, 1993. 73-96.

Jennings, Edward T. Jr., and Dale Krane. "Community-Level Coordination of the JOBS Program." *Welfare System Reform: Coordinating Federal, State, and Local Public Assistance Programs.* Eds. Edward T. Jennings Jr. and Neal S. Zank. Westport, CT: Greenwood, 1993. 211-27.

———. "State Government Coordination of the JOBS Program." *Welfare System Reform: Coordinating Federal, State, and Local Public Assistance Programs.* Eds. Edward T. Jennings Jr. and Neal S. Zank. Westport, CT: Greenwood, 1993. 123-142.

Jennings, Edward T., Jr., and Neal S. Zank, eds. *Welfare System Reform: Coordinating Federal, State, and Local Public Assistance Programs.* Westport, CT. Greenwood, 1993.

Jennings, Edward T., Jr., and Neal S. Zank. "The Coordination Challenge." *Welfare System Reform: Coordinating Federal, State, and Local Public Assistance Programs.* Eds. Edward T. Jennings Jr. and Neal S. Zank. Westport, CT: Greenwood, 1993. 3-19.

Jennings, Edward T., Jr., William Tracy, and Kathleen Wimer. "Plnning and Organizing to Coordinate Human Servie Delivery in the States." *Welfare System Reform: Coordinating Federal, State, and Local Public Assistance Programs.* Eds. Edward T. Jennings Jr. and Neal S. Zank. Westport, CT: Greenwood, 1993. 97-110.

Johnson, James H., Jr. "The Real Issues for Reducing Poverty." *Reducing Poverty in America: Views and Approaches.* Ed. Michael R. Darby. Thousand Oaks, CA: Sage, 1996. 337-363.

Jonas, Steven. "The U.S. Drug Problem and the U.S. Drug Culture: A Public Health Solution." *The Drug Legalization Debate.* Ed. James A. Inciardi. Newbury Park, CA: Sage, 1991. 161-182.

Jones, Jacqueline. "Southern Diaspora: Origins of the Northern 'Underclass.'" *The 'Underclass' Debate: Views From History.* Ed. Michael B. Katz. Princeton: Princeton University Press, 1993. 27-54.

"Juvenile Courts." *American Jurisprudence,* 2nd ed. Rochester, NY: Lawyers Cooperative Publishing, 1995.

Kantor, Harvey and Barbara Brenzel. "Urban Education and the 'Truly Disadvantaged': The Historical Roots of the Contemporary Crisis, 1945-1990." *The 'Underclass' Debate: Views From History.* Ed. Michael B. Katz. Princeton: Princeton University Press, 1993. 366-402.

Karel, Richard B. "A Model Legalization Proposal." *The Drug Legalization Debate.* Ed. James A. Inciardi. Newbury Park, CA: Sage, 1991. 80-102.

Kasarda, John D. "Urban Industrial Transition and the Underclass." *The Ghetto Underclass: Social Science Perspectives.* Updated edition. Ed. William Julius Wilson. Newbury Park, CA: Sage, 1993. 43-65.

Kates, Don B., Jr. *The Battle Over Gun Control.* Bellevue, WA: Second Amendment Foundation, n.d.

———. *The Second Amendment: Second to None.* Bellevue, WA: Second Amendment Foundation, 1982.

Katz, Michael B. "Reframing the 'Underclass' Debate." *The 'Underclass' Debate: Views From History.* Ed. Michael B. Katz. Princeton: Princeton University Press, 1993. 440-477.

———. "The Urban 'Underclass' as a Metaphor of Social Transformation." *The 'Underclass' Debate: Views From History.* Ed. Michael B. Katz. Princeton: Princeton University Press, 1993. 3-23.

Katz, Michael B., ed. *The 'Underclass' Debate: Views From History.* Princeton: Princeton University Press, 1993.

Kelly, Robin D.G. "The Black Poor and the Politics of Opposition in a New South City, 1929-1970." *The 'Underclass' Debate: Views From History.* Ed. Michael B. Katz. Princeton: Princeton University Press, 1993. 293-333.

Kelson, William A. *Poverty and the Underclass: Changing Perceptions of the Poor in America.* New York: New York University Press, 1994.

Kimenyi, Mwangi S. *Economics of Poverty, Discrimination, and Public Policy.* Cincinatti: South-Western, 1995.

King, Christopher T. "Federal Policy Changes to Enhance State and Local Coordination." *Welfare System Reform: Coordinating Federal, State, and Local Public Assistance Programs.* Eds. Edward T. Jennings Jr. and Neal S. Zank. Westport, CT: Greenwood, 1993. 55-67.

King, Michael and Christine Pipler. *How the Law Thinks About Children.* 2nd ed. Brookgate, VT: Ashgate, 1995.

Kirschenman, Joleen and Kathryn M. Neckerman. "'We'd Love to Hire Them, But. . . ': The Meaning of Race for Employers." *The Urban Underclass.* Eds. Christopher Jencks and Paul E. Peterson. Washington: Brookings, 1991. 203-232.

Klein, Malcolm W. *The American Street Gang: Its Nature, Prevalence, and Control.* New York: Oxford University Press, 1995.

Kleiman, Mark A.R. "The Optimal Design of Drug-Control Laws." *Searching for Alternatives: Drug-Control Policy in the United States.* Eds. Melvyn B. Krauss and Edward P. Lazear. Stanford, CA: Hoover Institution Press, 1991. 193-199.

Knopp, Fay Honey and Sandy Lane. "Program Development." *Juvenile Sexual Offending: Causes, Consequences, and Correction.* Eds. Gail D. Ryan and Sandy L. Lane. Lexington, MA: Lexington Books, 1991. 21-37.

Kodluboy, Donald W., and Loren A. Evenrud. "School-Based Interventions: Safety and Security." *The Gang Intervention Handbook.* Eds. Arnold P. Goldstein and C. Ronald Huff. Chamapign, IL: Research Press, 1993. 219-256.

Krane, Dale. "State Efforts to Influence Federal Policy." *Welfare System Reform: Coordinating Federal, State, and Local Public Assistance Programs.* Eds. Edward T. Jennings Jr. and Neal S. Zank. Westport, CT: Greenwood, 1993. 143-156.

Krauss, Melvyn B., and Edward P. Lazear eds. *Searching for Alternatives: Drug-Control Policy in the United States.* Stanford, CA: Hoover Institution Press, 1991.

Krisberg, Barry, Elliot Currie, David Onek, and Richard G. Wiebush. "Graduated Sanctions for Serious, Violent, and Chronic Juvenile Offenders." *Serious, Violent, & Chronic Juvenile Offenders.* Eds. James C. Howell, Barry Krisberg, J. David Hawkins, and John J. Wilson. Thousand Oaks, CA: Sage, 1995. 142-170.

Lane, Sandy. "Special Offender Populations." *Juvenile Sexual Offending: Causes, Consequences, and Correction.* Eds. Gail D. Ryan and Sandy L. Lane. Lexington, MA: Lexington Books, 1991. 299-332.

LeCompte, Margaret D. and Anthony Gary Dworkin. "Educational Programs: Indirect Linkages and Unfulfilled Expectations." *Beyond Welfare: New Approaches to the Problem of Poverty in America.* Ed. Harrell R. Rodgers Jr. Armonk, NY: M.E. Sharpe, 1988. 135-167.

Lehman, Jeffrey S. "Updating Urban Policy." *Confronting Poverty: Prescriptions for Change.* Eds. Sheldon H. Danziger, Gary D. Sandefur, and Daniel Weinberg. New York: Harvard University Press, 1994. 226-252.

Leighton, Barry N. "Community Policing in Canada: An Overview of Experience and Evaluations." *The Challenge of Community Policy: Testing the Promises.* Ed. Dennis P. Rosenbaum. Thousand Oaks, CA: Sage, 1994. 209-223.

Lenkowsky, Leslie. "Reducing Poverty: Will the New 'Services Strategy' Do Better Than the Old." *Reducing Poverty in America: Views and Approaches.* Ed. Michael R. Darby. Thousand Oaks, CA: Sage, 1996. 293-309.

Leonard, Kimberly Kempf and Henry Sontheimer. "The Role of Race in Juvenile Justice in Pennsylvania." *Minorities in Juvenile Justice.* Eds. Kimberly Kempf Leonard, Carl E. Pope, and William H. Feyerherm. Thousand Oaks, CA: Sage, 1995. 95-127.

Leonard, Kimberly Kempf, Carl E. Pope, and William H. Feyerherm, eds. *Minorities in Juvenile Justice.* Thousand Oaks, CA: Sage, 1995.

Leone, Peter E. "Toward Integrated Perspectives on Troubling Behavior." *Understanding Troubled and Troubling Youth.* Ed. Peter E. Leone. Newbury Park, CA: Sage, 1990. 15-22.

Leone, Peter E., ed. *Understanding Troubled and Troubling Youth.* Newbury Park, CA: Sage, 1990.

Leone, Peter E., Mary Bannon Walter, and Bruce I. Wolford. "Toward Integrated Responses to Troubling Behavior." *Understanding Troubled and Troubling Youth.* Ed. Peter E. Leone. Newbury Park, CA: Sage, 1990. 290-298.

Lerner, Richard M. *America's Youth in Crisis: Challenges and Options for Programs and Policies.* Thousand Oaks, CA: Sage, 1995.

Levitan, Sar A. *Programs in Aid of the Poor.* Baltimore: Johns Hopkins, 1990.

Levitsky, Melvyn. "U.S. Efforts in the International Drug War." Searching for Alternatives: Drug-Control Policy in the United States. Eds. Melvyn B. Krauss and Edward P. Lazear. Stanford, CA: Hoover Institution Press, 1991. 360-376.

Loury, Glenn C. "A Dissent From the Incentive Approaches to Reducing Poverty." *Reducing Poverty in America: Views and Approaches.* Ed. Michael R. Darby. Thousand Oaks, CA: Sage, 1996. 111-117.

Lovell, Rick and Carl E. Pope. "Recreational Interventions." *The Gang Intervention Handbook.* Eds. Arnold P. Goldstein and C. Ronald Huff. Chamapign, IL: Research Press, 1993. 319-332.

Lurigio, Arthur J., and Dennis P. Rosenbaum. "The Impact of Community Policing on Police Personnel: A Review of the Literature." *The Challenge of Community Policy: Testing the Promises.* Ed. Dennis P. Rosenbaum. Thousand Oaks, CA: Sage, 1994. 147-163.

Manski, Charles F. "Systemic Educational Reform and Social Mobility: The School *Choice* Controversy." *Confronting Poverty: Prescriptions for Change.* Eds. Sheldon H. Danziger, Gary D. Sandefur, and Daniel Weinberg. New York: Harvard University Press, 1994. 308-329.

Mare, Robert D., and Chrstopher Winship. "Socioeconomic Change and the Decline of Marriage for Blacks and Whites." *The Urban Underclass.* Eds. Christopher Jencks and Paul E. Peterson. Washington: Brookings, 1991. 175-202.

Martin, Teri K. "Determinants of Juvenile Detention Rates." *Reforming Juvenile Detention: No More Hidden Closets.* Eds. Ira M. Schwartz and William H. Barton. Columbus, OH: Ohio State University Press, 1994. 30-46.

Maxson, Cheryl L., and Malcolm W. Klein. "Street Gang Violence: Twice as Great, or Half as Great." *Gangs in America.* Ed. C. Ronald Huff. Newbury Park, CA: Sage, 1990. 71-100

Mayer, Susan E. "How Much Does a High School's Racial and Socioeconomic Mix Affect Graduation and Teenage Fertility Rates?" *The Urban Underclass.* Eds. Christopher Jencks and Paul E. Peterson. Washington: Brookings, 1991. 321-341.

McAdoo, John Lewis. "Understanding African-American Teen Fathers." *Understanding Troubled and Troubling Youth.* Ed. Peter E. Leone. Newbury Park, CA: Sage, 1990. 229-245.

McCully, Sharon. "Detention Reform from a Judge's Viewpoint." *Reforming Juvenile Detention: No More Hidden Closets.* Eds. Ira M. Schwartz and William H. Barton. Columbus, OH: Ohio State University Press, 1994. 162-175.

McLanahan, Sara and Irwin Garfinkel. "Single Mothers, the Underclass, and Social Policy." *The Ghetto Underclass: Social Science Perspectives.* Updated edition. Ed. William Julius Wilson. Newbury Park, CA: Sage, 1993. 109-121.

McVay, Douglas. "Marijuana Legalization: The Time Is Now." *The Drug Legalization Debate.* Ed. James A. Inciardi. Newbury Park, CA: Sage, 1991. 147-160.

Mead, Lwarence M. "The Logic of Workfare; The Underclass and Work Policy." *The Ghetto Underclass: Social Science Perspectives.* Updated edition. Ed. William Julius Wilson. Newbury Park, CA: Sage, 1993. 173-186.

————. *The New Politics of Poverty: The Nonworking Poor in America.* New York: Bsic Books, 1992.

————. "Raising Work Levels Among the Poor." *Reducing Poverty in America: Views and Approaches.* Ed. Michael R. Darby. Thousand Oaks, CA: Sage, 1996. 251-282.

Meese, Edwin III. "Drugs, Change, and Realism: A Critical Evaluation of Proposed Legalization." *Searching for Alternatives: Drug-Control Policy in the United States.* Eds. Melvyn B. Krauss and Edward P. Lazear. Stanford, CA: Hoover Institution Press, 1991. 283-291.

Messerschmidt, James W. *Capitalism, Patriarchy, and Crime.* Totowa, NJ: Rowman & Littlefield, 1986.

Miller, Andrew T. "Social Science, Social Policy, and the Heritage of African-American Families." *The 'Underclass' Debate: Views From History.* Ed. Michael B. Katz. Princeton: Princeton University Press, 1993. 254-289.

Miller, Jerome G. *Last One Over the Wall: The Massachusetts Experiment in Closing Reform Schools.* Columbus, OH: Ohio State University Press, 1991.

Miller, Walter B. "Why the United States Has Failed to Solve Its Youth Gang Problem." *Gangs in America.* Ed. C. Ronald Huff. Newbury Park, CA: Sage, 1990. 263-287.

Mincy, Ronald B. "The Underclass: Concept, Controversy, and Evidence." *Confronting Poverty: Prescriptions for Change.* Eds. Sheldon H. Danziger, Gary D. Sandefur, and Daniel Weinberg. New York: Harvard University Press, 1994. 109-146.

Miron, Jeffrey A. "Drug Legalization and the Consumption of Drugs: An Economist's Perspective." *Searching for Alternatives: Drug-Control Policy in the United States.* Eds. Melvyn B. Krauss and Edward P. Lazear. Stanford, CA: Hoover Institution Press, 1991. 68-76.

Model, Suzanne. "The Ethnic Niche and the Structure of Opportunity: Immigrants and Minorities in New York City." *The 'Underclass' Debate: Views From History.* Ed. Michael B. Katz. Princeton: Princeton University Press, 1993. 161-193.

Monkkonen, Eric H. "Nineteenth-Century Institutions: Dealing with the Urban 'Underclass.'" *The 'Underclass' Debate: Views From History.* Ed. Michael B. Katz. Princeton: Princeton University Press, 1993. 334-365.

Moore, Mark H. "Research Synthesis and Policy Implications." *The Challenge of Community Policy: Testing the Promises.* Ed. Dennis P. Rosenbaum. Thousand Oaks, CA: Sage, 1994. 285-299.

Morgan, John P. "Prohibition is Perverse Policy: What Was True in 1933 Is True Now." *Searching for Alternatives: Drug-Control Policy in the United States.* Eds. Melvyn B. Krauss and Edward P. Lazear. Stanford, CA: Hoover Institution Press, 1991. 405-423.

Mugford, Stephen K. "Drug Legalization and the 'Goldilocks' Problem: Thinking About Costs and Control of Drugs." *Searching for Alternatives: Drug-Control Policy in the United States.* Eds. Melvyn B. Krauss and Edward P. Lazear. Stanford, CA: Hoover Institution Press, 1991. 33-50.

Murnane, Richard J. "Education and the Well-Being of the Next Generation." *Confronting Poverty: Prescriptions for Change.* Eds. Sheldon H. Danziger, Gary D. Sandefur, and Daniel Weinberg. New York: Harvard University Press, 1994. 289-307.

Murray, Charles. "Reducing Poverty and Reducing the Underclass: Different Problems, Different Solutions." *Reducing Poverty in America: Views and Approaches.* Ed. Michael R. Darby. Thousand Oaks, CA: Sage, 1996. 82-110.

Nadelmann, Ethan A. "Beyond Drug Prohibition: Evaluating the Alternatives." *Searching for Alternatives: Drug-Control Policy in the United States.* Eds. Melvyn B. Krauss and Edward P. Lazear. Stanford, CA: Hoover Institution Press, 1991. 241-250.

———. "The Case for Legalization." *The Drug Legalization Debate.* Ed. James A. Inciardi. Newbury Park, CA: Sage, 1991. 17-44.

Nathan, Richard P. "Institutional Change and the Challenge of the Underclass." *The Ghetto Underclass: Social Science Perspectives.* Updated edition. Ed. William Julius Wilson. Newbury Park, CA: Sage, 1993. 187-198.

National Rifle Association. *Ten Myths About Gun Control.* Washington: National Rifle Association, 1987.

Neckerman, Kathryn M. "The Emergence of 'Underclass' Family Patterns, 1900-1940." *The 'Underclass' Debate: Views From History.* Ed. Michael B. Katz. Princeton: Princeton University Press, 1993. 194-219.

Nelson, C. Michael and Robert B. Rutherford, Jr. "Troubled Youth in the Public Schools: Emotionally Disturbed or Socially Maladjusted?" *Understanding Troubled and Troubling Youth.* Ed. Peter E. Leone. Newbury Park, CA: Sage, 1990. 38-60.

Nelson, Joel I. *Post-Industrial Capitalism: Exploring Economic Inequality in America.* Thousand Oaks, CA: Sage, 1995.

Osterman, Paul. "Gains from Growth? The Impact of Full Employment on Poverty in Boston." *The Urban Underclass.* Eds. Christopher Jencks and Paul E. Peterson. Washington: Brookings, 1991. 122-134.

Ostrowski, James. "Answering the Critics of Drug Legalization." *Searching for Alternatives: Drug-Control Policy in the United States.* Eds. Melvyn B. Krauss and Edward P. Lazear. Stanford, CA: Hoover Institution Press, 1991. 296-323.

Padilla, Felix M. *The Gang as an American Enterprise.* New Brunswick, NJ: Rutgers University Press, 1992.

Patterson, James T. *America's Struggle Against Poverty: 1900-1994.* Cambridge: Harvard University Press, 1994.

Perkins, Useni Eugene. *Explosion of Chicago's Black Street Gangs 1900 to the Present.* Chicago: Third World Press, 1987.

Peterson, Paul E. "The Urban Underclass and the Poverty Paradox." *The Urban Underclass.* Eds. Christopher Jencks and Paul E. Peterson. Washington: Brookings, 1991. 3-27.

Peterson, Robert E. "Legalization: The Myth Exposed." *Searching for Alternatives: Drug-Control Policy in the United States.* Eds. Melvyn B. Krauss and Edward P. Lazear. Stanford, CA: Hoover Institution Press, 1991. 325-355.

Peterson, Wallace C. *Silent Depression: The Fate of the American Dream.* New York: W.W. Norton, 1994.

Pope, Carl E. "Equity Within the Juvenile Justice System: Directions for the Future." *Minorities in Juvenile Justice.* Eds. Kimberly Kempf Leonard, Carl E. Pope, and William H. Feyerherm. Thousand Oaks, CA: Sage, 1995. 201-216.

Poupart, Lisa. "Juvenile Justice Processing of American Indian Youths: Disparity in One Rural County." *Minorities in Juvenile Justice.* Eds. Kimberly Kempf Leonard, Carl E. Pope, and William H. Feyerherm. Thousand Oaks, CA: Sage, 1995. 179-200.

Reischauer, Robert D. "Immigration and the Underclass." *The Ghetto Underclass: Social Science Perspectives.* Updated edition. Ed. William Julius Wilson. Newbury Park, CA: Sage, 1993. 137-148.

Reuter, Peter. "On the Consequences of Toughness." *Searching for Alternatives: Drug-Control Policy in the United States.* Eds. Melvyn B. Krauss and Edward P. Lazear. Stanford, CA: Hoover Institution Press, 1991. 138-164.

Rhodes, William C. "From Classic to Holistic Paradigm: The Troubled or Troubling Child as Environment Creator." *Understanding Troubled and Troubling Youth.* Ed. Peter E. Leone. Newbury Park, CA: Sage, 1990. 154-172.

Ribisl, Kurt M. and William S. Davidson II. "Community Change Interventions." *The Gang Intervention Handbook.* Eds. Arnold P. Goldstein and C. Ronald Huff. Chamapign, IL: Research Press, 1993. 333-355.

Roberg, Roy R. "Can Today's Police Organizations Effectively Implement Community Policing?" *The Challenge of Community Policy: Testing the Promises.* Ed. Dennis P. Rosenbaum. Thousand Oaks, CA: Sage, 1994. 249-257.

Rodgers, Harrell R., Jr. "Reducing Poverty through Family Support." *Beyond Welfare: New Approaches to the Problem of Poverty in America.* Ed. Harrell R. Rodgers Jr. Armonk, NY: M.E. Sharpe, 1988. 39-65.

Rodgers, Harrell R., Jr., ed. *Beyond Welfare: New Approaches to the Problem of Poverty in America.* Armonk, NY: M.E. Sharpe, 1988.

Rosenbaum, Dennis P., ed. *The Challenge of Community Policy: Testing the Promises.* Thousand Oaks, CA: Sage, 1994.

Rosenbaum, James E., and Susan J. Popkin. "Employment and Earnings of Low-Income Blacks Who Move to Middle-Class Suburbs." *The Urban Underclass.* Eds. Christopher Jencks and Paul E. Peterson. Washington: Brookings, 1991. 342-356.

Rosenbaum, Marsha, and Rick Doblin. "Why MDMA Should Not Have Been Made Illegal." *The Drug Legalization Debate.* Ed. James A. Inciardi. Newbury Park, CA: Sage, 1991. 135-146.

Rosenthal, Mitchell S. "The Logic of Legalization: A Matter of Perspective." *Searching for Alternatives: Drug-Control Policy in the United States.* Eds. Melvyn B. Krauss and Edward P. Lazear. Stanford, CA: Hoover Institution Press, 1991. 226-238.

Ross, Jonathan and Peter Loss. "Assessment of the Juvenile Sex Offender." *Juvenile Sexual Offending: Causes, Consequences, and Correction.* Eds. Gail D. Ryan and Sandy L. Lane. Lexington, MA: Lexington Books, 1991. 199-251.

Rossi, Peter H., and James D. Wright. "The Urban Homeless: A Portrait of Urban Dislocation." *The Ghetto Underclass: Social Science Perspectives.* Updated edition. Ed. William Julius Wilson. Newbury Park, CA: Sage, 1993. 149-159.

Rouse, John Jay and Bruce D. Johnson. "Hidden Paradigms of Morality in Debates About Drugs: Historical and Policy Sifts in British and American Drug Policy." *The Drug Legalization Debate.* Ed. James A. Inciardi. Newbury Park, CA: Sage, 1991. 183-214.

Royal, Marcella. *Youth Crime/Violence and the Cause.* Monroe, WA: Barrons, 1994.

Ryan, Gail. "Historical Responses to Juvenile Sexual Offenses." *Juvenile Sexual Offending: Causes, Consequences, and Correction.* Eds. Gail D. Ryan and Sandy L. Lane. Lexington, MA: Lexington Books, 1991. 17-20.

———. "Incidence and Prevalence of Sexual Offenses Committed by Juveniles." *Juvenile Sexual Offending: Causes, Consequences, and Correction.* Eds. Gail D. Ryan and Sandy L. Lane. Lexington, MA: Lexington Books, 1991. 9-16.

———. "Juvenile Sex Offenders: Defining the Population." *Juvenile Sexual Offending: Causes, Consequences, and Correction.* Eds. Gail D. Ryan and Sandy L. Lane. Lexington, MA: Lexington Books, 1991. 3-8.

———. "Perpetration Prevention: Primary and Secondary." *Juvenile Sexual Offending: Causes, Consequences, and Correction.* Eds. Gail D. Ryan and Sandy L. Lane. Lexington, MA: Lexington Books, 1991. 393-408.

Ryan, Gail D., and Sandy Lane. "Integrating Theory and Method." *Juvenile Sexual Offending: Causes, Consequences, and Correction.* Eds. Gail D. Ryan and Sandy L. Lane. Lexington, MA: Lexington Books, 1991. 255-298.

Ryan, Gail D., and Sandy L. Lane, eds. *Juvenile Sexual Offending: Causes, Consequences, and Correction.* Lexington, MA: Lexington Books, 1991.

Sadd, Susan and Randolph Grinc. "Innovative Neighborhood Oriented Policing: An Evaluation of Community Policing Programs in Eight Cities." *The Challenge of Community Policy: Testing the Promises.* Ed. Dennis P. Rosenbaum. Thousand Oaks, CA: Sage, 1994. 27-52.

Sanders, William B. *Gangbangs and Drive-Bys: Grounded Culture and Juvenile Gang Violence.* New York: Aldine De Gruyter, 1994.

Sanniti, Carl. "Controlling Juvenile Detention Population: Strategies for Reform." *Reforming Juvenile Detention: No More Hidden Closets.* Eds. Ira M. Schwartz and William H. Barton. Columbus, OH: Ohio State University Press, 1994. 97-107.

Schissel, Bernard. *Social Dimensions of Canadian Youth Justice.* Toronto: Oxford University Press, 1993.

Schneider, Anne L. *Deterrence and Juvenile Crime: Results from a National Policy Experiment.* New York: Springer-Verlag, 1990.

Schwartz, Ira M. "What Policymakers Need to Know about Juvenile Detention Reform." *Reforming Juvenile Detention: No More Hidden Closets.* Eds. Ira M. Schwartz and William H. Barton. Columbus, OH: Ohio State University Press, 1994. 176-182.

Schwartz, Ira M., and William H. Barton, eds. *Reforming Juvenile Detention: No More Hidden Closets.* Columbus, OH: Ohio State University Press, 1994.

Schwartz, Ira M., and Deborah A. Willis. "National Trends in Juvenile Detention." *Reforming Juvenile Detention: No More Hidden Closets.* Eds. Ira M. Schwartz and William H. Barton. Columbus, OH: Ohio State University Press, 1994. 13-29.

Shanker, Albert. "Mythical Choice and Real Standards." *Reducing Poverty in America: Views and Approaches.* Ed. Michael R. Darby. Thousand Oaks, CA: Sage, 1996. 154-172.

Simms, Margaret C. "Training, Work, and Poverty." *Reducing Poverty in America: Views and Approaches.* Ed. Michael R. Darby. Thousand Oaks, CA: Sage, 1996. 283-289.

Skocpol, Theda. "Targeting with Universalism: Politically Viable Policies to Combat Poverty in the United States." *The Urban Underclass.* Eds. Christopher Jencks and Paul E. Peterson. Washington: Brookings, 1991. 411-436.

Skogan, Wesley G. "The Impact of Community Policing on Neighborhood Residents: A Cross-Site Analysis." *The Challenge of Community Policy: Testing the Promises.* Ed. Dennis P. Rosenbaum. Thousand Oaks, CA: Sage, 1994. 167-181.

Snyder, James and Debra Huntley. "Troubled Families and Troubled Youth: The Development of Antisocial Behavior and Depression in Children." *Understanding Troubled and Troubling Youth.* Ed. Peter E. Leone. Newbury Park, CA: Sage, 1990. 194-225.

Soriano, Fernando I. "Cultural Sensitivity and Gang Intervention." *The Gang Intervention Handbook.* Eds. Arnold P. Goldstein and C. Ronald Huff. Chamapign, IL: Research Press, 1993. 441-462.

Spergel, Irving A. *The Youth Gang Problem: A Community Approach.* New York: Oxford University Press, 1995.

Spergel, Irving A., and G. David Curry. "The National Youth Gang Survey: A Research and Development Process." *The Gang Intervention Handbook.* Eds. Arnold P. Goldstein and C. Ronald Huff. Chamapign, IL: Research Press, 1993. 359-400.

———. "Strategies and Pereived Agency Effectiveness in Dealing with the Youth Gang Problem." *Gangs in America.* Ed. C. Ronald Huff. Newbury Park, CA: Sage, 1990. 288-309.

Steinhart, David. "Objective Juvenile Detention Criteria: The California Experience." *Reforming Juvenile Detention: No More Hidden Closets.* Eds. Ira M. Schwartz and William H. Barton. Columbus, OH: Ohio State University Press, 1994. 47-68.

Stephens, Ronald D. "School-Based Interventions: Safety and Security." *The Gang Intervention Handbook.* Eds. Arnold P. Goldstein and C. Ronald Huff. Chamapign, IL: Research Press, 1993. 219-256.

Stern, Mark J. "Poverty and Family Composition Since 1940." *The 'Underclass' Debate: Views From History.* Ed. Michael B. Katz. Princeton: Princeton University Press, 1993. 220-253.

Sugrue, Thomas J. "The Structures of Urban Poverty: The Reorganization of Space and Work in Three Periods of American History." *The 'Underclass' Debate: Views From History.* Ed. Michael B. Katz. Princeton: Princeton University Press, 1993. 85-117.

Sullivan, Mercer L. "Absent Fathers in the Inner City." *The Ghetto Underclass: Social Science Perspectives.* Updated edition. Ed. William Julius Wilson. Newbury Park, CA: Sage, 1993. 65-75.

———. *"Getting Paid" Youth Crime and Work in the Inner City.* Ithaca, NY: Cornell University Press, 1989.

Taubman, Paul. "Externalities and Decriminalization of Drugs." *Searching for Alternatives: Drug-Control Policy in the United States.* Eds. Melvyn B. Krauss and Edward P. Lazear. Stanford, CA: Hoover Institution Press, 1991. 90-111.

Taylor, Carl. S. *Dangerous Society.* East Lansing: Michigan State University Press, 1990.

———. "Gang Imperialism." *Gangs in America.* Ed. C. Ronald Huff. Newbury Park, CA: Sage, 1990. 103-115.

———. *Girls, Gangs, Women and Drugs.* East Lansing: Michigan State University Press, 1993.

Testa, Mark, ct al. "Employment and Marriage among Inner-City Fathers." *The Ghetto Underclass: Social Science Perspectives.* Updated edition. Ed. William Julius Wilson. Newbury Park, CA: Sage, 1993. 96-108.

Thomas, Jerry. "The Adolescent Sex Offender's Family in Treatment." *Juvenile Sexual Offending: Causes, Consequences, and Correction.* Eds. Gail D. Ryan and Sandy L. Lane. Lexington, MA: Lexington Books, 1991. 333-376.

Thornberry, Terrence P., David Huizinga, and Rolf Loeber, "The Prevention of Serious Delinquency and Violence: Implications From the Program of Research on the Causes and Correlates of Delinquency." *Serious, Violent, & Chronic Juvenile Offenders.* Eds. James C. Howell, Barry Krisberg, J. David Hawkins, and John J. Wilson. Thousand Oaks, CA: Sage, 1995. 213-237.

Thornburg, Kathy R. "Youth at Risk: Making a Difference at the Local Level." *Welfare System Reform: Coordinating Federal, State, and Local Public Assistance Programs.* Eds. Edward T. Jennings Jr. and Neal S. Zank. Westport, CT: Greenwood, 1993. 199-210.

Tien, James M., and Thomas F. Rich. "The Hartford COMPASS Program: Experiences With a Weed and Seed-Related Program." *The Challenge of Community Policy: Testing the Promises.* Ed. Dennis P. Rosenbaum. Thousand Oaks, CA: Sage, 1994. 192-206.

Tienda, Marta. "Puerto Ricans and the Underclass Debate." *The Ghetto Underclass: Social Science Perspectives.* Updated edition. Ed. William Julius Wilson. Newbury Park, CA: Sage, 1993. 122-136.

Tienda, Marta and Zai Liang. "Poverty and Immigration in Policy Perspective." *Confronting Poverty: Prescriptions for Change.* Eds. Sheldon H. Danziger, Gary D. Sandefur, and Daniel Weinberg. New York: Harvard University Press, 1994. 330-364.

Tienda, Marta and Haya Stier. "Joblessness and Shiftlessness: Labor Force Activity in Chicago's Inner City." *The Urban Underclass.* Eds. Christopher Jencks and Paul E. Peterson. Washington: Brookings, 1991. 135-154.

Tobin, James. "Poverty in Relation to Macroeconomic Trends, Cycles, and Policies." *Confronting Poverty: Prescriptions for Change.* Eds. Sheldon H. Danziger, Gary D. Sandefur, and Daniel Weinberg. New York: Harvard University Press, 1994. 147-167.

Trickett, Edison J., and Susan F. Zlotlow. "Ecology and Disordered Behavior: An Overview of Perspectives and Assuptions." *Understanding Troubled and Troubling Youth.* Ed. Peter E. Leone. Newbury Park, CA: Sage, 1990. 105-127.

Trojanowicz, Robert C. "The Future of Community Policing." *The Challenge of Community Policy: Testing the Promises.* Ed. Dennis P. Rosenbaum. Thousand Oaks, CA: Sage, 1994. 258-262.

Trostle, Lawrence C. *The Stoners: Drugs, Demons, and Delinquency.* New York: Garland, 1992.

Trotter, Joe William, Jr. "Blacks in the Urban North: The 'Underclass Question' in Historical Perspective." *The 'Underclass' Debate: Views From History.* Ed. Michael B. Katz. Princeton: Princeton University Press, 1993. 55-81.

Turner, David. "Pragmatic Incoherence: The Changing Face of British Drug Policy." *Searching for Alternatives: Drug-Control Policy in the United States.* Eds. Melvyn B. Krauss and Edward P. Lazear. Stanford, CA: Hoover Institution Press, 1991. 175-190.

Vigil, James Diego. "Cholos and Gangs: Culture Change and Street Youth in Los Angeles." *Gangs in America.* Ed. C. Ronald Huff. Newbury Park, CA: Sage, 1990. 116-128.

Vigil, James Diego, and John M. Long. "Emic and Etic Perspectives on Gang Culture: The Chicano Case." *Gangs in America.* Ed. C. Ronald Huff. Newbury Park, CA: Sage, 1990. 55-68.

Vigil, James Diego and Steve Chong Yun. "Vietnames Youth Gangs in Southern California." *Gangs in America.* Ed. C. Ronald Huff. Newbury Park, CA: Sage, 1990. 146-162.

Wacquant, Loic J.D., and William Julius Wilson. "The Cost of Racial and Class Exclusion in the Inner City." *The Ghetto Underclass: Social Science Perspectives.* Updated edition. Ed. William Julius Wilson. Newbury Park, CA: Sage, 1993. 25-42.

Walters, Glenn D. *Drugs and Crime in Lifestyle Perspective.* Thousand Oaks, CA: Sage, 1994.

Warboys, Loren M., and Carole B. Shauffer. "Protecting the Rights of Troubled and Troubling Youth: Understanding Attorneys' Perspectives." *Understanding Troubled and Troubling Youth.* Ed. Peter E. Leone. Newbury Park, CA: Sage, 1990. 25-37.

Waterston, Alisse. *Street Addicts in the Political Economy.* Philadelphia: Temple University Press, 1993.

Wattenberg, Ben. "No More Something for Nothing." *Reducing Poverty in America: Views and Approaches.* Ed. Michael R. Darby. Thousand Oaks, CA: Sage, 1996. 364-366.

Way, E. Leong. "Pharmacologic Assessment of Dependence Risks." *Searching for Alternatives: Drug-Control Policy in the United States.* Eds. Melvyn B. Krauss and Edward P. Lazear. Stanford, CA: Hoover Institution Press, 1991. 390-397.

Weatherly, Richard A. "Teenage Parenthood and Poverty." *Beyond Welfare: New Approaches to the Problem of Poverty in America.* Ed. Harrell R. Rodgers Jr. Armonk, NY: M.E. Sharpe, 1988. 114-134.

Webb, Margot. *Coping With Street Gangs.* New York: Rosen, 1992.

Weicher, John C. "A New War on Poverty: The Kemp Program to Empower the Poor." *Reducing Poverty in America: Views and Approaches.* Ed. Michael R. Darby. Thousand Oaks, CA: Sage, 1996. 199-223.

Weisburd, David. "Evaluating Community Policing: Role Tensions Between Practitioners and Evaluators." *The Challenge of Community Policy: Testing the Promises.* Ed. Dennis P. Rosenbaum. Thousand Oaks, CA: Sage, 1994. 274-277.

Weisel, Deborah Lamm and John E. Eck. "Toward a Practical Approach to Organizational Change: Community Policing Intiatives in Six Cities." *The Challenge of Community Policy: Testing the Promises.* Ed. Dennis P. Rosenbaum. Thousand Oaks, CA: Sage, 1994. 53-72.

Wiebush, Richard G., Christopher Baird, Barry Krisberg, and David Onek. "Risk Assessment and Classification for Serious, Violent, and Chronic Juvenile Offenders." *Serious, Violent, & Chronic Juvenile Offenders.* Eds. James C. Howell, Barry Krisberg, J. David Hawkins, and John J. Wilson. Thousand Oaks, CA: Sage, 1995. 171-212.

Wilkinson, Deann L., and Dennis P. Rosenbaum. "The Effects of Organizational Structure on Community Policing: A Comparison of Two Cities." *The Challenge of Community Policy: Testing the Promises.* Ed. Dennis P. Rosenbaum. Thousand Oaks, CA: Sage, 1994. 110-126.

Wilson, James Q. "Cultural Aspects of Poverty." *Reducing Poverty in America: Views and Approaches.* Ed. Michael R. Darby. Thousand Oaks, CA: Sage, 1996. 367-372.

Wilson, John J., and James C. Howell. "Comprehensive Strategy for Serious, Violent, and Chronic Juvenile Offenders." Serious, Violent, & Chronic Juvenile Offenders. Eds. James C. Howell, Barry Krisberg, J. David Hawkins, and John J. Wilson. Thousand Oaks, CA: Sage, 1995. 36-46.

Wison, William Julius. "Public Policy Research and The Truly Disadvantaged." *The Urban Underclass.* Eds. Christopher Jencks and Paul E. Peterson. Washington: Brookings, 1991. 460-481.

————. "The Underclass: Issues, Perspectives, and Public Policy." *The Ghetto Underclass: Social Science Perspectives.* Updated edition. Ed. William Julius Wilson. Newbury Park, CA: Sage, 1993. 1-24.

Wilson, William Julius, ed. *The Ghetto Underclass: Social Science Perspectives.* Updated edition. Newbury Park, CA: Sage, 1993.

Wiseman, Michael. "Workfare and Welfare Reform." *Beyond Welfare: New Approaches to the Problem of Poverty in America.* Ed. Harrell R. Rodgers Jr. Armonk, NY: M.E. Sharpe, 1988. 14-38.

Wolfe, Barbara L. "Reform of Health Care for the Nonelderly Poor." *Confronting Poverty: Prescriptions for Change.* Eds. Sheldon H. Danziger, Gary D. Sandefur, and Daniel Weinberg. New York: Harvard University Press, 1994. 253-288.

Woodson, Robert L., Sr. "What We Can Learn From Grassroots Leaders." *Reducing Poverty in America: Views and Approaches.* Ed. Michael R. Darby. Thousand Oaks, CA: Sage, 1996. 224-232.

Wordes, Madeline, and Timothy S. Bynum. "Policing Juveniles: Is There Bias Against Youths of Color." *Minorities in Juvenile Justice.* Eds. Kimberly Kempf Leonard, Carl E. Pope, and William H. Feyerherm. Thousand Oaks, CA: Sage, 1995. 47-66.

Wycoff, Mary Ann and Wesley G. Skogan. "Community Policing in Madison: An Analysis of Implementation and Impact." *The Challenge of Community Policy: Testing the Promises.* Ed. Dennis P. Rosenbaum. Thousand Oaks, CA: Sage, 1994. 75-91.

Young, J. Gerald and Colette Chiland. "Cultivating and Curing Violence in Children: A Guide to Methods." *Children and Violence.* Eds. Colette Chiland and J. Gerald Young. Northvale, NJ: Jason Aronson, 1994. 198-205.

Zank, Neal S., and Edward. T. Jennings, Jr. "Coordinating Public Assistance Programs in the United States" *Welfare System Reform: Coordinating Federal, State, and Local Public Assistance Programs.* Eds. Edward T. Jennings Jr. and Neal S. Zank. Westport, CT: Greenwood, 1993. 231-241.

Zeese, Kevin B. "Drug War Forever?" *Searching for Alternatives: Drug-Control Policy in the United States.* Eds. Melvyn B. Krauss and Edward P. Lazear. Stanford, CA: Hoover Institution Press, 1991. 251-268.

Zigler, Edward and Sally J. Styfco. "Reshaping Early Childhood Intervention to Be a More Effective Weaon Against Poverty." *Reducing Poverty in America: Views and Approaches.* Ed. Michael R. Darby. Thousand Oaks, CA: Sage, 1996. 310-333.

Zimring, Franklin E., and Gordon Hawkins. "The Wrong Question: Critical Notes on the Decriminalization Debate." *Searching for Alternatives: Drug-Control Policy in the United States.* Eds. Melvyn B. Krauss and Edward P. Lazear. Stanford, CA: Hoover Institution Press, 1991. 3-32.

Congressional Record

Bereuter, Doug. "Criminal Penalties for Crack Cocaine Possession." *Congressional Record* 28 November 1995: E2249.

"The Child Abuse Prevention and Treatment Act Amendments of 1995." *Congressional Record* 14 September 1995: S13612-S13613.

"Crime is Down But Drugs Are Up: Solutions Are No Mystery." *Congressional Record* 22 December 1995: S19271.

"Department of Commerce, Justice and State, the Judiciary and Related Agencies Appropriations Act, 1996." *Congressional Record* 28 September 1995: S14471-S14541.

"Department of Commerce, Justice and State, the Judiciary and Related Agencies Appropriations Act, 1996—Conference Report." *Congressional Record* 7 December 1995: S18127-S18179.

Dornan, Robert K. "Fighting Pornography on the Internet." *Congressional Record* 5 February 1996: E153-E154.

"Drug Legalization." *Congressional Record* 23 January 1996: S327-S329.

"Drug-Related Child Abuse." *Congressional Record* 25 January 1996: S361-S363.

"Drugs Legislation." *Congressional Record* 18 September 1995: S13738-S13740.

"Family Self-Sufficiency Act." *Congressional Record* 13 September 1995: S13481-S13489.

"Family Self-Sufficiency Act." *Congressional Record* 14 September 1995: S13558-S13561.

"Funding Earmarks for Dare America." *Congressional Record* 29 September 1995: S14688-S14689.

Hamilton, Lee H. "Television Violence." *Congressional Record* 1 February 1996: E124-E125.

"Kids Pay the Price." *Congressional Record* 3 November 1995: S16686.

"Mexico Legislation." *Congressional Record* 30 January 1996: S555-S559.

"Mexico Must Get Serious About Stopping Drug Trafficking." *Congressional Record* 1 February 1996: H1204-H1205.

"The Mysterious V-Chip." *Congressional Record* 10 August 1995: S12208-S12209.

"National Drug Policy." *Congressional Record* 12 December 1995: S18396-S18397.

"Prime Time Television—The New Fall TV Program Lineup." *Congressional Record* 19 September 1995: S13810-S13814.

"Prison, Probation Rolls Soaring." *Congressional Record* 27 September 1995: S14427-S14428.

"The Pros Know Why Prison Fails." *Congressional Record* 4 December 1995: S17928-S17929.

Rangel, Charles B. "Just Say 'Whoa.'" *Congressional Record* 5 February 1996: E180.

Solomon, Gerald B.H. "Drug Legalization." *Congressional Record* 19 December 1995: E2392-E2393.

"Some Second Thoughts on the First Amendment and Censorship." *Congressional Record* 27 October 1995: S16104-S16105.

"Time to Face the Truth on Prisons." *Congressional Record* 13 September 1995: S13549.

"Unanimous-Consent Agreement." *Congressional Record* 1 February 1996: S692-S720.

Vento, Bruce F. "Title I, An Educational Tool Meeting the Needs of Children." *Congressional Record* 21 December 1995: E2440-E2442.

"The Violent and Hard-Core Juvenile Offender Reform Act of 1995." *Congressional Record* 15 September 1995: S13656-S13659.

Documents

Anti-Recession Infrastructure Jobs Act of 1992. House Hearing, 12 and 18 March and 9 April 1992. Washington: Government Printing Office, 1992.

Before Dreams Disappear: Preventing Youth Violence. Senate Hearing, 17 May 1994. Washington: Government Printing Office, 1994.

Caught in the Crossfire: Kids Talk About Guns. House Hearing, 3 February 1994. Washington: Government Printing Office, 1994.

Contract With America: Hearing on Welfare Reform. House Hearing, 18 January 1995. Washington: Government Printing Office, 1995.

Drug Legalization—Catastrophe For Black Americans. House Hearing, 16 September 1988. Washington: Government Printing Office, 1989.

The Gang Problem in America: Formulating An Effective Federal Response. Senate Hearing, 9 February 1994. Washington: Government Printing Office, 1995.

Gun Violence: Problems and Solutions. Senate Hearing, 31 January 1994: Washington: Government Printing Office, 1995.

Hearing On Juvenile Crime and Delinquency: Do We Need Prevention? House Hearing, 22 March 1994. Washington: Government Printing Office, 1994.

Hearing Regarding the Department of Justice, Office of Juvenile Justice and Delinquency Prevention, Report Entitlted "A Cmprehensive Strategy for Serious, Violent, and Chronic Juvenile Offenders." House Hearing, 28 October 1993. Washington: Government Printing Office, 1994.

Hearings on H.R. 8, Child Nutrition Reauthorization. House Hearing, 17 November 1993, 24 March 1994, 12 and 14 April 1994. Washington: Government Printing Office, 1994.

Hearings on Training Issues. House Hearings, 1, 3, 7, 16 21, and 23 March 1995. Washington: Government Printing Office, 1995.

Hope For Tomorrow: Crime Prevention For At-Risk Children. Senate Hearing, 26 April 1994. Washington: Government Printing Office, 1995.

Implementation of the Television Program Improvement Act of 1990. Senate Hearings, 21 May and 8 June 1993. Washington: Government Printing Office, 1994.

Innovative Financing of Infrastructure Investment: The Use of Tax-Exempt Bonds. House Hearing, 30 June 1994. Washington: Government Printing Office, 1995.

Interim National Drug Control Strategy: Breaking the Cycle of Drug Abuse. Senate Hearing, 20 October 1993. Washington: Government Printing Office, 1995.

Joint Hearing on H.R. 4086, The Youth Development Block Grant Act. House Hearing, 4 August 1994. Washington: Government Printing Office, 1994.

Juvenile Courts: Access to Justice. Senate Hearing, 4 March 1992. Washington: Government Printing Office, 1993.

Legalization of Illicit Drugs: Impact and Feasibility. (A Review of Recent Hearings). House Report. Washington: Government Printing Office, 1989.

Legalization of Illicit Drugs: Impact and Feasibility, Part I. House Hearing, 29 September 1988. Washington: Government Printing Office, 1989.

Legalization of Illicit Drugs—Part II. House Hearing, 30 September 1988. Washington: Government Printing Office, 1989.

Minority Overrepresentation in the Juvenile Justice System. Senate Hearing, 25 June 1991. Washington: Government Printing Office, 1991.

Miscellaneous National Park System Measures. Senate Hearing, 19 May 1994. Washington: Government Printing Office, 1994.

National Drug Control Strategy: Strengthening Communities' Response to Drugs and Crime. Washington: Government Printing Office, February 1995.

Our Welfare System: What Can We Do to Fix It. House Hearing held in Cape Giradeau, Missouri, April 13, 1992. Washington: Government Printing Office, 1992.

Rebuilding America: Investing in Growth and Jobs. House Hearing, 16 November 1993. Washington: Government Printing Office, 1994.

Reforming the Present Welfare System. House Hearing, 7, 8, 9 and 14 February 1995. Washington: Government Printing Office, 1995.

Rethinking Poverty Policy. House Hearing, 2 October 1992. Washington: Government Printing Office, 1992.

Shaping Our Responses to Violent and Demeaning Imagery in Popular Music. Senate Hearing, 23 February 1994. Washington: Government Printing Office, 1995.

The State of Youth At Risk and the Juvenile Justice System: Prevention and Intervention. Senate Hearing in Atlanta, Georga, 21 October 1992. Washington: Government Printing Office, 1993.

Status Offenders: Risks and Remedies. Senate Hearing. 22 May 1991. Washington: Government Printing Office, 1991.

Urban Recreation and Crime Prevention. House Hearing, 10 March 1994.

Washington: Government Printing Office, 1994.

U.S. Advisory Commission on Intergovernmental Relations. *High Performance Public Works: A New Federal Infrastructure Investment Strategy for America.* November 1993.

Welfare Reform Proposals, Including H.R. 4605, The Work and Responsibility Act of 1994. House Hearings 14, 26, 27, and 28 July 1994. Washington: Government Printing Office, 1995.

Youth Development Community Block Grant Act of 1995. Senate Hearing, 8 June 1995. Washington: Government Printing Office, 1995.

Youth Violence: A Community Response. Senate Hearing in Phoenix and Tucson, Arizona, 1 and 2 June 1993. Washington: Government Printing Office, 1994.

Youth Violence Prevention. Senate Hearing, 31 March 1992. Washington: Government Printing Office, 1993.

Periodicals

Abraham, Spencer. ". . . And from the Senate." *National Review* 28 August 1995: 40.

"Alternatives to Violence." *Children Today* 23 (1994): 14-15.

Anderson, George M. "Juvenile Justice and the Double Standard." *America* 1 January 1994: 13-15.

Andrews, Lewis M. "Private Ratings." *National Review* 25 September 1995: 81-83.

Annin, Peter. "'We're Struggling to Keep Up.'" *Newsweek* 4 December 1995: 41.

Barkan, Steven E., and Stveven F. Cohn. "Racial Prejudice and Support for the Death Penalty by Whites." *Journal of Research in Crime and Delinquency* 31 (May 1994): 202-209.

Baumer, Eric. "Poverty, Crack, and Crime: A Cross-City Analysis." *Journal of Research in Crime and Delinquency* 31 (August 1994): 311-327.

Bazemore, Gordon and Mark Umbreit. "Rethinking the Sanctioning Function in Juvenile Court: Retributive or Restorative Responses to Youth Crime." *Crime & Delinquency* 41 (July 1995): 296-316.

Beckmann, David. "Assault on the poor." *Christian Century* 5 April 1995: 356-358.

Beger, Randall R. "Illinois Juvenile Justice: An Emerging Dual System." *Crime & Delinquency* 40 (January 1994): 54-68.

Bellafante, Ginia. "Locking Out Violence." *Time* 24 July 1995: 64.

Bergmann, Barbara R., and Heidi I. Hartmann. "A Program to Help Working Parents." *The Nation* 1 May 1995: 592-595.

"Bill Summary." *Congressional Digest* June/July 1995: 168-172+.

Blackwell, Brenda Sims, Harold G. Grasmick, and John K. Cochran. "Racial Differences in Perceived Sanction Threat: Static and Dynamic Hypotheses." *Journal of Research in Crime and Delinquency* 31 (May 1994): 210-224.

Boothe, James E., et al. "America's Schools Confront Violence." *USA Today* January 1994: 33-35.

Bower, Bruce. "Criminal Intellects: Researchers look at why lawbreakers often brandish low IQs." *Science News* 15 April 1995: 232, 233, 239.

———. "IQ Meets MQ." Science News 15 April 1995: 233.

Bradsher, Keith. "Low Ranking for Poor American Children." *The New York Times* 14 August 1995: A7.

Brezina, Timothy. "Adapting to Strain: An Examination of Delinquent Coping Responses." *Criminology* 34 (February 1996): 39-60.

Bridges, Linda. "Home Lessons from Abroad." *National Review* 26 June 1995: 41-42.

Brown, Lee P. "Eight Myths About Drugs: There Are No Simple Solutions." *Vital Speeches of the Day* 15 July 1994: 578-580.

Buerger, Michael E. "A Tale of Two Targets: Limitations of Community Anticrime Actions." *Crime & Delinquency* 40 (July 1994): 411-436.

Butterfield, Fox. "Study Finds a Disparity in Justice for Blacks." *The New York Times* 13 February 1996: A8.

Cannon, Carl M. "Honey, I Warped the kids: The argument for eliminating movie and TV violence." *Utne Reader* May/Jne 1994: 95-96.

Cherne Anderson, Michelle Lea. "The High Juvenile Crime Rate: A Look At Mentoring as a Preventive Strategy." *Criminal Law Bulletin* 30 (January/February 1994): 54-75.

Chisman, Forrest P. "Can the States Do Any Better." *The Nation* 1 May 1995: 600-602.

Clark, Charles S. "Sex, Violence and the Media." *CQ Researcher* 17 November 1995: 1017-1040.

Conley, Darlene J. "Adding Color to a Black and White Picture: Using Qualitative Data to Explain Racial Disproportionality in the Juvenile Justice System." *Journal of Research in Crime and Delinquency* 31 (May 1994): 135-148.

Cox, Stephen M., William S. Davidson, and Timothy S. Bynum. "A Meta-Analytic Assessment of Delinquency-Related Outcomes of Alternative Education Programs." *Crime & Delinquency* 41 (April 1995): 219-234.

Crutchfield, Robert D, George S. Bridges, and Susan R. Pitchford. "Analytical and Aggregation Biases in Analyses of Imprisionment: Reconciling Discrepancies in Studies of Racial Disparity." *Journal of Research in Crime and Delinquency* 31 (May 1994): 166-182.

Cullingford, Cedric. "Children's Social and Moral Claims." *Society* November/December 1993: 52-54.

"Current Programs." *Congressional Digest* June/July 1995: 166-167.

"D'Angelo, Ed. "The Moral Culture of Drug Prohibition." The Humanist September/October 1994: 3-7.

DeParle, Jason. "Welfare, End of." *The New York Times Magazine* 17 December 1995: 64-65.

Dewar, Helen. "$30.2 Billion Package Appproved, 61 to 38, Despite GOP Assault." *Washington Post* 26 August 1994: A1, A14.

Dorn, James A. "The Rise of Government: The Decline of Morality." *Vital Speeches of the Day* 15 October, 1995: 10-13.

Eisenman, Russell. "Society Confronts the Hard-Core Youthful Offender." *USA Today* January 1994: 27-28.

Eitzen, D. Stanley. "Violent Crime: Myths, Facts, and Solutions." *Vital Speeches of the Day* 15 May 1995: 469-472.

Elsea, Kelly Keimig. "The Juvenile Crime Debate: Rehabilitation, Punishment, or Prevention." *Kansas Juournal of Law and Public* Policy 5 (Fall 1995): 135-146.

Engler, John. "No Devil in Devolution." *National Review* 28 August 1995: 38-40.

Esbensen, Finn-Aage and David Huizinga. "Gangs, Drugs, and Delinquency in a Survey of Urban Youth." *Criminology* 31 (November 1993): 565-589.

Fagan, Patrick. "The Real Root Cause of Violent Crime." *Vital Speeches of the Day* 15 December 1995: 157-158

Farnsworth, Clyde. "Canada Likes Chip to Block TV Violence." *The New York Times* 28 February 1996: A1, A2.

Fox, James Alan and Glenn Pierce. "American Killers Are Getting Younger." *USA Today* January 1994: 24-26.

Garron, Barry. "Yet another view on violence on television." *Kansas City Star* 8 April 1996: D1, D2.

Gest, Ted and Dorian Friedman. "The new crime wave." *U.S. News & World Report* 29 August and 5 September 1994: 26-28.

Gilder, George. "End Welfare Reform As We Know It." *The American Spectator* June 1995: 24-27.

Gitlin, Todd. "Imagebusters: The hollow crusade against TV violence." *Utne Reader* May/June 1994: 92-93.

Glazer, Sarah. "Juvenile Justice." *CQ Researcher* 25 February 1994: 169-191.

———. "Preventing Teen Drug Use." *CQ Researcher* 28 June 1995: 657-680.

Gordon, Charles. "The trouble with doing the right thing." *Macleans* 16 October 1995: 15.

Gottfredson, Denise C., and William H. Barton. "Deinstitutionalization of Juvenile Offenders." *Criminology* 31 (November 1993): 591-610.

Gredrickson, George M. "Land of Opportunity." *New York Review of Books* 4 April 1996: 4-7.

Greenspan, Alan. "Key Economic Issues Facing the Nation." *Vital Speeches of the Day* 15 November 1995: 79-82.

Grinc, Randolph M. "'Angels in Marble': Problems in Stimulating Community Involvement in Community Policing." *Crime & Delinquency* 40 (July 1994): 437-468.

Griset, Pamala L. "Determinate Sentencing and the High Cost of Overblown Rhetoric: The New York Experience." *Crime & Delinquency* 40 (October 1994): 532-548.

Guest, Ted and Dorian Friedman. "The new crime wave." *U.S. News & World Report* 29 August and 5 September 1994: 26-28.

"Guns Are No. 2 Cause of Death Among the Young, Data Show." *The New York Times* 9 April 1996: A8.

Hagan, John. "The Social Embeddedness of Crime and Unemployment." *Criminology* 31 (November 1993): 465-491.

Hagedorn, John M. "Homeboys, Dope Fiends, Legits, and New Jacks." *Criminology* 32 (May 1994): 197-219.

Harris, Patricia M. "Client Management Classification and Prediction of Probation Outcome." *Crime & Delinquency* 40 (April 1994): 154-174.

Healey, Jon. "Exon Wants Shield for Children." *Congressional Quarterly* 18 March 1995: 803.

Herbert, Bob. "City Job, Minimum Wage." *The New York Times* 28 July 1995: A13.

———. "Daytime TV's Child Porn." *The New York Times* 1 March 1996: A15.

———. "Strength in Numbers." *The New York Times* 3 November 1995: A11.

———. "Trouble After School." *The New York Times* 4 March 1996: A15.

———. "Welfare Stampede." *The New York Times* 13 November 1995: A13.

Hetter, Katia. "Can she censor the mayhem?" *U.S. News & World Report* 9 May 1994: 45.

Hobbs, Fay Wilson. "Building Bridges: A Personal Reflection on Race, Crime, and the Juvenile Justice System." *Washington and Lee Law Review* 51 (Spring 1994): 535-545.

Howell, James C. "Recent Gang Research: Program and Policy Implications." *Crime & Delinquency* 40 (October 1994): 494-515.

Hundt, Reed. "Serving Kids and the Community." *Vital Speeches of the Day* 1 September 1995: 674-676.

Impoco, Jim. "The Bundys meet the censors at Fox." *U.S. News & World Report* 11 September 1995: 68-69.

"Issue: Crime." *Congressional Quarterly* 6 January 1996: 40-41.

Jencks, Christopher. "Housing the Homeless." *The New York Review of Books* 12 May 1994: 39-46.

Jensen, Eric L., and Linda K. Metsger. "A Test of the Deterrent Effect of Legislative Waiver on Violent Juvenile Crime." *Crime & Delinquency* 40 (January 1994): 96-104.

Johnson, Bruce D., Andrew Golub, and Jeffrey Fagan. "Careers in Crack, Drug Use, Drug Distribution, and Nondrug Criminality." *Crime and Delnquency* 41 (July 1995): 275-295.

Jourdan, Jeanne. "A Community's Answer to Teen Violence." *Children Today* 23 (1994): 20-24.

Kalogerakis, George. "Stoned Again." *New York* 1 May 1995: 41-47.

Kates, Don B. "Gun Control: Separating Reality From Symbolism." *Journal of Contemporary Law* 20 (1994): 353-379.

————. "The Value of Civilian Handgun Possession as a Deterrent to Crime or a Defense Against Crime." *American Journal of Criminal Law* 18 (Winter 1991): 113-167.

Kates, Don B., et al. "Guns and Public Health: Epidemic of Violence or Pandemic of Propaganda." *Tennessee Law Review* 62 (Spring 1995): 513-596.

Knipps, Susan K. "What is a 'Fair' Response to Juvenile Crime?" *Fordham Urban Law Journal* 20 (Spring 1993): 455—466.

Koretz, Gene. "Treat Junkies, Save Money: Therapy proves to be cost-effective." *Business Week* 14 August 1995: 26.

Kotlowitz, Alex. "Their Crimes Don't Make Them Adults." *New York Times Magazine* 13 February 1994: 40-41.

Lacayo, Richard. "When Kids Go Bad." *Time* 19 September 1994: 60-63.

Lattimore, Pamela K., Christy A. Visher, and Richard L. Linster. "Predicting Rearrest For Violence Among Serious Youthful Offenders." *Journal of Research in Crime and Delinquency* 32 (February 1995): 54-83.

LaVelle, Avis. "Should Children Be Tried As Adults?" *Essence* September 1994: 85-88.

Leo, John. "Punished for the sins of the children." *U.S. News & World* Report 12 June 1995: 18.

Leonard, John. "Why blame TV?: The Boob tube has little to do with our violent culture." *Utne Reader* May/June 1994: 90-94.

Leuchtag, Alice. "The Culture of Pornography." *The Humanist* May/June 1995: 4-6.

Levine, Suzanne Braun. "Caution: Children Watching." *MS* July/August 1994: 22-25.

Lewis, Anthony. "First, Do Less Harm." *The New York Times* 1 March 1996: A15.

————. "End the War." *The New York Times* 3 November 1995: A11.

Lewis, Neil . "President Foresees Safer U.S." New York Times 27 August 1994: A6.

Littlefield, Kinney. "The amazing V-chip." *Kansas City Star* 28 March 1996: F1, F5.

Lokeman, Rhonda Chris. "Kids As Criminals: young offenders are geting more prevalent and more violent." *Kansas City Star* 31 March 1996: I1, I4.

Luks, Allan. "Advice From Welfare Mothers." *The New York Times* 24 August 1995: A15.

Lurigio, Arthur J., and Wesley G. Skogan. "Winning the Hearts and Minds of Police Officers: An Assessment of Staff Perceptions of Community Policing in Chicago." *Crime & Delinquency* 40 (July 1994): 315-330.

MacKenzie, Doris Layton and Alex Piquero. "The Impact of Shock Incarceration Programs on Prison Crowding." *Crime & Delinquency* 40 (April 1994): 222-249.

MacKenzie, Doris Layton, Robert Brame, David McDowall, and Claire Souryal. "Boot Camp Prisons and Recidivism in Eight States." *Criminology* 33 (August 1995): 327-337.

Marris, Michael. "Young, Angry and Lethal." *Newsweek* 18 December 1995: 122.

Marvell, Thomas B., and Carlisle E. Moody. "Determinate Sentencing and Abolishing Parole: The Long-Term Impacts on Prisons and Crime." *Criminology* 34 (February 1996): 107-128.

————. "The Impact of Enhanced Prison Terms for Felonies Committed With Guns." *Criminology* 33 (May 1995): 247-281.

Masci, David. "The Modified Crime Bill." *Congressional Quarterly* 27 August 1994: 2490.

————. "$30 Billion Anti-Crime Bill Heads to Clinton's Desk." *Congressional Quarterly* 27 August 1994: 2488-2493.

Mauser, Elizabeth, Kit R. Van Stelle, and D. Paul Moberg. "The Economic Impact of Diverting Substance-Abusing Offenders Into Treatment." *Crime & Delinquency* 40 (October 1994): 568-588.

Mayer, Susan and Christopher Jencks. "War on Poverty: No Apologies, Please." *The New York Times* 9 November 1995: A15.

McCormick, John. "Missing the Point on Welfare." *Newsweek* 14 August 1995: 32-33.

McLarin, Kimberly. "Foster Care Plan Provides a Model for New York." *The New York Times* 20 November 1995: B12.

Mifflin, Lawrie. "New Plan to Simplify Rating of TV Shows." *The New York Times* 4 April 1996: B1, B4.

————. "Top TV Executives Agree, and Disagree, on Rating System." *The New York Times* 1 March 1996: A7.

Minerbrook, Scott. "A generation of stone killers." *U.S. News & World Report* 17 January 1994: 33-37.

Minow, Newton M., and Craig L. Lamay. "Making Television Safe for Kids." *Time* 26 June 1995: 70, 72.

Mitchell, Alison. "TV Executives Promise Clinton a Violence Ratings System by 97." *The New York Times* 1 March 1996: A1, A7.

————. "White House Sees a Dire Result But May Accept Plan on Welfare." *The New York Times* 10 November 1995: A1, A11.

Morganthau, Tom. "The Lull Before the Storm." *Newsweek* 4 December 1995: 40-42.

Murray, Charles. "Welfare Hysteria." *The New York Times* 14 November 1995: A10.

Nelson, James F. "A Dollar or a Day: Sentencing Misdemeanants in New York State." *Journal of Research in Crime and Delinquency* 31 (May 1994): 183-201.

Offner, Paul. "So Now You Know." *The New Republic* 10 July 1995: 11-12.

————. "Welfare Dads." *The New Republic* 13 February 1995: 12-14.

Olasky, Marvin. "Welfare States." *National Review* 23 October 1995: 44-48.

Pagnozzi, Amy. "When Good Kids Kill." *New York* 23 October 1995: 24-25.

"Parental Responsibility Laws: Cure for Crime or Exercise in Futility?" *Wayne Law Review* 37 (Fall 1990): 161-187.

Pate, Antony M., and Penny Shtull. "Community Policing Grows in Brooklyn: An Inside View of the New York City Police Department's Model Precinct." *Crime & Delinquency* 40 (July 1994): 384-410.

Paternoster, Raymond and Paul Mazerolle. "General Strain Theory and Delinquency: A Replication and Extension." *Journal of Research in Crime and Delinquency* 31 (August 1994): 235-263.

"Planning Grants Awarded to Combat Youth Violence/Gang Activity." *Children Today* 23 (1994-1995): 2-3.

Polakow, Valerie. "On a Tightrope Without a Net." *The Nation* 1 May 1995: 590-592.

Pollitt, Katha. "Subject to Debate." *The Nation* 18 December 1995: 777.

Prothrow-Stit, Debora. "The Power of Nonviolence." *Technology Review* August/September 1994: 31.

Purdum, Todd S. "Clinton Takes on Violence on TV." *The New York Times* 11 July 1995: A1, A12.

"Recent Action in the Congress." *Congressional Digest* June/July 1995: 173.

Rich, Frank. "The V-Chip G-String." *The New York Times* 28 February 1996: A13.

"Right Questions, Wrong Answers." *America* 7 October 1995: 3-5.

Rodriguez, Luis J. "Turning Youth Gangs Around." *The Nation* 21 November 1994: 605-609.

Rosenbaum, Dennis P., and Arthur J. Lurigio. "An Inside Look at Community Policing Reform: Definitions, Organizational Changes, and Evaluation Findings." *Journal of Research in Crime and Delinquency* 40 (July 1994): 299-314.

Ruefle, William and Kenneth Mike Reynolds. "Curfews and Delinquency in Major American Cities." *Crime & Delinquency* 41 (July 1995): 347-363.

Samuelson, Robert J. "The Politics of Ignorance." *Newsweek* 18 December 1995: 45.

Sanborn, Joseph B. "Remnants of Parens Patriae in the Adjudicatory Hearing: Is a Fair Trial Possible in Juvenile Court?" *Crime & Delinquency* 40 (October 1994): 599-615.

Schoolfield, Susan H. "Can Children and Guns Coexist in the Home?" *USA Today* January 1994: 40-41.

Sherman, Lawrence W. "Defiance, Deterrence, and Irrelevance: A Theory of the Criminal Sanction." *Journal of Research in Crime and Delinquency* 30 (November 1993): 445-473.

"Should Good Parents Be Jailed When Bad Children Break Laws?" *Jet* 27 June 1994: 14-16.

"Should the House Pass H.R. 4, the Personal Responsibility Act?" *Congressional Digest* June/July 1995: 174-191.

Silver, Marc. "Sex and Violence on TV." *U.S. News & World Report* 11 September 1995: 62-68.

Simons, John. "A Wayward Boys' 'Shock Incarceration' Camp." *U.S. News & World Report* 9 May 1994: 20.

Smith, Carolyn and Terence P. Thornberry. "The Relationship Between Childhood Maltreatment and Adolescent Involvement in Delinquency." *Criminology* 33 (November 1995): 451-481.

Smolowe, Jill. "Going Soft on Crime." *Time* 14 Novmeber 1994: 63-64.

———. "Out of the Line of Fire." *Time* 25 July 1994: 25.

Spelman, William. "The Severity of Intermediate Sanctions." *Journal of Research in Crime and Delinquency* 32 (May 1995): 107-135.

Stephens, Ronald D. "Gangs, Guns, and School Violence." *USA Today* January 1994: 29-32.

"Stevens, Jane Ellen. "A Media Campaign to Squash Violence." *Technology Review* August/September 1994: 28.

———. "Treating Violence as an Epidemic." *Technology Review* August/September 1994: 23-30.

Strossen, Nadine. "The Perils of Pornophobia." *The Humanist* May/June 1995: 7-9.

Tapia, Andres. "Healing Our Mean Streets." *Christianity Today* 18 July 1994: 46-48.

Teitelbaum, Lee E. "Youth Crime and the Choice Between Rules and Standards." *Brigham Young University Law Review* (1991): 351-402.

Uchitelle, Louis. "Some Cities Pressuring Employers to Pay a Higher Minimum Wage." *The New York Times* 9 April 1996: A1, C9.

Villani, Edward D. "Risk and Opportunities: A Rapidly Changing World." *Vital Speeches of the Day* 15 November 1995: 82-85.

Wall, James M. "Hang time, not gang time." *Christian Century* 9 November 1994: 1035.

Wallach, Lorraine B. "Breaking the Cycle of Violence." *Children Today* 23 (1994-1995): 26-31.

"Washing Their Hands." *The Progressive* November 1995: 8-9.

"Welfare Overview." *Congressional Digest* June/July 1995: 163-165+.

"Welfare Reform." *Congressional Digest* June/July 1995: 162.

Welsh, Wayne N., Philip W. Harris and Patricia H. Jenkins. "Reducing Overrepresentation of Minorities in Juvenile Justice: Development of Community-Based Programs in Pennylvania." *Crime & Delinquency* 42 (January 1996): 76-98.

White, Mary Jo. "Collecting Child Support Is a Federal Matter." *The New York Times* 14 August 1995: A11.

Whitman, David. "Compleat Engler." *The New Republic* 6 February 1995: 13-15.

Wordes, Madeline, Timothy S. Bynum, and Charles J. Corley. "Locking Up Youth: The Impact of Race on Detention Decisions." *Journal of Research in Crime and Delinquency* 31 (May 1994): 149-165.

"Work Fear." *The New Republic* 17 and 24 July 1995: 7-8.

Wyatt, Edward. "Stocks Tumble on Jobs Data, and Rates Hit 8-Month High." *The New York Times* 9 April 1996: C1, C8.

Yu, Jiang and Allen E. Liska. "The Certainty of Punishment: A Reference Group Effect and Its Functional Form." *Criminology* 31 (August 1993): 447-464.

Zuckerman, Mortimer B. "Scary Kids Around the Corner." *U.S. News & World Report* 4 December 1995: 96.